What Is a Person?

What Is a Person?

An Ethical
Exploration

James W. Walters

Foreword by

Lawrence J. Schneiderman

♦ ♦ ♦ ♦ ♦ ♦ ♦ ♦ ♦ ♦

University of Illinois Press

Urbana and Chicago

© 1997 by the Board of Trustees of the University of Illinois
Manufactured in the United States of America
C   5   4   3   2   1

This book is printed on acid-free paper.

Library of Congress Cataloging-in-Publication Data
Walters, James W. (James William), 1945–
What is a person? : an ethical exploration / James W. Walters ;
foreword by Lawrence J. Schneiderman.
p.   cm.
Includes bibliographical references and index.
ISBN 0-252-02278-5 (acid-free paper)
1. Personalism. I. Title.
B828.5.W35   1997
126—dc20   96-9991
                                    CIP

To Jack W. Provonsha

Contents

Foreword

Lawrence J. Schneiderman

In this lucidly written book, James W. Walters takes the reader on an excursion that perhaps only he could lead. Trained in the ethereal realms of theology and philosophy, he is also grounded in the clinical setting as a medical ethicist at the Loma Linda University Medical Center, which is renowned for its pioneering and controversial work in neonatal organ transplantation. It was here that a baboon heart was transplanted into an infant with a lethal congenital abnormality of the heart and here also that some of the first efforts were made to find medically and ethically acceptable approaches to using organs obtained from anencephalic infants.

Walters discusses these tempestuous issues in a way that exemplifies civilized discourse. Theologian Walters is by no means a single-minded religious chauvinist. On the contrary, religion, he holds, "like other forces in modern society must make a public case for its views." And any particular theological interpretation must be "argued in the classroom and finally on the town square along with other contenders." He invites us to join him by suggesting that although religion does not possess definitive answers to ethical dilemmas, "it consists of many rich traditions that have grappled with the meaning of life and as such it has something valuable to offer the contemporary discussion."

Philosopher Walters is equally gracious; for he is no Absolute Truth chauvinist either. Contending rather that "good philosophy includes sensitivity to historical and social context," Walters then displays that very sensitivity as he leads the reader from the classical period through centuries of Catholicism into contemporary American Christianity, giving a fair hearing to arguments defining the moral rights of a human being from both the physicalists' and personalists' viewpoints. These two disputational trajectories, he acknowledges, are like "colliding moral galaxies" when it comes to deciding how to treat "marginal" human life such as the embryo, the fetus, or the permanently vegetative patient.

Thus, Walters constantly keeps both the lofty sky and the hard ground in sight when he prepares us for his arguments regarding "proximate personhood" and the use for anencephalic organ donors. Indeed, he presents and reviews arguments of philosophers, theologians, sociologists, and medical ethicists with such subtlety and detail that he even includes thoughtful side trips into animal rights and the moral rights of a sleeping person—topics that would not ordinarily be of compelling interest to a practical clinical ethicist like me. But he makes these subjects relevant as background and preparation for arguments.

Simply stated, Walters holds that "the more a fetus or newborn approximates—or is proximate to—personhood, the greater his or her claim to life. Likewise the further beyond the threshold of uncontestably personal life an adult individual is (for example, a patient with severely advanced Alzheimer's disease is beyond that threshold), the less clear is that individual's claim to protectable life." Thus, Walters sees an evolving moral status of the newborn, particularly the severely handicapped newborn, a kind of sliding scale (adversaries will see a slippery slope, of course) gradually gaining weight against competing claims such as parental liberty.

Walters provides an exceedingly fair discussion of the ethical issues and conflicting opinions regarding anencephalic infants as organ sources, setting this specific issue in the context of the broader, philosophical question: (1) What constitutes a person, so to give her or him a unique claim to life? (2) In determining protectable human life, what are the respective roles of medical, legal, and social considerations? (3) Does every legally alive human individual possess an equal claim to medical resources and continued life? (4) What role should cerebral life/death play in determining which individuals deserve common protection?

For Walters the arguments lead in a logical progression to a set of conclusions: If terminally and seriously ill patients have the right to discontinue life-sustaining treatment, they should also have the right to donate organs, even if they are not yet dead (by current standards) but only permanently unconscious. If organs can be taken from those whose higher brain functions are irreversibly lost, then by logical extension, a surrogate should be able to implement the patient's wishes regarding organ donation. By further logical extension, a newborn infant whose higher brain is anatomically absent ought to be considered also as a suitable organ donor if designated surrogates, such as parents, so decide. Walters furthers his case by pointing to the large numbers of parents of anencephalic infants who have contacted the Loma Linda University Medical Center asking for the chance to give life to another child and meaning to the brief existence of their own offspring through organ donation.

Throughout this book Walters provides unexpected discoveries. My personal favorite is learning that legal statutes protecting animals against abuse and cruelty antedated statutes protecting children. Indeed the Society for the Prevention of Cruelty to Children was founded in New York City in 1871 following a neighborhood's frustration at being powerless to protect a young girl who was regularly beaten by her adoptive parents. No legal mechanism existed to counteract the parents' right to chastise their children as they saw fit. Fortunately for the girl, a shrewd and inventive interpretation of the law allowed her to be rescued. She was removed from the home under the auspices of the Society for the Prevention of Cruelty to Animals on the ground that the young girl belonged to the animal kingdom.

Whether or not you agree with Professor Walters's analyses and proposal, I recommend that you join him on this excursion. He is an excellent guide and companion.

Acknowledgments

The basic idea of this volume—proximate personhood—arose in a National Endowment for the Humanities seminar led by James F. Childress at the University of Virginia in the summer of 1986. A bioethicist at Loma Linda University, where Baby Fae had received a baboon heart transplant in 1984, I attended the seminar while the chair of a committee working on a protocol for the use of anencephalic infants as organ sources. The question of the relative value of primate and marginal human life had practical implications, but more importantly I found and continue to find it of great social importance and significant philosophic interest.

Most of the work in this book is original, but three chapters are based on essays that appeared in various journals. Chapter 3, "Proximate Personhood," which contains the core of my argument, is an elaboration of two published essays: "Proximate Personhood as a Standard for Making Difficult Treatment Decisions: Imperiled Newborns as a Case Study" (*Bioethics* 6 [Jan. 1992]: 12–22) and "Approaches to Ethical Decision Making in the Neonatal Intensive Care Unit" (*American Journal of Diseases of Children* 142 [Aug. 1988]: 825–30. Copyright 1988, American Medical Association). James Childress, Tristram Engelhardt Jr., Clifford Grobstein, David Larson, Michael Lockwood, and Peter Singer provided particularly helpful criticisms of earlier formulations of key ideas in this chapter. Also, at various stages of development, Lawrence D. Longo, Richard R. McCarty, and Anthony Shaw made constructive suggestions.

Chapter 5, "The Moral Status of Anencephalic Infants," is based on two essays that arose out of my involvement as chair of the Loma Linda interdisciplinary committee on anencephalic infants: "Organ Prolongation in Anencephalic Infants: Ethical and Medical Issues" (*Hastings Center Report* 18 [Nov. 1988]: 19–27. Reproduced by permission. © The Hastings

Center), coauthored with Stephen Ashwal, and "Anencephalic Infants as Organ Sources: Report from North America" (*Bioethics* 5 [Oct. 1991]: 326–41). This chapter benefited from the criticism of the Kennedy Institute staff and friends who heard it in part at one of their weekly noon bioethics sessions. In this connection I am particularly thankful to Tom L. Beauchamp and Robert Veatch. Statistician Floyd Petersen was invaluable in collecting and interpreting the survey data reported in the chapter.

Chapter 6, "Anencephalic Infants and the Law" is based on three earlier essays on social policy: "Yes, the Law on Anencephalic Infants as Organ Sources Should be Changed" (*Journal of Pediatrics* 115 [Nov. 1989]: 825–28); "Anencephalic Organ Procurement: Should the Law Be Changed?" (*BioLaw,* special section [Dec. 1987]: S83–89); and "Anencephalic Infants as Organ Sources: Current Attitudes and Prospects" (*BioLaw* 2 [May 1992]: S834–37).

The remaining chapters—and important additions to the aforementioned chapters—were written to complement the work I had already done on proximate personhood and anencephalic infants. For instance, knowing what we do about nonhuman animals, I believed that it would be unconscionable to write on "proximate" persons without significantly delving into the animal rights debate. David DeGrazia was very helpful in correcting some obvious errors in the chapter on animal issues.

William Winslade and an anonymous reader for the University of Illinois Press provided invaluable insights into and criticisms of the project as a whole. Also, my secretary, Gayle Foster, provided most careful proofreading and saved me from a multitude of errors. Finally, I thank my wife, Priscilla, and daughters, Wendy and Christina, for putting up with their father who spent too many long evenings working at his Macintosh.

What Is a Person?

Introduction

Are persons and humans equivalent terms? Are all persons human? And are all humans persons?

In a medically simpler time, it was easy to hold the view that all human life—precisely because it is *human*—is valuable or sacred. But today much of the mystery about life has disappeared. Today medical science takes four-color photographs of the developing fetus. Further, it tells us that we all begin our lives as single-celled organisms the size of a pencil dot. And each of those pencil dots is a *human being*. That is, each of us, just after conception, is indisputably human in our genetics, and each of us at that primitive stage is a being—a living thing.

But whether the term *person* aptly applies to the human conceptus is highly debatable. If person is defined as the equivalent of human—a simple synonym—then of course it applies to the conceptus. But if by person we mean an individual who possesses a degree of self-consciousness, for example, then the newly conceived human being does not qualify to be called a person.

The dilemma of human/person raises questions: Given the elemental nature of a conceptus, is a morning-after pill moral? Is an IUD morally permissible, since it strips the days-old blastocyst from the uterine wall? Is RU-486 a godsend or a great evil since it is most often used to thwart pregnancies after five or six weeks of gestation?

At the other edge of life, consider an elderly patient with terminal illness who lapses into a comatose state. Whether this condition is viewed by society and the patient as a significant aspect of living or as a meaningless part of dying depends much on where the patient is placed along the human-to-person continuum. To an increasing degree patients are incompetent as they lie dying in medical centers, and others must make the crucial decisions. Today in the modern hospital, fully three quarters of deaths occur because of a conscious decision made by care givers that the therapies being used to sustain the patient should be discontinued. Whether the patient's life is viewed as merely *human* existence or as meaningful *personal* living is crucial to the decision.

This book is an exploration into the enigmatic moral status of human—and yes, animal—lives. I argue that the possession of self-consciousness is a necessary and sufficient condition to be a person of full moral status. Unless otherwise qualified, my use of the term person denotes an individual who possesses self-consciousness and is thus entitled to maximal moral standing. There are certain individuals, such as normal newborns, who should be and are considered persons because they show significant development toward realizing their potential for self-consciousness.

The concern that prompts this study is not the ethical status of readers of this page—an elevated status that we do and should take as a given. Rather, my interest is in grappling with the moral standing of "marginal" personal life—the Karen Ann Quinlans, the Kokos, the Baby Michelles, the Nancy Cruzans of society.

Karen Ann Quinlan, in a persistent vegetative state, survived for over eleven years, first on a hospital ventilator and then on artificial nutrition in a nursing home, despite her parents' wishes that she be allowed to die. Finally on June 13, 1986, she was pronounced dead, because her heart stopped due to increasing respiratory congestion and because her parents' request that no antibiotics or blood pressure medication be given was heeded.

Koko, the "talking" gorilla made the front cover of the National Geographic. This educated ape is reported to use five hundred words in sign language and understand five hundred additional words. Koko so mourned the accidental death of her pet kitten that another was given to her.

Canadian Baby Michelle was born in 1986 with the diagnosis of anencephaly—absence of the neocortex and most of the cerebrum. Doctors later found that even the lower portions of her brain had died, and it was determined that she met the criteria for whole-brain death. Subsequently the baby was used as a controversial source for a heart that saved the life of baby Paul Holc.

Nancy Cruzan, a young Missourian whose case went to the U.S. Supreme Court, was left in a vegetative state after an auto accident. To thwart the will of Nancy Cruzan's parents to let their permanently unconscious daughter die peacefully and legally, militant pro-life advocates literally attempted to steal her body from a hospital and sustain her in their own quarters.

The all-humans-are-sacred and the only-persons-are-maximally-valuable groups are colliding moral galaxies. The strengths of the "humanist" approach are tradition and clarity: Western society has long seen human life as possessing a categorically privileged moral status. The strength of the personalist view is that its rational assessment of valuable beings fits more easily with the complexity of modern knowledge and life. Neither approach can be "proven." Thoughtful individuals will not easily label either position right or wrong. Both are held for deep-seated social, philosophical, or, indeed, religious reasons. In his recent book on abortion and euthanasia, Ronald Dworkin is correct to contend that abortion and such issues as we are discussing here are "essentially religious."[1] I have the deepest respect for those in the all-humans-are-sacred camp, but for my own philosophical and religious reasons I argue for the adequacy of the personalist approach.

It is my opinion that human and person are not equivalent terms. For example, I do not think that a human conceptus qualifies as a person and neither does a human who is irretrievably beyond consciousness—say, a patient in a truly permanent coma. That is, neither a conceptus nor a permanently comatose patient possesses self-consciousness and therefore neither qualifies for the moral status of person. And just as not all humans are persons, all persons are not human. For instance, Koko is at least a quasi-person, and ET in the Speilberg movie, angels, and God Himself are surely persons. Each is portrayed as intelligently self-conscious in ways similar to us—individuals who are indisputably persons, that is, entities with full moral status.

The distinction between human and person is important and will become even more significant as medical technology gallops ahead and resources shrink. A conceptus slowly evolves toward personhood, and just how one defines the human/person issue is crucial for determining the permissibility of interrupting a pregnancy. As medicine allows patients with less and less quality of life to be sustained longer and longer, the issue of mere human existence versus meaningful personal life increases in importance.

Here I argue that an entity's unique moral claim to life is primarily dependent on that individual's higher mental capacities. The individual being that will never possess—or is forever beyond possession of—neocortical functioning does not have a special moral claim to life. Thus, for example, I view an anencephalic infant or a permanently comatose patient as lacking the special claim to existence that you or I possess.

Even more difficult than issues surrounding upper-brain-absent patients is the question of aggressive treatment for the severely handicapped newborn or the nursing home resident with advanced senility. There is no simple answer to these dilemmas. However, a failure to decide on such borderline cases itself constitutes a decision because the technology to sustain life is readily available and will be used unless predetermined limits are set. Decisions on marginal human life are made every day in the modern medical center and their number and difficulty will only increase. Hence the importance of grappling with the issue of what it is about an individual's life that gives him or her or "it" a distinctive moral right to existence.

The big question is, How do we decide who has a special moral claim to life and scarce medical resources? And this question, made more urgent by modern medicine's powers, prompted the writing of this book. My argument, in just a sentence, is that *the more nearly an individual human or animal approximates a life of self-consciousness (such as yours or mine), the greater the claim of that individual to maximal moral status.*

My rationale for viewing life as I do is not merely my own personal opinion but emerges from a particular tradition. Philosophical and religious traditions have long determined fundamental views about life, and today they continue to inform us on big existential issues. In chapter 1, I trace two opposing philosophical/religious traditions. The first, physicalism, emphasizes genetic status; the second, personalism, stresses the capacity for self-consciousness. Chapter 2 continues the physicalism versus personalism theme by analyzing contemporary apologists, specifically Cardinal Joseph Bernardin and philosopher Tristram Engelhardt. I argue that both positions, although sensitive and nuanced, are incomplete.

In chapter 3, I argue for a proximate personhood perspective that takes into account but advances beyond both the physicalist and the personalist positions. I advocate a point of view that recognizes a patient's claim to full moral standing as proportionate to that patient's proximity to a life that all would agree is morally valuable and legally protectable. Developed in the context of the treatment of handicapped newborns, the proximate personhood model contends that the greater the *potentiality for* and the greater the *development toward* uncontested personhood and the greater the *binding of* persons to the baby, the greater the newborn's moral standing.

Some animals have greater mental capacities than certain human beings, and this fact raises significant ethical issues. In chapter 4, I argue that every animal, regardless of its size or complexity, has an interest in living. This translates into its possession of at least a minimal moral status. The greater the animal's capacity for at least minimal self-consciousness, the higher its moral status.

Chapters 5 and 6 explore the concept of using anencephalic infants as organ sources and its relationship to the larger issue of the possession of moral status. First, the case of Baby Gabrielle of Canada, the only anencephalic infant to be used successfully as a heart donor, is studied for its ethical, legal, and medical appropriateness. Second, the question of brain death is examined, both in regard to anencephalic infants and a broader class of patients. Here the primary concern is whether absence of autonomic brain functioning or of the mental capacity for self-consciousness should be the primary standard for the determination of death.

I conclude with a look at public policy on anencephalic infants as organ sources. I argue that it is time for the law to be changed to allow for their use as donors. No individual harm would be done to anencephalic newborns if direct procurement of organs were legally permissible. And because much public discussion has already occurred on this issue, the time has come to move forward on a state-by-state basis.

1 ❖ Modern Bioethics
and Religious Roots

Nancy Beth Cruzan, involved in a tragic auto accident in January 1983, survived in a persistent vegetative state for eight years without hope of recovery. She stayed in a condition, now legally defined as alive, through artificial nutrition and hydration. Nancy had told friends that she would not want to exist as a "vegetable" or continue her life unless she could live "halfway normally," but she had never completed an advance directive or formally stated her desires in writing.

Nancy's Roman Catholic parents were convinced that their daughter would not want to live in her condition and sought removal of life support. A trial court ruling authorizing removal was overturned by the Missouri Supreme Court in November 1988. A year-and-a-half later the United States Supreme Court, in its first ever termination of medical treatment case, decided that the Missouri Supreme Court did not violate federal constitutional rights in demanding "clear and convincing" evidence for Nancy's reported desires to refuse medical care. A heated debate in the country ensued, and subsequently the Missouri courts acknowledged that reports of Nancy's wishes not to live under certain conditions were indeed valid. Joe and Joyce Cruzan's petition was granted, and life-sustaining medical treatment was withdrawn from their daughter.

Why does one individual staunchly believe that a Nancy Cruzan possesses life of full moral status? And why does another individual with identical information think that a Nancy Cruzan is merely an artificially sustained corpse? There are many factors that contribute to why people possess certain moral beliefs—parents, peers, neighborhood, education. However, despite talk of our living in a post-Christian era, it is religion—often in subconscious ways—that frequently plays a formative role in determining deep-seated convictions.

In this chapter I argue that religious reasons lie behind many of our beliefs about the moral status of an individual's life. (For our purposes religion is a life-informing ultimate belief. A leading scholar recently defined religion as: "the organization of life around the depth dimensions of experience.")[1] Consider the high value we place on *individual* human life. In America it is popularly held that we would rather see ten guilty people go free than send one innocent individual to jail; and in the 1980s scores of "million dollar babies" were treated in intensive care units only to survive in a near vegetative state of being. Be it good or bad, the Christian religion, building on an Hebraic foundation, has been largely responsible for influencing the West toward a high valuation of individual life generally and of newborn life in particular.[2]

My contention is not that contemporary America is devoutly religious. Given our high levels of suicide, crime, and materialism, the United States may be viewed as less religious than most peoples of the world. Nevertheless, eighty million Americans attend worship services on any given weekend (roughly 40 percent of Americans over the last fifty years have reported that they regularly go to church or synagogue), and 89.5 percent of Americans openly claimed a religious preference in the recent National Survey of Religious Identification (NSRI) involving 113,000 representative citizens.[3]

Such religious attraction—the highest in the Western world—does suggest that despite our widespread higher education and advanced technology, we regard institutions that stand for transcendent values as having something significant to offer. If this is true today, it was even more true in former eras when the church and synagogue played a dominant role. Where we look to the scientist, our forebears looked to the theologian. In fact some of the first "modern" scientists were also theologians, such as Sir Isaac Newton who published works in both religion and science.[4]

I mention this sociological and historical data on America's religiousness to suggest that religious views of human life have been passed on, often stripped of their religious garb or underpinning, and significantly influence how modern America values human life today. This statement is meant to be merely descriptive, not prescriptive or normative. I am simply contending that society's values have some origin, and that many fundamental values in the Western world have been handed down via a Judeo-Christian belief system. (The NSRI reports that 88 percent of Americans identify themselves as Christian [86.2] or Jewish [1.8].)

The Judeo-Christian tradition, however, does not speak with one voice on basic views of life, particularly regarding bioethics. With respect to the moral status of human life, there are completely opposing views in Western religion and philosophy. In the latter part of this chapter I explore the development of these views utilizing two models—the physicalist and the personalist. [5]

The physicalist model is based on the idea that embodied human nature is of paramount value. Here, all individuals, by virtue of their live physical presence, share in the nature of humanness and therefore possess full moral standing. The personalist model is premised on the idea that certain intellectual and emotional capacities are the basis for valuing individual life. Here, only those individuals who possess particular higher capacities of the brain deserve full moral status.

Religion and Ethics

Religious people of the physicalist and personalist persuasions come down very differently, of course, on the issue of "marginal" human life—be that life the embryo, the fetus, or a permanently vegetative patient. The physicalist thinker would view Nancy Cruzan as a very ill individual but as one possessing a moral standing equal to all other humans. The personalist thinker would see Ms. Cruzan as one of diminished moral standing—if she was indeed *permanently* unconscious.

These opposing views of Nancy Cruzan's moral status are alternate ethical universes and fundamentally different views of the human individual. They differ at ethics' most basic level—that of metaethics, presuppositions that undergird questions of right and wrong. For example, one cannot merely ask whether personalism is right or wrong. This question would be on the level of normative ethics, and normative questions only make sense when a common philosophical basis can be assumed. Such a common basis is missing for personalism and physicalism; they themselves are alternate bases for normative ethics. They found contrasting philosophical systems and contrasting religious worldviews.

Religious worldviews are of fundamental importance to ethics in three ways. First, a knowledge of the presence of such worldviews and of their impact on society helps us *descriptively;* that is, it aids us in describing the historical background of our ethical views. Second, religious worldviews contribute *normatively;* they provide bases for our norms of right and wrong. Third, recognition of differing religious worldviews is the first step toward fulfilling our need for *public reasoning* about our common moral life. These three elements deserve further treatment.

Descriptive Contributions of Religion

Once theology was the queen of the sciences; now it is lucky to be a servant. This demotion of religion is the case in the modern world, at least. It never was and is still not the case in the premodern world. There religion still reigns—often in increasingly fundamentalist garb. But, interestingly, as the West enters the postmodern era—a time full of self-doubt and ambiguity at the deepest levels of conceptualization—religion may once again gain in respectability, or at least recognition. Early modernism's notion that calculated reason could bring about universal morality and world community has yielded to the postmodern view that there are no objectively "best" ideas and that all ideas—even those of philosophy itself—are conditioned by the accidents of history.

Does recognition of historical conditionedness mean that religious claims are suspect? Yes. But such an admission does not mean that religious views are therefore untrue—or less important than ever in people's lives. Regardless of the final philosophical status of basic worldviews, what people believe—or disbelieve—about life profoundly informs their ethics. Contending religious claims, such as arguments about the moral status of a Nancy Cruzan, make a great difference in how one views bioethics. This is starkly evident in the contrast between the physicalist and personalist models of life. Which model one choses is likely to have far-reaching consequences for decisions about such controversial dilemmas as abortion and euthanasia. My point is a descriptive one: underlying religious views can profoundly influence contemporary ethical decisions.

Most people in this country—to say nothing of most of the rest of the world—continue to be overtly religious. The investigators from City University of New York who conducted the National Survey of Religious Identification found Americans ready to discuss their religious views, with a "remarkably low 2.3 percent refusing to participate."[6] As was previously indicated, some 90 percent of the population identifies with the Judeo-Christian tradition. It is reasonable to expect that religious beliefs will affect one's fundamental moral views. So if an individual accepts the physicalist approach to human life, a particular set of ethical mandates and prohibitions quite logically follows.

Organized religion's sway in contemporary Western society is still considerable, and it was previously all-pervasive. For this reason, it is no surprise that many of our society's most fundamental moral views are rooted in religion. Such correlation of morality and religion goes back at least to the time of the ancient Hebrews and Babylonians with their Ten Commandments and Code of Hammurabi, respectively, which indiscriminately combined what today we separate into legal and moral norms.

However, despite statistics about belief in America, our society—and what we know about our universe and our psyches—is profoundly different from that of ancient times and even far different from a century ago. Today a growing number of people are agnostic or have unorthodox or non-Western beliefs. Still, Judeo-Christian religious beliefs and derivative ideas pervade our society, even the society of unbelievers.

I know of no better exposition on the far-reaching societal impact of religion than that developed at the turn of the century by the German sociologist Max Weber. Weber traced the powerful effect of Calvinist theology on the rise of capitalism. He argued that the Calvinistic doctrine of predestination gave believers hope for and concomitant anxiety about eternal life. To discover whether they were predestined for heaven or hell, believers examined their lives for a sign of what God had foreordained. If examination revealed good works, heaven was their destination. Although not meant as a basis for works-righteousness, such was the result. Believers worked hard at their religion and consequently were able to view their righteous lives as a *sign*—not the *cause*—of salvation.

Two centuries later when many in the Calvinist tradition retained only a dim theology, an established pattern of diligence, thrift, sobriety and prudence was unabated. These qualities comprised the seedbed for capitalism. To use a different metaphor, they were an economic aftershock of Calvinistic theology. Benjamin Franklin epitomized the ascetic Puritan work ethic, largely stripped of its religious underpinning, in his admonition that "time is money," "credit is money," and "the good paymaster is lord of another man's purse." The pursuit of material goods as ends in themselves reached its zenith in the United States. "In the field of its highest development, in the United States, the pursuit of wealth, stripped of its religious and ethical meaning, tends to become associated with purely mundane passions, which often actually give it the character of sport."[7] Thus Weber explained how old, even jettisoned, religious worldviews could illuminate contemporary dispositions and practices in ethics.

Normative Claims of Religion

James Gustafson has defined an ethicist as "a former theologian who does not have the professional credentials of a moral philosopher."[8] He acknowledges that although the ethical questions in the life sciences have become quite clear, the theological questions have not. As a result many interested theologians neither attempt to clarify them nor answer the ones that are apparent.[9] For example, to the question of whether contemporary Christians can continue to believe in a God who personally intervenes in natural processes, Gustafson answers no. He further laments the rift between theology and bioethics and criticizes the theologians who write in bioethics—and primarily theologians began the discipline—for failing to contribute from their unique position as theologians. Paul Ramsey, a leading conservative bioethicist, was an exception, once declaring, "I always write as the ethicist I am, namely a Christian ethicist, and not as some hypothetical common denominator."[10]

Without difficulty or embarrassment, televangelists proclaim the normative benefits for morality that come from religion. However, not only fundamentalists recognize the benefits of absolutes and near-absolutes for society. So do some theologians and philosophers, but the academics are a bit more sophisticated in how they invoke such absolutes, and their language recognizes the difficulties in such an enterprise.

Paul Ramsey, for instance, cited the Nuremberg Code authors' warning that Nazi medical crimes "started with small beginnings . . . with the acceptance of the attitude . . . that there is such a thing as a life not worthy to be lived."

Ramsey himself contended that "any boundaries (preventing infanticide) that can be fixed or preserved today are precious, and should be cherished and strengthened—however nonrational they may be."[11] Note that Ramsey did not say "irrational," perhaps suggesting that the ban on infanticide does not go against reason even if it may need to surpass reason in bolstering its claim to rightness. Evidently, Ramsey here implicitly appealed to revealed Christian norms on the sanctity of human life, which he evidently saw as transcending mere reason.

Not only do duty-oriented ethicists such as Ramsey appeal to "nonrational" absolutes, but some philosophers share similar perspectives in their contentions for other norms. Scientist-philosopher Hans Jonas and bioethicist Daniel Callahan are examples.

Jonas is concerned about the ethics of technology, particularly the ethics of a genetic technology that could produce autonomous organisms. "If it is a categorical imperative for mankind to exist, then any suicidal gambling with that existence is categorically forbidden, and technological bets with even remotely this at stake are ruled out in their first beginnings." The old sorcerer could command, "'In the closet, / broom! broom! / As you were,'" and there the broom would stand motionless, comments Jonas. But "the creations of technology are no longer brooms but new living creatures."

The long trial of evolution has produced a genetic heritage that ought to be respected, says Jonas. But the lure of technology to remedy human ills is so strong that initial efforts to repair genetic nature—legitimate in themselves—will inevitably open Pandora's box. It is against humans playing as "creators at the roots of our being, at the primal seat of its mystery" that Jonas protests. Ironically, Jonas's admittedly godless lament invokes Judeo-Christian images: "We must rediscover fear and trembling, even without God, and awe of what is holy." The playful imaginings of biologists include such notions as interchange of genetic material between animals and humans—"a concept which calls to mind such ancient, forgotten terms as 'blasphemy' and 'abomination.'" "Our world, so completely stripped of its taboos, must voluntarily establish new ones to match the new types of power it possesses." According to Jonas, modern technology is something new in the history of existence and it calls for a new ethics of limits, even an ethics of cessation. Jonas mentions, but cannot invoke, the notion of humans being created in God's image. But for him the integrity of the "human image" is "inviolable."[12]

In 1983 Daniel Callahan disclosed his "stubborn emotional repugnance" against removal of artificial nutrition. He granted the cogency of the rational arguments for removing sustenance in certain circumstances. However, for him the battle between "head and heart" was unresolved. At that time he leaned toward continuance of artificial feedings, even when they might "under legitimate circumstances" be discontinued. He allowed that "No doubt some people will live on in ways beneficial neither to them nor to others. No doubt a good bit of money will be wasted indulging rationally hard-to-defend anti-starvation policies. That strikes me as a tolerable price to pay to preserve—with ample margin to spare— one of the few moral emotions that could just as easily be called a necessary social instinct."[13] Several years later Callahan altered his position. He conceded that in particular circumstances there might be good reasons for pulling a feeding tube and allowing an underlying disease to take a patient's life.[14]

Jonas and Callahan, in discussing genetic engineering and artificial nutrition, are not advocating religious norms, per se. But their insightful cautions amount to as much. They themselves must be conscious of this, considering their respectful invocation of religious terms such as "taboo." Fundamental legal/moral concepts such as rape or incest are not as far removed from religious views of life as many would suppose. And this is no criticism of society—far from it. The very notion of a "society" presupposes social norms. We must have norms dealing with everything from autos at intersections to definitions of death. The more profound the issue, the more likely the regulatory norms are rooted in religion or its secular equivalent.

Religion, as I am using the concept, is any ultimate belief that provides significant meaning to one's existence. For most Western peoples such belief includes a deity. A clear demarcation between a philosophy of life and religion is not always evident or perhaps necessary. The close relationship of religion and philosophy was vividly illustrated in 1992 when the U.S. Senate's judicial affairs committee conducted hearings on Judge Clarence Thomas, nominee to the Supreme Court. Thomas held to the notion of "natural law," a traditional Christian belief that God created the natural world in a particular and stable form that is sacred. The senators engaged Thomas in an extensive debate over this concept and how his belief could influence his vote on the Court regarding issues such as human rights. These hearings were a fascinating discussion of the interpenetration of civil religion, the Constitution, and contemporary social policies.

The Need for Public Reasoning

This brief summary of the descriptive and normative contributions of religion provides two insights. First, our beliefs about the moral world have some origin and, given the pervasiveness of religion—particularly in the past, knowledge of the religious and philosophical influences in our backgrounds can help us describe how we came to our present convictions, attitudes, and actions.

Second, the realization that all ethics is influenced by historical contingency need not blunt our search for the superiority of one position over others. Regardless of the insights of postmodern philosophy, society inevitably must live by some norms, and theologians and philosophers adamantly contend for certain norms and inveigh against others. Three thinkers advocate positions on contemporary issues that they themselves label as possibly "nonrational" (Ramsey), "holy" (Jonas), or "instinct(ive)" (Callahan).

Advocates of different normative positions on such issues as infanticide, genetic engineering, or artificial nutrition—or the proponents of different ethical bases such as physicalism and personalism—do not see themselves as bedfellows, but in a sense they *are*. They belong to the same professional societies and they are in conversation. This is no mean accomplishment. Evidently these scholars recognize that as different as their positions may be, there is an assumed civility in academic interchange that is basic. This civility includes reasoned discussion—sometimes cool, other times intense. Further, the very notion of a society demands a fundamental civility, one which our society has detailed in various legal statutes. By necessity, societal norms require compromise among opposing positions.

Compromise is inevitable in a pluralistic society that prizes democracy. Hence, for the good of social order and respect for differing individuals, the physicalists are willing to abide a government that allows abortion on demand. And for similar reasons, the personalists are willing to follow laws that prohibit the use of anencephalic infants as organ sources even though such laws mean that other infants will die for lack of transplantable organs.

However important a final compromise may be, advocates of distinctive religious views need not be defensive. And those holding minority views may support their positions with a new respectability in the eyes of the intelligentsia—a traditional bastion for criticism of religion. Western intellectuals, for the first time, are now beginning to recognize that no individual, discipline, or philosophy is beyond the conflicting histories of cultures and movements. No person and no philosophy begins from scratch, and no one has the final word. Formerly, analytical philosophers largely disregarded religious ethics. And what attention was paid to religion tended to be derisive. It was believed that logic could neatly divide the purely moral from the essentially religious and that the former had no logical dependence on the latter. But now many philosophies of language and theories of knowledge are realizing that there is no neutral, abiding morality that is untouched by history. No longer does logical positivism and its dismissal of religion hold the field.[15]

This is not to say that religious propositions are welcomed by philosophers with open arms. But the ground is being leveled—at least in theory—so that religious claims may be taken seriously without immediate rejection. However, the same postmodern or antifoundationalist movement in the humanities that levels the ground, thus favoring religion, also keeps religion from being able to assume any "high ground" in our pluralistic society. So religious insights, regardless of the assumptions of transcendence that the believer may hold, must be advanced on the basis of public criteria if they are to gain a hearing. The coinage of human experience and rationality must be utilized and the offered propositions must "make sense" in the public arena.

Religion has long offered and continues to offer fundamental perspectives that influence society's dilemmas. For example, the Judeo-Christian tradition possesses a long history of fighting for justice for the orphan, homeless, alien, and poor. This tradition is certainly reflected in Western governments' quest for secular justice. Surely it would be unwise for a secular government to adopt or reject certain perspectives of right and wrong solely because their antecedents are religious. The criteria for open democracies in pluralistic societies include notions of the good and of humaneness and reasonableness. Because, as has been argued, religion has previously gone far toward defining the good in society, it is in a strong position to advance tradition-rich perspectives. But it, like other forces in modern society, must make a public case for its views; that is, the case must make sense to average citizens, to society at large.

Religion influences society, but happily the street is two-way. The abolitionist movement of the mid-nineteenth century was vehemently opposed by many Bible-quoting Christians. And we cannot say that these sincere believers were merely citing passages out of context. It must be admitted that the whole Biblical era and the writers of holy writ condoned gross inequality, including slavery. Similarly, Christianity and other world religions were obviously founded in and influenced by a common sexist past, one which unfortunately continues in varying degrees to live in and through them. So society has and can positively influence religion. This is necessary unless religion is to retreat to prerational forms of argument and support an absolutism that today claims limited respect. John Cobb Jr. shows insight in his modest contention that "in addition to grounding and motivating the ethical concern it shares with secular humanism, religious faith provides an ethos and a world view, and it affects the people and communities involved."[16]

Religion does not possess a definitive answer to the difficult issues raised by bioethics. But it consists of many complex traditions that have grappled with the meaning of life and, as such, it has something valuable to offer the contemporary discussion. Today's discussion would indeed be bland, even vapid, if there were no religious traditions, or remnants of such traditions and the positions derived therefrom, upon which we could cast our analytical eyes. Society has increased richness and depth because of the various religious traditions from which our citizenry come. These traditions have bestowed on their adherents the sensibilities, opinions, values, and commitments that inform their moral lives—even if indirectly in some cases.

Now we turn to a brief discussion of the religious and intellectual roots of the two opposing camps in Western thought on the value of human life.

The Physicalist Model of Human Life

By physicalism I mean the view that the human individual is structurally constituted to live according to a pattern that is both essential and natural. To deviate from this pattern is sin.

This view was first formulated by St. Thomas Aquinas, a thirteenth-century Dominican friar who has emerged as the patron philosopher of Roman Catholic theology and has influenced Christian theology in general. Aquinas was particularly dependent on ideas of the Greek philosopher Aristotle (384–322 B.C.).

However, Aristotle's writings were not available to Christians for many centuries, and it was Aristotle's teacher Plato who through his writings profoundly influenced early Christian thinking. Platonic thought was thoroughly dualistic: spiritual life was good and material life was evil. Authentic life was that of the "eternal forms"—perfect, ideal, changeless entities in a realm beyond the material world. According to Plato all that exists in our earthly sphere is but a faint, defective replica of the ideal. For example, a chair here on earth is defective in multiple ways, including the fact that it will eventually deteriorate into dust. It is but an inferior replica of the ideal chair that exists in the heavenly realm. Influenced by Platonic philosophy, early Christian thinkers developed a dualistic view of reality that contrasted the body and the soul, the earthly and the heavenly. (To the medieval theologians enjoyment of sexual intercourse was suspect because of its transience, whereas debate about the number of angels that could alight on a pinhead had genuine significance because it dealt with ideal concerns.)

This was the world into which Aquinas was born, but he took a step beyond it. The writings of Aristotle had recently been discovered, and they diverged significantly from Plato's. Aristotle was a scientist-philosopher who studied biological life and created an elaborate taxonomy. For Plato the "soul" was an immaterial psyche trapped in many material bodies longing to escape. However, according to Aristotle every living thing possesses a soul—the vital principle of life that animates each organic entity to achieve its unique potential, its own natural end or *telos*.[17]

Aquinas followed Aristotle in believing that by carefully studying human life we could discover its proper end or purpose and taxonomically define it. For Aquinas life's "natural" purpose is to live, to reproduce, and to worship God. Thus he developed the rich and influential doctrine of "natural law." And in accordance with classical Greek thought, Aquinas, too, thought in terms of the immutable, the unchanging, the ideal. As was characteristic of his era Aquinas approached life in an a priori fashion; his logic was essentially deductive. Thus he formulated what would become in Christian tradition an absolute norm of nature. In sum, the doctrine of natural law holds that God created rational human beings to live in a particular manner, that the knowledge of "natural" life is available to all honest inquirers, and that one is morally obligated to follow natural law.

Thus traditional Roman Catholic moralists, following Aristotle's idea of a natural *telos* for each particular created object, pushed natural law to its logical conclusion. They viewed every aspect of a human as contributing to a commonsense pattern revealed in nature. For example, the purpose of the reproductive system is the reproduction of humankind; and many concluded that it is therefore sinful—actively or passively—to impede this function. This thinking led to an emphasis on having a large family and a ban on sexual intercourse for purposes other than procreation. In more recent times, it has meant a ban on contraceptive devices and humanly devised forms of human reproduction.

The Vatican's statement of doctrine, "Respect for Human Life in Its Origins and on the Dignity of Procreation," promulgated in 1987, strongly affirms the church's traditional physicalist approach to human sexuality, and it contends that all humans possess full moral status—totally aside from the issue of self-consciousness. The document speaks of the embryo as "the unborn child" who "must be cared for, to the extent possible, in the same way as any other human being as far as medical assistance is concerned." The Church is unflinchingly consistent in reasoning that the embryo "must be treated as a person." Even in-vitro fertilization, which utilizes the husband's sperm, is banned because, among other objections, unused embryos might be used for experimentation or destroyed outright.[18]

Contemporary Physicalist Philosophy

Physicalism is not merely an official position of the Roman Catholic church. It is cogently argued for by theologians and philosophers. One thinker who has articulated a coherent physicalist view of human life is theologian Peter Byrne of Kings College, London.

Professor Byrne uses traditional physicalist thinking to criticize those who would define human individuals in terms of their unique personal capacities, not in terms of their biological nature. He argues in terms of a "rational nature" and "humanity itself": "The unconscious adult, the infant and the aged comatose or non-comatose patient all possess the nature of rational beings. They share in rational nature even though they have lost or not yet acquired the present ability to express that nature. They have the constitution of beings of their kind who are able to display the qualities of a rational existence even though the expression of this nature be impaired or undeveloped."[19] Byrne is explicit. The boundaries delineating rational beings are synonymous with those of "humanity itself"; "valuing rational nature is not a matter of valuing the human being as mere occasion for the display or existence of rationality." Such is labeled "occasionalism." "We value the substance which possesses this nature."[20]

The Personalist Model of Human Life

Ethical personalism focuses on the concrete individual as a feeling and thinking subject who is of highest moral value. Personalism and its roots must be understood as a post-Enlightenment development. The Enlightenment, says Kant, "*is man's emergence from his self-imposed immaturity.*

Immaturity is the inability to use one's understanding without guidance from another. . . . 'Have the courage to use your own understanding!'—that is the motto of enlightenment."[21] Personalism, along with so many other post-Enlightenment movements, breaks with authoritarian, heavy-handed claims of traditional religion—religion that posits supernatural truth as existing quite apart from the individual.

Personalism affirms "self-conscious experience to be the irreducible synoptic key to reality and defines value as of, by, and for persons-in-community. The person is the ontological ultimate, and personality is the fundamental explanatory principle."[22] A twentieth-century American philosophy developed at the Boston University School of Theology, personalism is characterized by several traits: a belief in reason, an appreciation for interdisciplinary studies, a commitment to theism, a nondogmatic view of moral truth, and a belief in freedom.

Personalism is characterized by a passion for the experience of the particular person. This sense is communicated in a 1908 letter from William James to Boston University's B. P. Bowne, the father of American personalism: "It seems to me that you and I are now aiming at exactly the same end. . . . The common foe of both of us is the dogmatist-rationalist-abstractionist. Our common desire is to redeem the concrete personal life."[23]

These and related ideas are not radical today. Because such notions have prevailed in modern consciousness, many of them are part of the contemporary Western intellectual worldview. However, we must realize that viewed through the spectrum of history, they are novel. Today the personalist movement of the late nineteenth and early twentieth centuries has lost its sheen, and the more recent "children" of the Enlightenment, such as existentialism, phenomenology, process thought, and now antifoundationalism are more influential. These schools of thinking, however, have supplemented rather than supplanted personalism.

Armenian Methodism in Early America

Personalism in America is best understood against the intellectual background of the English settlers. The New World was ready for a fresh perspective on the human individual.

A boatload of Puritans, the first English settlers in the new world, found themselves in increasing disagreement with High-Church Anglicanism. "The first Puritans, sure in their own hearts that they were the elect of God, found the doctrine (of election) necessary to sustain them in the tremendous struggles through which they passed."[24] But the settlers soon became quite self-sufficient. Further, as life settled into routine colony existence, the Puritans found that their traditional emphasis on divine power and control made little headway in converting the wayward colonists—folk who relished their new-found frontier freedom. The preaching of divine sovereignty and human inability "produced sluggishness, apathy, self-distrust, despair. It has never been a good way to induce men to repent to tell them that they cannot."[25]

The classic "doctrine of inability" was not well received in New England from the start. The Plymouth Colony settlers had come from England via Holland, where they resided for a short period. There the liberal and liberating thinking of the Dutch theologian Jacobus Arminius[26] was very influential. He was preaching and teaching an unorthodox exalted view of individual freedom and responsibility. Arminius argued for reason and tolerance and insisted on the dignity and freedom of all people. His vision of salvation was not only for the future but also for the present in both an individual and social dimension.[27]

Given the close association of these Puritans with the Netherlands, it is understandable how the seeds of Arminian thought may have come to the New World. In any event, Arminianism was to have a significant effect on American theology. Arminius's emphasis on human free will (a focus very different from divine sovereignty) and the related belief in Jesus Christ's death as *universally* efficacious (as opposed to divine predestination of only the elect) gave his theology a democratic character that rode well in the American saddle.

The Arminian emphasis on human freedom and moral responsibility was good news on the American frontier. Here a strong sense of individualism had emerged as people moved out to explore and possess new lands. Methodism was significantly influenced by Arminian ideas and placed a heavy emphasis on human responsibility.[28] The Methodist church was the most self-consciously Arminian of all the Christian groups in America. According to Gerald McCulloh, "Because of both its polity and its doctrine Methodism was remarkably suited for the new country. Methodism developed a ministry that was itinerant, extempore, and hardy enough to keep up with the westward expansion of American settlement. With the Methodist expansion went one of the most significant prongs of Arminian penetration in America."[29]

The frontiersmen readily heard the circuit riders with their gospel of free will, free grace, and individual responsibility. The rugged frontier where every man was master of his fate seemed tailor-made for a message of freedom of the will. These notions—from very different viewpoints—bolstered a fundamental sense of equality, the basis for the American experiment in democracy.[30] Methodism's congenial theological tenets and also its adaptability to frontier needs helped to quickly make it a major American denomination. The Arminian seed of personal freedom and responsibility took root in the American frontier soil and blossomed into a robust American Methodism that yielded the Boston Personalist Tradition, an urbane offshoot of this person-centered theology.

Contemporary Personalist Philosophy

Uniquely American religious roots have significantly contributed to the free, rational, and morally nondogmatic personalism of modern America. One American theologian and philosopher who champions personal freedom and is broadly in the personalist school of thought is Charles Hartshorne.[31] Hartshorne taught at the University of Chicago for most of his long career and was most recently a professor emeritus at the University of Texas at Austin.

In 1981 Hartshorne wrote an essay on abortion that well demonstrates his high valuation of the human person, freedom, rationality, and responsibility.[32] Such American traits as pragmatism and individuality are also prominent in his writing.

Hartshorne is adamant in arguing against the contention that because the fetus is human and alive, it deserves respect equal to that of persons. Of course, a fetus is genetically human, but so is "every unfertilized egg in the body of a nun." Yes, a fetus is alive, but so are bacteria and mosquitoes—and all plants. Realistically, in its first weeks the fetus is not even comparable to an individual animal. It is "an organized society of single-celled individuals" with a particular origin and a "possible or probable destiny." Fundamental to Hartshorne is the distinction between "possible individual person" and "actual person." Only actual persons, he repeatedly emphasizes, have the capacity to speak, reason, and judge between right and wrong. Hartshorne applies similar reasoning to "hopelessly senile" humans. He recognizes that such an individual may have to be treated as a person for symbolic reasons.

◆ ◆ ◆

This chapter is the first in my argument for a nuanced "proximate" personhood—a position that highly values but is not limited to appreciating the higher functioning of the mind. Religion, broadly understood, is profoundly involved with the argument, for it provides a final grounding. However, it is incumbent upon religious thinkers—and all who would enter the conceptual arena—to marshall public reasons and common data to support their claims. Therefore, in addition to the religious perspective, I include a variety of fields such as law, medicine, philosophy, and history. Finally, I appeal to common reasoning about our shared human experience of contemporary life.

2 Vying Models: Physicalism and Personalism

The physicalist and personalist models of the last chapter were traced through specific historical developments.[1] However, the basic positions represented in those models are not limited to individuals possessing the particular histories sketched above. For example, today the physicalist view attracts people with diametrically opposed opinions on religion and politics—Jews, Catholics, evangelical Protestants, agnostics, atheists, feminists, peace activists, and political conservatives, moderates, and liberals.[2] Similar diversity is also seen among adherents to personalism.

Not only is the general public divided along the physicalist/personalist break, but so are bioethicists. In a perceptive analysis of the concept of "personhood" in bioethics literature, Ruth Macklin found that philosophers, theologians, physicians, and attorneys writing on the notion of personhood easily fall into two camps: "low standard" and "high standard" personhood.[3] In her categorization, low standard personhood is typified by those who contend that from conception on an individual is inherently of high moral value, quite aside from brain function. Low standard personhood corresponds to physicalism, whose historical development was described in the last chapter. High standard personhood, on the other hand, describes the position of thinkers who believe that some form of self-consciousness is necessary for personhood to be achieved—a development that occurs after birth. High standard personhood corresponds to personalism.

Macklin emphasizes that a thinker's position on the moral status of human life is profoundly influenced by his or her antecedently held moral values. That is, one's view of a human and what one selects—or inherits—as criteria for determining the presence of moral status is largely determined by preexisting personal, religious, or philosophical views.

Writers on abortion, euthanasia, and genetic engineering often argue from an assumed consensus on the criteria that supposedly determine moral status. But no such consensus exists. There is even confusion over whether the concept of personhood is something that is discovered or decided. For example, philosopher Mary Ann Warren, clearly in Macklin's "high standard" camp, acknowledges that personhood is a morally weighted, and therefore normative, term. However, in enthusiasm for her own position she confuses empirical discovery of personhood with moral decision about personhood. "I consider [my] claim to be so obvious that I think anyone who denied it, and claimed that a being which satisfied none of [my criteria] was a person all the same, would thereby demonstrate that he had no notion at all of what a person is—perhaps because he had confused the concept of a person with that of genetic humanity."[4] Macklin cites this sentence from Warren and concludes that personhood is of limited, if any, value in resolving arguments in bioethics because of the inconsistent use of the term and the ad hoc arguments advanced by both low and high personhood proponents.

It may be that we should retreat to less grand issues, to subordinate our discussion to secondary notions for which a consensus may be developed on quite pragmatic grounds. There is a precedent for unanimity on specific cases despite great diversity on metaethical foundations: members of a recent national commission on bioethics found uncanny agreement on specific policy recommendations but little agreement on the philosophical bases for those policy positions.[5] Admittedly, it is a challenge to make coherent use of the term person because it has a variety of connotations. But I am convinced that the effort is worthwhile. Further, although anyone can claim to be a personalist, because of the recent philosophical and popular use of the term,[6] I will continue to use *personalism* to designate one camp, Macklin's high standard view; and because an individual's physical nature is of such great importance to the other camp, *physicalism* will continue to be its designation.

In order to understand the philosophical differences and search for areas of agreement, I want to explore and critique the contemporary viewpoints of the opposing personalist and physicalist camps. It is significant that neither takes its theoretical position to its logical conclusion, and I will argue that both of these models have something valuable to contribute to the discussion and to public policy. Personalism may be rationally compelling, but physicalism speaks to society at the important affective level of being.[7]

My own use of the term *person* should be clearly stated. First, I and many others use the word person as a normative term that denotes an individual who possesses maximal moral status. Second, I join other mainstream personhood thinkers in contending that only individuals who possess certain capacities of the higher brain inherently lay claim to the designation of person (although in chapter 3 on proximate personhood I add an important nuance to this claim). The higher-brain capacity that I see as especially crucial is *self-consciousness.*

Much has been written about human consciousness of late, such as Daniel Dennett's ambitiously titled *Consciousness Explained,* Owen Flanagan's *Consciousness Reconsidered,* Colin McGinn's *The Problem of Consciousness,* William Seager's *Metaphysics of Consciousness,* and John Searle's *The Rediscovery of Mind.*[8] Consciousness remains a pressing conundrum to both scientists and philosophers. As Dennett states, "human consciousness is just about the last surviving mystery."[9] My use of the term self-consciousness is just a more precise way of stating human consciousness, since not all humans possess consciousness.

Other higher-brain capacities, rather than self-consciousness, could have been chosen: consciousness, reasoning, language or symbol use, cerebral function, and so forth. I use self-consciousness because it is, by its very nature, so fundamental, and because the term is both clear and practical. *Self-consciousness is the capacity to be aware of one's distinctive self as a relatively autonomous being among other such selves.* Self-consciousness, beyond the other capacities mentioned, is seen as a necessary and sufficient criterion for an individual to be called a person, that is, to possess maximal moral standing. Mere consciousness itself is important, but this capacity is shared with lesser animals that can be sensitively aware of and deeply affected by their peers' or humans' expressed feelings toward them. Similarly, as discussed in chapter 4, many animals are capable of some reasoning and some are very adept at using a type of language. And of course, any creature endowed with an alive cerebrum possesses cerebral function.

In a word, it seems to me that self-consciousness is the most adequate single concept to capture what most of us have in mind when we assign maximal moral standing and, therefore, use the term person. We might say that self-consciousness is the key trait that characterizes persons in a descriptive, nonmoral sense. A related argument is that only individuals who are persons in the nonmoral sense are persons in a moral sense as well, individuals with full moral standing. But explicit attention to this further argument belongs after the discussion of the considerable capacities of animals.

It could be argued that in an ideal universe, all creatures with any higher-brain function would be treated as possessing maximal moral status. However, given the number of humans in the world who are not now treated as indisputably possessing full moral status (one thinks of the millions of malnourished, even starving people), limited financial and political resources cannot practicably be spread equally to serve additional billions of creatures who are but quasi-persons. But proximate personhood thinking contends that we ought to show increased respect to animals of ascending grades of moral status.

Modern Physicalism

The Roman Catholic Church, with its hierarchical structure and nearly one billion adherents, is a formidable proponent of physicalist views. The Vatican strongly promulgates tenets rooted in the physicalist tradition, but an evolution in Catholic bioethics is underway.

David F. Kelly, in his *The Emergence of Roman Catholic Medical Ethics in North America,*[10] identifies three Catholic approaches to medical ethics and the undergirding question of the status of the humans:

- "Physicalism." This approach determines the morality of an act or the status of a human by focusing on the subject and its physical characteristics.
- "Ecclesiastical positivism." Here moral norms and positions are determined by conformity to God's will as expressed by the church's hierarchical magisterium.
- "Personalism." This position is currently emerging and emphasizes "human dimensions, circumstances, and consequences" as it develops ethical principles and perspectives.

The three approaches are historical phases, says Kelly. Physicalism was the dominant mode for doing ethics before Pope Pius XII, ecclesiastical positivism ruled from Pius XII until the Second Vatican Council, and since the Council "personalism" has been on the ascendance.

I use Kelly's historical scheme as a way of systematically describing the breadth of thinking within Catholic bioethical thought today, with major attention devoted to Cardinal Joseph Bernardin's magisterial position. Before proceeding to Bernardin's ethic, I examine the larger context for American Catholic bioethics by briefly dealing with the thought of divergent Catholic moralists William E. May and Benedict Ashley, on the one hand, and Charles Curran, on the other.

Divergence in Catholic Ethics

William E. May is a notable conservative who has articulated a coherent position on the religious and moral status of humans, based on the notion of an eternal human spirit or soul. In his "What Makes a Human Being to Be a Being of Moral Worth?" he deliberately develops a position in answer to those who hold that personhood requires self-consciousness.[11] May distinguishes "moral beings" from "beings of moral worth," but *both* categories are in the physicalist camp. He argues that moral beings are those who are "capable of performing acts of understanding, of choice, and of love." These humans are moral beings because they are "minded" entities. Not all humans are "minded" moral beings (for instance, newborns) but all humans are "beings of moral worth" because all share "something rooted in their being human beings to begin with." This "something" is "the principle immanent in human beings, a constituent and defining element of their entitative makeup, that makes them to be what they and who they are: beings of moral worth capable of becoming minded entities or moral beings; it is a principle of immateriality or of transcendence from the limitations of materially individuated existence" (425). Significantly, "neonates, infants, raving maniacs and fetuses" are not "moral beings," but they are "beings of moral worth." And as such they possess "inalienable rights" and are "valuable, precious, irreplaceable just because [they exist]" (416).

Benedict Ashley, a moral theologian at the Aquinas Institute of Theology, St. Louis, is in basic agreement with May but uses different language in developing his own perspective and is more charitable toward other views. Ashley employs the notions of objectivism and subjectivism.[12] The former holds that one determines human nature by studying human beings as simply objects among other objects. Subjectivism, on the other hand, views humans as self-conscious subjects that are ultimately beyond objective, empirical study.

Ashley articulates these definitions and chooses objectivity as his basis for ethics. However, he sees objectivity and true subjectivity as finally complementary. He arrives at this conclusion by positing that self-consciousness (the basis of subjectivity) is one merely *objective* fact about human nature. But regardless of one's self-consciousness and its importance, there are "basic human needs" that are objectively known and that "define the person throughout time and space, [and therefore] no essentially new ethical problems can arise."[13] Ashley believes that subjectivist theologians are developing forceful positions that "will enrich moral theology and make it more sensitive and compassionate," but that the Catholic church will maintain its prophetic mission and avoid cultural relativism by grounding ethics "in an understanding of human nature that is transcultural and objectively verifiable."[14]

Charles Curran, a professor at Southern Methodist University, is possibly one of the subjectivist Catholic theologians Ashley has in mind. Curran writes approvingly of the contemporary emphasis on the human person as subject. He appreciates how certain Vatican II documents recognize personal dignity and responsibility.[15] Curran sees two different ways of developing the subjective emphasis: "The emphasis on the personal subject and the freedom and dignity of the person could be exaggerated into a liberalistic individualism unless one remembers that the individual person lives in relationship with other persons and communities."[16] Curran is sensitive to the dangers of pure subjectivism and isolated individualism. He sees the individual person in relation to community and with openness to the Infinite.

Such a view of the subject is very different from that of traditional Catholic theology that sees humans in terms of a natural order, an order that mandates that individuals make sense of their lives by assuming stable roles within existing patterns and structures. Curran further describes this shift in worldview as that of "classicism" yielding to historical consciousness: "Classicism thought in terms of the immutable, the eternal and the unchanging; whereas historical consciousness emphasizes evolution, growth, change and historicity. A classicist approach concentrates on order and tries to put things into an order that tends to be conceived in an a priori way; whereas historical consciousness reflects the reality of growth, movement and tension that defies complete order and categorization."[17] Curran holds that often Roman Catholic theology has proclaimed as an absolute norm of nature that which was merely a culturally and historically conditioned reality.

Bernardin's "Seamless Garment" Ethic

Cardinal Bernardin has brought a freshness in approach to his church's traditional pro-life stance. Bernardin is a gifted Catholic leader who is a conceptualizer, diplomat, and effective promoter. He was one of the authors of the U.S. bishops' 1983 pastoral letter, "The Challenge of Peace." That same year he was elected chairman of the bishops' pro-life activities committee and set out a new pro-life agenda in his call for a "consistent ethic of life," more popularly dubbed the "seamless garment" ethic.

In a major address at Fordham University in 1983 Bernardin articulated his consistent ethic,[18] and at two other church universities over the following two years defended and amplified his vision.[19] At Fordham, Bernardin boldly stated that the bishops' pastoral letter on peace

links the questions of abortion and nuclear war. The letter does not argue the case for linkage; that is one of my purposes today. It is important to note that the way these two issues are joined in the pastoral places the American bishops in a unique position in the public-policy discourse of the nation. No other major institution presently holds these two positions in the way the Catholic bishops have joined them. This is both a responsibility and an opportunity. I am convinced that the pro-life position of the church must be developed in terms of a comprehensive and consistent ethic of life.[20]

Bernardin sees multiple threats to the "sacredness of life" in modern society. The bishops' peace pastoral was a defense of human life in the context of potential nuclear annihilation; the cardinal's expanded context includes concern about abortion, euthanasia, genetics, hunger, human rights, capital punishment, and care for the underprivileged.

Just as the bishops intended to impact the national debate on nuclear armaments through their pastoral, so Bernardin at Fordham announced his intention to shape a consistent ethic of life for common culture. The backdrop for Bernardin's proposal is what he sees as an unprecedented challenge to fragile human life presented by new technologies in both modern warfare and modern medicine.

Bernardin is clear about what he is calling for: a profound respect for human life. He uses broad strokes in portraying a vision that he invites others to think through further and implement. He summons poets, theologians, technicians, scientists, politicians, and "plain citizens" and articulates the need for "detailed balancing, distinguishing and connecting of different aspects."

Bernardin has been criticized by anti-abortion forces for his seamless garment approach because some feel it weakens the focus on abortion.[21] Bernardin defends his inclusive proposal with the argument that Catholicism possesses a broad and profound moral vision concerned with all innocent human life. A variety of issues are interrelated and must be addressed with strength and subtlety. The tradition is concerned with protecting and promoting life along a continuum—from the womb to the terminally ill. Not content to merely protect fetal life in his church's popular anti-abortion efforts, Bernardin expands his call to include the provision of shelter for the homeless, education for the illiterate, and care for the undocumented immigrant, the unemployed worker, and the disabled individual. He refuses to separate right-to-life concerns from quality-of-life issues, seeing the seamless-garment principle translating into specific political and economic positions on issues such as tax policy, generation of employment, feeding programs, and health care.

Bernardin's Theological Anthropology

Cardinal Bernardin, in yet a fourth address in the mid-1980s, expanded on his view of humanity.[22] Speaking to Illinois health care professionals the cardinal explicitly delineated his religious view of the human individual. Ironically, this address on theological anthropology given to hospital executives rivaled, if it did not surpass, his previous university lectures in philosophical sophistication and political subtlety.

Bernardin calls for an "authentic medical humanism." It is appropriate for modern medicine to look to the philosophy of humanism for guidance in light of the challenges provided by advanced technology and constrained budgets. Humanism itself is praised by Bernardin as recognizing human potential and seeking to foster human progress and civilization. However, he criticizes "pragmatic" medical humanism in favor of what he terms "personalist humanism."

Pragmatic humanism, Bernardin argues, is a secular, purely utilitarian philosophy—the greatest good for society regardless of individual claims of the weak and voiceless. "Implicit in pragmatic humanism is the fact that society may diminish the value and dignity of non-productive persons for the sake of the common welfare . . ."(47). The cardinal lists fetuses, newborn babies, the comatose, and the hopelessly senile as "not enjoying full human dignity" in the eyes of pragmatic humanists. What dignity these individuals have is merely "extrinsically attributed," and what may be done with such patients is subject to cost-benefit analysis and manipulation. More than once Bernardin uses the slogan "might makes right" to describe pragmatic humanism.

Bernardin's Catholic option stands in contrast to pragmatic humanism. This perspective follows "a higher moral law" and affirms the "inherent value and dignity of every living human person, even if unwanted or undervalued by others." The cardinal claims that every human, regardless of "age, intelligence, degree of social adaptability, state of health or social usefulness" has the right to life found in the Declaration of Independence, a document he cites as normative (48). Bernardin rejects the pragmatists' interest in "the seeming efficiency of abortion and euthanasia" because such solutions erode human dignity. Bernardin portrays the two camps as diametrically opposite: One holds that human dignity is rooted in "being human"; the other believes that human dignity is found in "doing human things" such as acting and thinking.

An Ambiguous Ethic

Cardinal Joseph Bernardin performed a valuable service to his church and to the nation by his forceful proclamation of a consistent ethic of life. However, it appears that the cardinal is attempting to hold old wine in new wine skins, and the result is an ambiguous ethic.

Bernardin appears to set pragmatic and Catholic humanism in clear opposition. However, the diplomatic cardinal muddies the water. Two sources of abivalence—ideology and money—affect Bernardin's insightful thinking. The way he deals with them makes what would otherwise be a sacred/profane standoff into a soft-edged theology.

In regard to ideology, Bernardin does not want to be read as a vitalist. Catholic humanism "does not constitute an idolatrous worship of human life as an absolute good." He recognizes that there must be "reasonable limits to society's obligation to prolong lives." Yet in the next paragraph a tension arises as he asserts that "human equality stems from being human rather than from any given threshold of human achievement. . . . Though no two of us are exactly equal in anything because of our individual heredity and environment, we are equal in the fundamental fact of our humanness" (48). So what prohibits medicine from morally viewing every human life—regardless of condition—as an absolute good?

Bernadin is also preoccupied with high-technology medicine, its proven effectiveness, and its high cost. He recognizes that modern medicine can keep the bodies of dying patients alive for a long time at great expense, and although the logic of his threshholdless notion of valuable human life would push him to commit enormous resources for every patient, he backs away:

Health care personnel cannot do all things for all persons. They cannot provide all services to all members of the human family. The question they daily encounter, therefore, is how to serve people best. Making those concrete judgments often involves a painful struggle. Health care providers daily find themselves having to balance a variety of values, seeking to respond to the competing claims of different populations and different perspectives. They must often perceive themselves as the great compromisers.[23]

The cardinal shows himself to be quite adept at compromise in this address to health care executives. But Bernardin's hearers and readers legitimately may expect the cardinal to offer more guidance than mere acknowledgment of difficult, competing claims.

A further problem in Cardinal Bernardin's several addresses is his ambiguous use of key concepts. In view of Kelly's description of Catholic bioethics evolving from physicalism to personalism and in light of my own analysis of these terms in chapter 1, what is one to make of Bernardin's espousal of "personalist humanism"? No one would quarrel with Bernardin's emphasis on the importance of the human person (that is, the importance of those with maximal moral standing), but is it an advance beyond traditional thinking and should the ethic be cast solely in anthropomorphic terms?[24] A basic issue is the cleric's understanding of the term "person." Is "person" to be seen in pre-Pius XII terms of objectivity or in the post-Vatican II terms of a more responsible, self-determining subject? Bernardin appears to embrace both views simultaneously. Although this move may be a religious and political necessity, it is a serious conceptual flaw in his fine addresses.

Obviously in his rhetoric (personalist humanism) and in his manner (nondogmatic and dialogical) Bernardin is in the modern personalist camp. However, in far-reaching statements of substance (such as, "human dignity is rooted in 'being human' rather than 'doing human things'") the cardinal comes across as a physicalist. And what resolution is offered? Here Bernardin dons his pastoral, diplomatic hat rather than his creative, conceptual one. In speaking to hospital executives he cites the challenges of practicing modern medicine, appeals for "reasonable limits to society's obligation to prolong lives," and readily acknowledges the need for compromise in balancing a variety of values.[25]

As has been mentioned, Bernardin recognizes that he does not have the expertise to work out definitively the vision he proclaims. But his basic vision is conflictual and he offers no resolution at fundamental junctures. He does point to the seemingly interminable conflict of basic values facing medicine, but his answer appears to be that practitioners should do their conscientious best. This answer is true but insufficient.

Bernardin would have done his hearers and all of society a favor had he been clearer in his use of two key terms—*human person* and *respect for life*. In regard to persons, Bernardin "affirms the inherent value and dignity of every living human person"(48). Intelligence, age, and supposedly factors such as deformity of newborns and health of the dying in no way dilute that inherent value. Yet he says that he does not want to make "dignity of life" a "taboo" principle. He suggests that some individual lives need not be prolonged if such endeavors strain either society's limited resources or our "reasonable limits." So evidently some lives may be allowed to wane even if more could be done to sustain them. Perhaps Bernardin has in mind such cases as advanced Alzheimer's patients of old age who are near death but could be sustained through IV feedings for a few more months. But why should another ten or twenty thousand dollars not be spent on nursing care while advanced Alzheimer's patients are artificially fed, if every human life, simply as human life, possesses inherent dignity? Would we withhold such feedings from a conscious cancer patient who desired to live out her last three months of precious earthly existence? Bernardin's failure to grapple with the distinctive features of human life on which we base our high valuing of personal existence is unfortunate. Surely his appeal for respect for the dignity of every human life from "womb to tomb" is of little help, if not a detriment to this end. Finally, he seems to rely on our basic human intuitions, which tell us that it is unreasonable to try to prolong every day of life in every patient.

Cardinal Bernardin speaks of the need for America to develop a "respect life" attitude that can mobilize and sustain a comprehensive and consistent pro-life ethic in this nation. As a slogan, "respect life" is good. But in the real world of hard bioethical decisions, it is at best ambiguous.

Columnist Ellen Goodman wrote about an eighty-five-year-old terminally ill man who decided to end his life by ceasing to eat. Goodman said his choice deserved "respect."[26] Respect for choice is a rationale used by a variety of people: those who want their nation to have nuclear weapons as long as any potential enemy has them, those who believe a woman has a basic right to control her reproductive processes, and those Oregonians who voted for physician-assisted dying as a legal possibility for the terminally ill. Bernardin must give further reasons why all life as such must be respected or he must be clearer about what qualities of life deserve respect. Whether his rationale is finally rooted in the physicalist camp, as it appears to be, or whether it is genuinely personalist makes a significant difference.

Bernardin has succeeded in affecting public consciousness with his notion of Catholicism's pro-life stance as a "seamless garment." Whether he succeeds in setting the agenda for public policy is another matter.[27]

Personhood

The story of baby John Pearson is the British equivalent of America's original Baby Doe case. Born in 1980, Baby Pearson was an apparently uncomplicated Down syndrome infant whose parents decided that they did not want their newborn to live. (A post-mortem examination revealed a damaged heart and lungs but these defects were not known during the newborn's life.) The attending pediatrician, Dr. Leonard Arthur, complied with the parents' wishes and prescribed nursing care only and large dosages of adult pain medication. Dr. Arthur faced murder charges in this highly publicized case and after supportive testimony from leading physicians was finally acquitted. A BBC poll showed that the public by a margin of 86 to 7 favored a "not guilty" verdict if a physician was charged with murder because, with parental consent, "he sees to it that a severely handicapped baby dies."[28]

Raanan Gillon, writing in the *British Medical Journal,* justified Dr. Arthur's use of euthanasia on the pivotal basis of personhood: "I believe that the issue turns on the question of personhood and that it is because the newly born infant is not a person that it is justifiable in cases of severe handicap to 'allow it to die' in the way Dr. Arthur allowed baby Pearson to die."[29]

The perspective limiting personhood to self-conscious beings is gaining increased attention and prominence.[30] The essential claim is that only individuals with capacities for significant cerebral functioning possess a morally unique claim to existence. Persons are defined (analytically) as living entities with full moral standing. Defenders of personhood claim (synthetically) that only those with significant cerebral functioning have full moral standing, and that therefore only they are persons. Significant cerebral functioning is variously perceived: individuals who are self-conscious and capable of self-direction (Engelhardt), able to enter meaningful relationships (McCormick), capable of minimal independent existence (Shelp), and in possession of a minimal 20–40 I.Q. (Fletcher). Underlying these definitions is the assumption that newborns—*all* newborns—are not, strictly speaking, persons. That is, newborns do not possess maximal moral standing because they are not self-conscious, intentionally choosing individuals. These theorists deal with the status of newborns in various ways, from allowance of early infanticide (Tooley) to the positing of an imputed personhood (Engelhardt).

Michael Tooley is a philosopher now based in Colorado who comes close to taking a pure personalist philosophy to its logical conclusion. Tooley has long argued a personhood position that leads him to advocate a liberal policy on abortion and a "radical" (Tooley's word) permission for infanticide. According to Tooley, only a being "possessing the concept of a self as a continuing subject of experience and other mental states" and that believes "it is itself such a continuing entity," qualifies for uniquely personal status.[31] In his *Abortion and Infanticide* he gives a full-fledged elaboration of his concept of person. At one point in his extensively and closely argued volume Tooley appeals to what he sees as common sense, suggesting that most people would agree

that anything that has, and has exercised, all of the following capacities is a person, and that anything that has never had any of them is not a person: the capacity for self-consciousness; the capacity to think; the capacity for rational thought; the capacity to arrive at decisions by deliberation; the capacity to envisage a future for oneself; the capacity to remember a past involving oneself; the capacity for being a subject of non-momentary interests; the capacity to use language.[32]

Engelhardt's Ethic

Tristram Engelhardt is a free-thinking physician-ethicist who has systematically worked out a more moderate philosophy of personhood.In his important *The Foundations for Bioethics,* Engelhardt accepts Tooley's basic criteria for personhood but places emphasis on the social role that newborns fill in society. Newborns are not persons in the strict sense, argues

Engelhardt, but, in a deeply held social, cultural sense, they are. We treat newborns as if they were persons; recognition and appreciation of this role is imperative.[33]

Engelhardt begins his discussion of personhood with the statement, "Not all humans are equal." It goes without saying that not all humans are persons, at least in the strict sense of that word. Fetuses are prime examples. Further, in a theoretical sense, not all persons are human. For instance, ET of Hollywood fame is surely a person but is not human. That ET is a person by virtue of self-consciousness is evident enough, but whether a human society would grant full moral standing is less obvious.

Persons in the "strict sense," says Engelhardt, are those individuals who are self-conscious, rational, free-to-choose, and capable of moral concern. Such individuals and only these individuals have an "absolute" right to respect and to existence itself. Engelhardt has taken his cue from Kant, who wrote that morality is the consequence of autonomous human beings inhabiting the intelligible world: "'We think of ourselves as free, we transport ourselves into the intelligible world as members of it and know the autonomy of the will together with its consequence, morality. . . .'"[34] Because only persons are capable of reflecting on the world and rationally determining accounts of meaning from a moral point of view, respect for persons is of highest importance.[35] The moral importance of persons derives from our capacity for self-reflection, which itself "requires us to treat ourselves as moral agents," says Engelhardt. In other words, the rulemakers, that is, individuals who are capable of conceiving of moral rules in the first place, deserve special moral standing. There is a sort of commonplace logic to such reasoning.

But Engelhardt realizes that we treat with respect humans who do not share in these rational capacities, and he creatively grapples with this dilemma. He takes seriously our human experience of treating infants, retarded individuals, and the senile as we treat those who have undisputed moral standing.

Infants, for instance, are not persons in any strict sense, but nevertheless we treat them as such. We "impute" to these individuals a certain moral status, despite their obvious lack of self-consciousness. They do not intrinsically have a right to it, but we give it for other good reasons. Engelhardt points to Kant's contention that at times it is good to adopt practices that in general lead to protection of persons even if no concrete person's autonomy is directly at stake. Engelhardt adapts Kant's perspective to his own model of personhood and the dilemma of dealing with such individuals as the senile and the retarded. These individuals are not themselves "moral agents" and therefore do not have "intrinsic moral standing." But Engelhardt argues that we usually ought to treat such individuals "as if" they were persons. Such an individual has the role of "being a person for social considerations."

Similarly, the fetus does not possess intrinsic moral standing. However, a person may value a fetus as if the "entity" were a person and do so for good reasons. Engelhardt contends that there should be rules against maiming and injuring but not killing fetuses because of the "future person" the fetus will likely become. "Future persons can have the standing of actual persons who we know will in the future exist."[36] This is so because the act of maiming a fetus, which will likely be a person in a certain number of months or years, has moral implications akin to injuring an extant person because the result is identical.

Engelhardt suggests various senses of person as important:

person$_1$ is a moral agent who is a person in the strict sense;

person$_2$ is a person in the social sense and as such is treated with "nearly full rights" (an infant is given as an example);

person$_3$ applies to neonates, a class of individuals whose moral status is not yet as strong or secure as that of infants;

person$_4$ refers to individuals who once were persons$_1$, but are capable of only minimal interaction as found in senile or retarded individuals;

person$_5$ pertains to the severely and profoundly retarded individuals who never were and never will be persons.[37]

Engelhardt sees a categorical difference of intrinsic significance between persons "in a strict sense" and persons "in a social sense." The "basic grammar of morality" pertains to the former whereas only extrinsic moral reasoning can be used in justifying actions regarding the social persons. Engelhardt appears a bit defensive here: "Some may find it disquieting that the strongest rights claims that can be advanced in favor of humans who are not persons in the strict sense depend on consequentialist, if not indeed on utilitarian, considerations. These conclusions do not represent an assault on those who are not persons in the strict sense. The circumstances reflect the limits of secular philosophical reasoning. Only some of our prejudices can be justified."[38]

In concluding his definitions of person, Engelhardt deals with the problem of sleep and embodiment. The issue is the moral status of the sleeping person. Why, for instance, does an individual classified as person$_1$ retain his or her moral status when temporarily oblivious to and out of conscious control of the capacities that bestow unique personal status? He gives two replies. First, our self-conscious minds are embodied in spatiotemporally extended brains and bodies that by their nature experience periods of rest. Throughout the day a normal brain will experience brief pulsations of inattention, and at night there will be prolonged inattention by the conscious mind. The important point, says Engelhardt, is whether a person's self-conscious identity can "reasonably be presumed to span" the temporal discontinuities. Engelhardt's second point is consequentialist. If strict continuity of self-consciousness were required, the "minimum moral fabric of the peaceable moral community would be set aside. . . . In the case of competent adults not only does one know whose embodiment is at stake (unlike fetuses and infants, whose bodies are not yet anyone's embodiment), but taking a view that would allow the killing of sleeping persons would make a coherent portrayal of a moral community of spatiotemporally extended persons impossible."[39] Finally, beyond the arguments about intrinsic moral worth and its relationship to self-consciousness, Engelhardt acknowledges that if persons$_1$ linked their identity to continuous self-consciousness so that they morally could be terminated in their sleep, the very idea of a civilized society would be impossible.

Religious vs. Secular Ethics

Engelhardt's *The Foundations of Bioethics* is a significant contribution to the field. He grapples with the moral status of marginal persons and other issues against the larger backdrop of conflicting religious contentions in our essentially secular era. He is clear throughout his book that he is not against religious views but that no one of them can claim general allegiance. Engelhardt sees himself as advocating and pursuing a secular bioethics, which he defines as "the attempt to find those understandings that can be justified across particular moral communities, traditions and ideologies, including not only particular religious communities, but particular secular communities of thought as well."[40]

On the one hand, Engelhardt sees secular ethics as performing essentially a mediatory role in light of the moral claims of conflicting camps.

On the other hand, his own ethics comes through as substantive, making moral claims in its own right. For instance, in discussing his view of humans, Engelhardt asserts that individuals who are persons in only a social sense cannot be justified as persons by "the basic grammar of morality" because "such entities do not have intrinsic moral standing."[41] However, this category of social persons includes infants and very young children. And to assert that ethics' basic grammar does not apply to such individuals clearly goes beyond utilizing ethics as a mediator merely seeking common ground. In sum, Engelhardt's avowedly secular ethics is but another formulation of ethics, be it called religious or secular. This is not bad or even unfortunate; it is inevitable for any theorist who gets beyond mere description of others' views.

Engelhardt's writing on personhood is very helpful in its clear description of the rudiments that underlie the very idea of human morality. However, taken to its logical conclusion in normative ethics, his thinking leads to questionable ends. For instance, he argues that infanticide is permissible, at least theoretically. Only secondary, consequentialist considerations override this allowance. The lack of respect for neonatal life is not moral meanness, but rather reflects, in Engelhardt's words, "the limits of secular philosophical reasoning." Strictly speaking "*years* go by before there is evidence of the life of a person."[42]

Are we to believe that it may be intrinsically moral—albeit coldhearted and wrong for consequentialist reasons—to allow an infant to die because the child is not yet the subject of a developed self-consciousness? Such thinking would be morally questionable to most religious and secular people. Although secular philosophical reasoning may appear to be a logical common denominator in our pluralistic society, it is not. Most Americans are neither thoroughly secular nor adept at classically liberal philosophical reasoning. The concept of proximate personhood, developed in chapter 3, is offered as a move beyond and an answer to Engelhardt's theoretical openness to infanticide, a position so opposed by our moral intuitions.

An Enlightenment Ethic

What type of ethic does Engelhardt develop? His basic grammar appears to be an essentially Kantian ethic of reason, which he champions as a common basis for societal ethics, regardless of what religious peculiarities some may wish to add. Kant made great contributions to ethical theory and normative ethics, and Engelhardt is a very fine Kantian ethicist. But no Kantian ethics or any single ethical system is "*the* language of morals."[43] No one language of morals is available, including that of secular ethics. Engelhardt, following Kant and to some degree Hegel, appears to assume that all persons, if truly rational, would come to similar conclusions. After all, Kant was a leading Enlightenment figure, thinking like others in his era that reason could unite humankind in common pursuit of peace, harmony, and beauty.

Engelhardt is unabashedly Kantian in his approach. Yet as he develops his substantive arguments for particular and unique positions (such as the moral status of various humans) he seems to lose sight of the fact that he is working from a certain framework—with the assets and liabilities that accompany all particular points of view. Engelhardt's fine volume would be even better if the normative positions he argues for later in the book were nuanced by epistemological points made early on. For instance, in his early discussion of the emergence of secular bioethics he states that this philosophy may occasion disappointment "when final answers are not forthcoming." Further, he recognizes that there may be many "human realities" and that "the portrayal of the conditions of reality in any detail is itself conditioned by the perspective of a particular historical period."[44] These qualifications get lost along the way as Engelhardt argues for his own ethical vision.

Who—or *What*—Is a Person?

To the question "Who is a person?" the answers of Engelhardt and Bernardin, to say nothing of Tooley and May, are far apart. Even if they all defined personhood in similar ethical fashion (such as, that only persons have full moral status), they surely differ on the characteristics that an entity must possess to be called a person. One might expect that there would be unanimity on something as basic as criteria for determining personhood and merely division on the particulars. As the above discussion shows, such is not the case. A peculiarity of bioethics, alluded to in the early pages of this chapter, is that among religiously and philosophically diverse people agreement on an answer to a particular ethical dilemma is more probable than agreement on the undergirding reasons that support the answer.

The neologism personhood serves as a convenient rubric under which one may determine the moral status of various beings. If we were content to follow the dictionary, we could be somewhat clearer than we are at present in our use of *person* and related words.

Just consider the two words, human and person. *The Random House Dictionary of the English Language* lists *human* first as an adjective and second as a noun. *Person,* on the other hand, is listed only as a noun. *Human* pertains primarily to the nature of humankind; *person* generally connotes a socially developed and self-conscious human subject. But current usage of the words human and person is ambiguous on all sides—left and right. Joseph Fletcher speaks of "indicators of humanhood." Paul Lehmann writes about "what it takes to make and to keep human life human."[45] Cardinal Bernardin talks of the inherent value of every human person regardless of extenuating considerations. Dictionary usage follows actual usage in a society, and if contemporary usage of such terms as human and person are any indication, tomorrow's dictionaries will give even broader definitions of these terms than they currently do.

The generic term *life* is similarly used in a loose manner. Witness the opposing ideologies that include the term in their slogans sanctity of life and quality of life. In the former life stands for all human life and in the latter it means strictly self-conscious life. But our lack of terminological precision belies the deeper conceptual conflict about how we perceive our humanity, our very existence.

We all possess gut-level responses to the question of moral status and human life. An animal or human individual that looks or acts like us is quite naturally given a higher ranking than entities that do not. But just because we can sustain marginal human beings does not necessarily mean we should. Take, for instance, a fetus that will die without experimental intrauterine surgery. Or consider a million-dollar baby in a neonatal intensive care unit, who, because of profound retardation, will never gain self-consciousness. Or think about the terminally ill patient who is ready to die and wants to expire naturally but who must by law be revived by paramedics summoned by nonaccepting relatives.[46] Not all human lives—even self-conscious personal lives—should be sustained in certain circumstances. For example, there could be a functioning, socially productive member of the moral community who is excluded from an intensive care unit through a morally legitimate triage mechanism. Where the line should be, and who should draw it, are pressing issues.

In the landmark 1973 *Roe v. Wade* decision on abortion, the Supreme

Court said that it had no intention of settling the difficult question of when "human"[47] life begins. But it declared that a bold line should be drawn at the point of viability and that the pregnant woman and her physician could decide on abortion at any time before then. Whether and how long the viability threshold will continue is an open question, given the Reagan and Bush administration appointments that continue to dominate the Court. However, we all would benefit if we could agree on the facts. Certain facts should be incontrovertible. For example, human life is that life belonging to the species *Homo sapiens* and begins in an individuated form at conception or shortly thereafter. A human begins as a single-celled entity one to two hours after a sperm begins to successfully wiggle its way into the nucleus of an ovum. *The controversial question is when that developing human embryo/fetus/newborn/infant/child possesses a life of full moral status such as the life of any reader of this page.*

This question, which is at the core of this book's concerns, is today commonly viewed in quite an individualistic or particularistic manner. That is, the focus is limited to the status of a particular human being or class of humans or merely the human species. Thus the arguments of Engelhardt and Bernardin, along with most other Western perspectives, are essentially particularistic. A particular person, for instance, is of great importance in his or her own self. Every individual, merely as an individual, possesses basic human rights. And the Western concern for individual human rights has brought many benefits to modern life.

However, the person—and our definition of a person as having full moral status—possesses great symbolic significance beyond any individual. From this we construe all of life and its meaning or lack thereof. And for this reason our discussion of personhood must transcend talk of mere existence. Our discussion is catapulted beyond the merely particularistic realm of the individual into the social and religious arenas. It is only in society and finally in religion where a determination of the moral status of individuals and classes of beings is rooted. The particularistic, social, and religious dimensions of this discussion warrant further comment.

The Particularistic Dimension

First, both personalism and physicalism are essentially particularistic in outlook. Personalism holds that the actual possession of higher-brain capacities is all important. From this position, it follows that infanticide may be inherently moral, since there is no self-conscious subject whose life is at stake. Personalists focus on the singular, particular individual. Engelhardt, who gives some attention to persons-in-a-social-sense, is an exception.

Although the Vatican, as the leading physicalist advocate, is diametrically opposed to the personhood school of thinking, including its nuanced forms, it, too, is essentially particularistic. The human species is the only important issue at stake. May views every particular embryo as a manifestation of an eternal essence that inhabits all members of the species. Bernardin speaks of the "inherent value and dignity of every living human person, even if unwanted or undervalued by others." This value exists regardless of "age, intelligence, degree of social adaptability, state of health or social usefulness."

It is not unusual that physicalism and personalism—although diametrically opposed—are both particularistic. Contemporary Western society, whether manifest in left, right, or centrist political parties, is dominated by particularism. It is not happenstance that the value of every marginal human being—be it an unwanted fetus, a disabled newborn, or a terminally ill patient—is being questioned most rigorously in the advanced Western world. There are at least two reasons for this phenomenon. First, it is primarily in the developed world that the technology exists to sustain the lives of marginal human beings—be they young or old. Second, the seeds of modern individualism and particularism were planted long ago by Judeo-Christian beliefs and nurtured by the Enlightenment. But in regard to this second development, the road to Western individualism has not been straight.

Suspicion of individual rights, if not downright disregard for them, has characterized much of Western history. For instance, the ancient Hebrew people and their God were primarily concerned with the *nation* of Israel, not with particular Israelites. In the Middle Ages individuals were secondary to society and religion. Particular lives would soon die, but the divine laws that gave life its form and meaning were eternal and hence preeminent. Walter Ullman writes that in the Middle Ages the "individual was so infinitesimally small a part that his interests could easily be sacrificed at the altar of the public good, at the altar of society itself, because nothing was more dangerous to society than the corrosion and undermining of the very element which held it together, that is, the faith."[48] Hence, collective punishment and even the death penalty for doctrinal disagreement were not unusual. Even two hundred years ago conservative critics of the Enlightenment such as Edmund Burke scorned the particular person's "private stock of reason" and feared lest "the commonwealth itself would, in a few generations, crumble away, be disconnected into the dust and powder of individuality, and at length dispersed to all the winds of heaven."[49]

Yet, beyond strong state interests, or, more accurately, because of revamped notions of these interests, a systemic and strong emphasis on the value of the particular citizen developed in the West. In bioethics today that development is seen in the unprecedented swing of the pendulum from physician paternalism to patient autonomy. Interestingly, autonomy of the patient and important contemporary emphases such as freedom of speech and religious liberty have their ancient precursors:

> In the Hebrew scriptures, attitudes toward the importance of the individual evolve. For instance, the exilic prophet Ezekiel called for a change in traditional thinking: "What do you mean by repeating this proverb concerning the land of Israel, 'The fathers have eaten sour grapes, and the children's teeth are set on edge'? As I live, says the Lord God, this proverb shall no more be used by you in Israel. Behold, all souls are mine; the soul of the father as well as the soul of the son is mine: the soul that sins shall die." (18:2–4)

> The supreme worth of the individual is extolled in the Gospels. Jesus stated, "in as much as ye have done it unto one of the least of these my brethren, ye have done it unto me." (Matthew 25:40)

> The Greeks had their city-states in which each man (no women or slaves) directly voted on corporate affairs.

> Immanuel Kant, the son of a Lutheran clergyman and a leading exponent of the Enlightenment, profoundly influenced Western life and philosophy with his categorical imperative: "Act in such a way that you always treat humanity, whether in your own person or in the person of any other, never simply as a means, but always at the same time as an end."[50]

It is simplistic to suggest that particularism, per se, is good or bad. At this point we may conclude that giving value to each individual is mandatory but that personalism's interest in an individual's mental capacity or physicalism's special concern for fetal life may be too restricted a focus. In light of our increased knowledge of the mental span of humans in their lifetimes and the mental capacity of other animal life, mere repetition of the mantra "human life is sacred" will no longer do. No simple slogan will resolve the debate over moral status.

The Social Dimension

Traditional societies have been and remain more concerned with social well-being (the welfare of family, community, or nation) than with particular individuals and their unique desires. For example, the Bantu culture of central Africa is fundamentally different from that of the West in that most Bantu languages possess no term corresponding to the English word "person." Many traditional Africans are not aware of themselves as separate beings but see themselves as part of a larger whole. Of course they have particular names and this signifies that they do distinguish themselves one from another. However, these names often signify the individual's status in a particular group and usually her or his relationship to kin and the larger village.[51]

Life within traditional societies has had great problems. The excesses of religion and the stifling of individual voices by this century's statism and communism are egregious. The spirit of democracy, which recently has flowered or is budding in Latin and South America, Eastern Europe, the former USSR, and in the People's Republic of China are signs that the particular person throughout the world may be coming into his and her own. However, lest we become too preoccupied with individual initiative, rights, and production, we must remember an enduring truth: individual life only assumes a richness of meaning—indeed, any meaning at all—in a social context. As social scientists have long said, humans are social beings.[52] A particular human finds life's basic meaning in her or his relationship to others—usually in the family unit and in various voluntary, civic, and religious communities.

Renee Fox believes that medicine is serving modern society as its "primary symbolic media" for dealing with a series of "metaquestions" such as, What is life? What is death? When does life end? Is it better not to have been born at all than to have been born with severe defects? The fundamental questions in such debates as that over genetic engineering are much more in the realm of morals and metaphysics than they are in the domain of biology and science.[53]

The biomedical sciences are making such breakthroughs that important bioethical issues, with their deep existential roots, can no longer remain essentially private matters, if indeed they ever were. Society, through its courts, legislatures, and commissions, is debating and deciding on matters such as surrogate motherhood, voluntary euthanasia, and abortion. And on what grounds—be they cultural, moral, religious—are government officials deciding these issues? Perhaps the answer is that democratic governments look to no ideology but to the popular mind for direction on difficult issues. But in modern states, where the reigning principles of separation of church and state and particularly civil rights have spawned ubiquitous pluralism and individuality, there is an increasingly thin cultural consensus upon which society can form its fundamental judgments about right and wrong, good and bad.

Robert Bellah and colleagues, in their *Habits of the Heart: Individualism and Commitment in American Life,* are eloquent in their analysis of the breakdown of community in America. "In our desperate effort to free ourselves from the constrictions of the past," they contend, "we have jettisoned too much."[54] The authors rightfully criticize the prevalent individualism in the United States, but they do not espouse going back to premodern social views that were blind to individual rights. Although they offer no simplistic solution for our modern "culture of separation," they believe that a regained sense of the importance of family, religious community, and political involvement is a first step.

Not only intellectuals but also some elected officials are calling for greater commitment to social well-being. For example, Los Angeles county's sheriff, Sherman Block, has called for improved educational programs, more job training, and more recreational opportunities for citizens. Block believes that solutions to crime are more complex than just applying punishment and says that "society has been asking its police to deal with the outgrowth of years of neglect of the more basic needs of education, health care, transportation, and human resources."[55]

A great need in contemporary society is for citizens to regain a sense of belonging and a sense of meaning in life. It may not be that this need is greater than before, but today our socially fractured and economically polarized country provides little opportunity for many underprivileged persons to become functional components of the community. And even some of the privileged members of society suffer boredom and seek some greater meaning for their lives.

The modern quest for meaning is illustrated and analyzed in the renowned Viennese psychiatrist Viktor Frankl's best selling *Man's Search for Meaning*. Frankl views a person "as a being whose main concern consists in fulfilling a meaning and in actualizing values, rather than in the mere gratification and satisfaction of drives and instincts."[56]

Because persons are so essentially social beings, the question of personal status and protectable human life must include the indispensable social dimension of personal life. Precisely because human life is not merely an aggregate of individuals, neither of the contending schools—the physicalists and the personalists—can legitimately avoid grappling with life's social dimension. Physicalist thinkers must not separate discussion of the moral value of the embryo from the larger social context in which that human life form exists. Likewise, personalist theorists must not abstract higher-brain functioning from the rich social context in which we humans slowly develop and gradually lose brain capacities.

The Religious Dimension

Throughout history, the social and religious dimensions of human existence have been deeply interwoven. In a sense, a religious system is but an ultimate "society" envisaged in eternal or cosmic terms.

Humankind is *homo religiosus*. Religion is as old as personal consciousness, and a number of scholars are again awakening to its normative importance. One thinker, philosopher Leszek Kolakowski, wonders if civilization can survive without it:

It is obviously possible for individuals to keep high moral standards and be irreligious. I strongly doubt whether it is possible for civilizations. Absent religious tradition, what reason is there for a society to respect human rights and the dignity of man? What is human dignity, scientifically speaking? A superstition? Empirically, men are demonstrably unequal. How can we justify equality? Human rights is an unscientific idea. . . . these values are rooted in a transcendent dimension.[57]

Clifford Geertz has distinguished himself among cultural anthropologists because he is not content merely to analyze the psychological and sociological aspects of religion but has spent a lifetime probing the systems of meaning embedded in religious symbols and rituals. Geertz portrays religion as socially powerful: "It alters, often radically, the whole landscape presented to common sense, alters it in such a way that the moods and motivations induced by religious practice seem themselves supremely practical, the only sensible ones to adopt given the way things 'really' are."[58]

Geertz has described the normative role that religion has long played in human life.[59] Until recently mainline analytic philosophy dismissed any normative status for religion and religious ethics as nonrational at best and superstitious at worst. However, much has now changed in philosophy. And Jeffrey Stout is right to suggest rethinking the logical relation between religion and morality. There is no longer a consensus that morality is autonomous and that it is a merely rational system that speaks with one voice.[60] And because morality does not and never has started from some neutral position, it is only reasonable that present moral positions are recognized as interlaced with traditional religious and philosophical doctrines. Philosophy in its purest form is not exempt from historical contingency, and therefore not even the tenets of this discipline, which critiques all others, are beyond fundamental criticism.[61]

Therefore, it is understandable why philosopher Basil Mitchell, in his 1974–75 Gifford lectures, might survey the pervasive moral disagreement in society and call for a justification, indeed a theological justification, of "traditional conscience." Similarly Alisdair Macintyre calls for a return to Aristotelian-Aquinian morality as the option of choice.[62] These critical thinkers are not alone in their recognition of a transcendent dimension to life.

Martin Buber, whose existentialist Jewish humanism was influenced by nineteenth- and twentieth-century Continental philosophy, sought the divine and transcendent dimension of life in the mundane event of a genuine meeting between persons. For Buber, "The fundamental fact of human existence is man with man."[63] Fundamental to Buber's philosophy—most fully elaborated in his classic, *I and Thou*[64]—is his contention that the reality of life does not lie in each of us individually, in our collectivities, or in our religions. These are finally abstractions. Beyond the realms of subjectivity and objectivity Buber posits the concrete realm of reality that he calls the *Zwischen*, the between.

The personal interaction between individuals is where life is fundamentally and meaningfully lived. "'Between' is not an auxiliary construction, but the real place and bearer of what happens between men; it has received no specific attention because, in distinction from the individual soul and its context, it does not exhibit a smooth continuity, but is ever and again re-constituted in accordance with men's meetings with one another; hence what is experienced has been annexed naturally to the continuous elements, the soul and its world."[65]

Buber rejects the label "theologian" for he has no dogma. Rather he sees himself as a philosophical anthropologist and a religious thinker. In every genuine person-to-person meeting, for Buber, one also approaches the divine. A true I-Thou encounter is open to being simultaneously an I eternal-Thou meeting as well.

James M. Gustafson, a Protestant theologian and bioethicist, grapples with the question of what truth-claims one can make in this age of science. He concludes that there is little propositional content from Christian tradition that can unquestionably stand, but he confesses a religious "piety" based on his own and many others' human experience. "Religion, it has been argued, is a matter of the affections or the emotions. This I shall defend."[66] The burden of Gustafson's nuanced argument is that he senses a universal power forcing down upon him, and his chosen response is awe and respect—a response he calls piety. Piety, as opposed to an uncritical "faith," is a thoughtful, settled, appreciative disposition toward God and the world.[67]

Stout applauds Gustafson's bold restatement of the Christian faith in light of modern knowledge, but he questions why anyone would desire to worship his demythologized god. Stout himself embraces a "secular piety." He takes his cue from Mary Midgley who chides certain theologians for claiming that God is dead but continuing to "dress up in his clothes."[68] Both Stout and Midgley espouse a piety that marvels at a sublime universe that we are only beginning to explore.[69] Novelist Salman Rushdie asks whether the "religious mentality" can survive outside religious dogma and hierarchy. He believes it can and that great literature, particularly the novel, is a contemporary means of secular transcendence. "Not only is [the novel] the art involving least compromises, but it is also the only one that takes the 'privileged arena' of conflicting discourses *right inside our heads*."[70]

Beyond the Rational Individual

The purpose of this brief excursion into a variety of contemporary social and religious perspectives is to show how many serious thinkers are exploring areas that transcend those of particularity and individualism. The individualism implicit in the personhood thinking of Engelhardt puts a premium on self-consciousness and equates Kantian ethics with a supposedly neutral and foundational "secular" morality. Kant wrote much about rational and autonomous individuals freely willing to do their duty. Whether Kant's focus on the strictly rational individual would have shifted had he to deal with barely sustainable disabled newborns and unconscious patients in persistent vegetative states, no one knows. However, personhood affirms that all newborns and all permanently comatose patients are not humans deserving of unique moral respect. My point is not complex. This view is simply one of many views of the human person and is not sacred because of its philosophical or ideological pedigree. If this ethic is correct, and I believe that it makes an essential point, it must be argued in the classroom and finally on the town square along with other contenders.

Physicalism is also particularistic. Ironically, however, its particularity is cloaked by its breadth. For example, debate over the status of a single embryo is conducted under a right-to-life rubric. An analogy is illustrative: An individual may be easily identified as self-obsessed, but the self-preoccupation of a large group is less easy to recognize. A mere defense of the fetus or the disabled newborn by citing the need to "respect life" is exceedingly particularistic in its insensitivity to larger, social dimensions of the issue. Physicalism can be just as particularistic as personalism; they are just on opposite ends of the modern spectrum of particularity. To the credit of traditional Catholic thinking about the fetus, the invocation of an eternal soul that inhabits all humans who are biologically alive gives the question a coherent religious framework through which to view oneself and every human entity.

As I argued in chapter 1, personhood had roots in a liberal Protestant focus on the rational, choosing believer. Further, the tenets of personhood, focusing on self-consciousness, are in keeping with modernity's high valuation of the strong and independent individual. On the other hand, physicalism, with its attention on generic humanity and immaterial essences and its downplaying of concrete circumstances, appears somewhat alien to the modern mind. Does this mean that personalism is therefore right and physicalism wrong? By no means. We may agree that a set of facts is descriptively correct (for example, a fetus is not self-conscious); we may not agree on what normative judgment is implied by or drawn from those facts. Strictly speaking, we do not logically deduce an *ought* from an *is*. That is, it is not good moral logic to reason that a society ought to accept policy A merely because many people accept policy A. However, a reasonable relationship should exist between ought and is.

The majority position on an issue counts in democratic states. But even if personhood has immediate intuitive appeal to most of us, we do not follow it to its logical conclusions. That is, we do not perform or even allow infanticide merely because the newborn does not possess the higher-brain capacity of self-consciousness. No doubt society behaves thus for many reasons, but at least some of our reasons are basically emotional. Regardless of other considerations we find it revolting to even think of killing a newborn baby whose anatomical features are so like our own and who after normal development will be a person like us in a few short years.[71] The *theory* of personhood has little to do with normal initial emotions about infanticide when we consider the welfare of a baby unwanted by its parents.

It is interesting that our theories and our emotions are not as distant as is often supposed. In fact, theories and principles need not be seen as abstract concepts apart from personal emotions. Jonathan Bennett views principles as "embodiments of one's best feelings, one's broadest and keenest sympathies."[72] J. B. Schneewind makes a related point:

Moral philosophers, whatever their theoretical programmes, have in practice always recognized that allegedly basic moral principles depend no less on fairly specific moral propositions than on the other sorts of grounds that have been offered for them; a principle that led to the conclusion that truth-telling was usually wrong, and torturing children normally permissible would be rejected, no matter what kind of proof it might have.[73]

Sidney Callahan is insightful in pointing out that some psychopaths possess a high I.Q. and are well able to articulate society's moral rules, but they are deficient in emotional responsiveness. "A good case can be made that what is specifically moral about moral thinking, what gives it its imperative 'oughtness,' is personal emotional investment."[74]

The implication of these comments for our purposes is that neither the theory of personalism nor that of physicalism is right and appropriate in and of itself. Their basic logic is very different, but both perspectives are profoundly influenced by the fact that they are conceptualized by feeling and thinking persons in a given time and place. And it is this common social centeredness of persons, recognized and appreciated or not, that is the human experience that should moderate both. This social commonality checks both camps from carrying their theories to logical conclusions. For example, the physicalist group does not hold funerals for spontaneously aborted fetuses and the personalist camp does not treat non-self-conscious babies as being of inconsequential moral worth.

Theories emerge from lived communal experience and must be examined continually and perhaps modified in light of further experience. In the next chapter I advance a position that steers between the Scylla and Charybdis of personalism and physicalism by advocating a "proximate personhood" perspective. It is derived from personhood thinking in that it recognizes the unique capacities of higher levels of brain functioning. But I attempt to take into full account our natural and growing affinity for the developing human fetus/newborn.

3 Proximate Personhood

One of the most vexing right-to-die issues facing modern society concerns severely imperiled newborns. Unlike adults—competent or otherwise—infants have never registered their desires on quality of life, and some other individual must decide their fate. Who should decide? What options are legitimate? The following case illustrates the quandary of ethical decision making in regard to newborns:

A couple in their early twenties expect their first child. The wife begins labor at approximately thirty-four weeks' gestation. Ultrasonography is performed at a small community hospital, and the prenatal diagnosis is diaphragmatic hernia—inadequate lung development because of the presence of intestines in the thoracic cavity. When the family arrives at the tertiary care center, the parents confer with the obstetrician and neonatologist. The physicians plan to document lung maturity and, if premature labor cannot be stopped, to deliver the infant under controlled circumstances so that surgery for the hernia may be done immediately.

Two days later the infant is born and found to have gross limb deformities, including absent forearms bilaterally, no lower leg on the right side, and a deformed left foot. A diaphragmatic hernia is also confirmed. The parents decide to withhold surgery because of concern that their son would suffer too much from gross physical abnormalities.

An infant care review committee is immediately called. The subspecialties of surgery, physical therapy, neonatology, pediatrics, nursing, and respiratory care are represented, and a clergyman also attends. The consensus is that it is impossible to predict the quality of this infant's life and that since prostheses might be made available to render the subject a somewhat independent individual, surgery for the hernia should be recommended. When the parents still refuse, the committee reconvenes. At this meeting the question is whether the consensus is strong enough to try to obtain a court order to perform surgery against the parents' wishes. At this point, consensus fails. Most of the physicians feel a sense of outrageous arrogance at the prospect of forcing such an action on the parents.

In a bygone era, parents—usually in their own homes—decided the fate of their very sick newborn, if indeed there was anything to decide. Today, hospital health care professionals are playing an increasingly vital role in these neonatal decisions.

Medical center subspecialists, utilizing high technology, can and usually do fan a spark of life into a vital flame. Life-saving technology, unfortunately, is also capable of transforming an infant's spark of life into a distorted, flickering flame. Many question who has the right to determine when neonatal intensive care unit (NICU) equipment can be used for severely disabled newborns.

Both medicine and society increasingly recognize that assumptions of value underlie NICU moral decisions but find a cacophony of voices in the ethical, religious, and legal communities. Ethicists are rooted in philosophical and moral traditions nearly as diverse as society's religious perspectives. The judicial system, trying to build upon a societal consensus, finds little explicit agreement and thus, unsurprisingly, produces conflicting opinions.[1]

Four Decision-Making Approaches

Nevertheless, from these conflicting voices emerge at least four identifiable approaches to deciding morally difficult neonatal cases. Each of these, which I call value of life, parental authority, best interests, and personhood, makes a plausible contribution to the discussion but is finally inadequate. After analyzing these options, I propose a theory of proximate personhood that takes into account insights in each of the other positions but attempts to overcome some of their inadequacies.

Value of Life

C. Everett Koop, former U.S. Surgeon General, commenting on the Baby Jane Doe case stated, "We're not just fighting for this baby but for the principle that every life is sacred." Koop, like many value-of-life[2] advocates, roots his position in the Judeo-Christian heritage: "Each newborn infant, perfect or deformed, is a human being with unique preciousness because he or she was created in the image of God."[3] In the United States, where Christianity continues to be a vital presence, the high-valuation-of-life position is a part of the larger culture. The breadth of value-of-life thinking is reflected in the joint policy statement on treatment of disabled infants, voted in 1983 by the American Academy of Pediatrics and eight national associations of the disabled, which begins: "Discrimination of any type against any individual with a disability/disabilities, regardless of the nature or severity of the disability, is morally and legally indefensible."[4]

The high-valuation-of-life stance has at least two distinct lines of argument. First is the substantive, duty-oriented conviction that human nature qua human nature is precious. The degree of life's potential to be realized in an imperiled child is of secondary importance. To possess a minimal degree of life is superior to no human life. Even severely disabled children do not often choose to end their lives because of an alleged wrongful birth.[5] Hence, their lives, as judged by themselves and not by whole-bodied others, are deemed worth living. It is discrimination for society's able-bodied majority population to deny existence to members of the disabled minority, according to this position. Disabled humans possess a rightful human claim to existence.

Although the basic right to life is quite naturally the crux of this position, an interesting consequentialist reasoning surfaces in some of its defenses. Paul Ramsey, in a version of the slippery slope argument referred to earlier, cites the Nuremberg Code warning that Nazi medical crimes "'started with small beginnings . . . with the acceptance of the attitude . . . that there is such a thing as a life not worthy to be lived.'" Ramsey himself contends that "any boundaries (preventing infanticide) that can be fixed or preserved today are precious, and should be cherished and strengthened—however nonrational they may be."[6]

Allusions to medical practices of the Third Reich may be overly dramatic,[7] but the argument takes a more subtle turn. It involves the effect that authorized withholding of treatment from nondying newborns may have on society's esteem for the medical profession and ultimately itself. Medicine possesses a preeminent position in society because it is perceived as dedicated to the saving of human life. If the medical community seems to hold an ambiguous position on life's value, a deeply entrenched social ethos of caretaking may erode and all society would lose. Such is the thinking of law professor Robert Burt, who argues that there are severely disabled newborns whose lives mercifully should be allowed to ebb, but the decision making should not be formalized. The myth that everyone's life can and should be saved has a powerful and socially constructive hold on our collective imagination and, though excessive, contributes to the "social ideal" of viewing the physician as caretaker, an image that must be preserved, says Burt.[8]

Would society's self-esteem, a communal sense of well-being important for any culture, be threatened by an explicit and publicly disclosed process of neonatal decision making? For example, consider a newborn with major physical abnormalities and likely to be profoundly retarded, never aware of its own existence. Should the present ad hoc basis for such decisions be purposely kept secret so society may maintain a formal stance of highly valuing life, perhaps even "valuing each life infinitely"?[9]

The Baby Doe directives, which forbade quality-of-life considerations and essentially banned allowing newborns to die except those who were comatose or whose treatment was deemed "virtually futile," were a de jure method of avoiding the formalization of decision making for the *marginal* newborns.[10] Both neonatal and societal benefits, say value-of-life advocates, thus obtain. However that may be, even Koop, who was instrumental in drafting the Baby Doe regulations, cannot himself avoid quality-of-life judgments. In defending these regulations he granted that an infant born with essentially no intestine could be sustained with artificial feedings for perhaps eighteen months—but need not be.[11] Supposedly the baby's life would not be intolerable, if this makes a difference; but such life is certainly of short duration and subject to lengthy hospitalizations. The point is that a value judgment was made; indeed, such a judgment is unavoidable because of our vast capability to sustain physical life. Should we deal with this case and even more difficult ones in a deliberate and systematic manner? Would acknowledgment of the value judgments we make about neonatal life threaten our own humanity? This is a pivotal but unresolved issue raised by the value-of-life position.

In regard to the infant case cited above, the value-of-life advocate would argue that the newborn should receive immediate surgery for the diaphragmatic hernia. None of the Baby Doe criteria for forgoing treatment (it merely prolongs the dying, it would be virtually futile and its provision is inhumane, the infant is irreversibly comatose)[12] are met.

Parental Authority

When a sick baby is born the presumption is that treatment should be given. But if the newborn requires extensive, multiple surgeries over a prolonged period and the long-term prognosis is ambiguous, a decision must be made whether to continue aggressive treatment. Who should decide?

The argument for parental decision-making is strong. It is supported by the history of parent-child relations and by the continuing belief in parental responsibility for the well-being of their offspring.

Throughout most of Western history children have had few rights independent of their parents and were treated as mere chattel. (Plato denied children the right of self-defense against a life-threatening parent.[13]) However, since the seventeenth century children have been increasingly valued in their own right. Philosophers such as Rousseau and Bentham were influential in their emphasis on the role of feeling and natural affection in child rearing.[14] The parental role was thus not so much weakened as enriched and broadened.

Today parental affection for children is assumed and underlies our belief that parents can best make family decisions. Although children possess an important separate existence, parents continue to make both crucial and trivial decisions, ones that significantly determine the person their child will become. Parents decide to conceive and to continue the pregnancy. They are expected to provide adequate food and housing, but the quality of food and type of shelter is left to parental discretion. Although basic education and care are mandatory, the type of schooling (good or bad) and upbringing (religious or secular) are open. Parents have always made and continue to make basic decisions in behalf of their families.

The right of parents to make decisions regarding their imperiled newborn, it is contended, is even enhanced today because of our society's increasing moral pluralism. But whatever moral pluralism denotes, it does not mean a national disavowal of fundamental norms. Recent historic enactment of laws on child abuse and sexual and racial equality—laws for which there is widespread consensus—suggest the opposite. However, pertinent to our discussion, no similar consensus exists on the moral claim to life of a severely disabled newborn—as demonstrated by the controversy begun over Baby Doe. Precisely because of the difference of opinion over newborns' welfare, the parents should be the presumed surrogates, claims the parental-authority position. When society is so divided, parents must not have a disputed ideological (religious?[15]) belief about life forced upon them. It would be ironic if parents could make decisions ranging from conception to college and be denied authority during the neonatal period. On the topic of foregoing the treatment of sick newborns, the President's Commission cites common and Constitutional law in stating its position that "there is a presumption, strong but rebuttable, that parents are the appropriate decision maker for their infants."[16]

Parental autonomy is strong but not unlimited. For example, Jehovah's Witnesses may educate their child against receiving transfusions but are not allowed to make him or her a child-martyr. Neither do parents have the right to refuse routine life-saving surgery for their uncomplicated Down syndrome infant, according to the President's Commission. Further, whether parents who are emotionally distraught at bearing a disabled baby are capable of making good decisions and whether they should be saddled with decisions for which they may suffer lifelong guilt are poignant issues. The case for parental decision making is strong but not unchallenged.

If the couple cited in the initial case study gave an informed denial of consent to the diaphragmatic hernia surgery required to save their newborn, they were deciding within their legitimate role.[17] In this case, whatever the decision, according to the doctrine of parental authority, it should be made finally by the parents.

Best Interests

A strong consensus exists in favor of the best interests of the infant as the chief criterion for decision making. James Childress,[18] Robert Weir,[19] Norman Fost,[20] and others concur with the President's Commission that treatment should be based on a reasonable assessment of the burdens and benefits that are likely to accompany the child's life. A life—all medical factors considered—that results in a "net benefit" to the infant should be aggressively treated.[21]

This stance has two particular strengths. First, the best-interests standard is substantive rather than merely procedural. Its substance is the conferred moral value of the newborn that, logically, is integrally related to the person this baby is in the process of becoming. Second, best-interests thinking is a common sense, moderate position. It assumes the high value of neonatal life but recognizes that tragic circumstances can turn the normal good of existence into a life that, on balance, does not warrant the candle's flicker. Life cannot be seen as precious only in an abstract sense and the life of another cannot be left—at worst—to whim; the best interests of the baby are the standard.

As eloquent as this position may be in theory, it is not problem-free in practice. The "best interests" of the infant are difficult to assess both medically and intellectually.

Some newborns—such as anencephalic and trisomy 13 and 18 infants—can be clearly diagnosed at birth as possessing a physical condition that is incompatible with personal life.[22] Other newborns—such as those affected by Down syndrome without further anomalies—can be diagnosed as having a physical disability that is most unfortunate but likely compatible with a life in the child's best interests. However, there are severely ill newborns with multiple congenital handicaps and premature, low birth weight infants with inadequately developed vital organs whose best interests in continued life are problematic. A five-hundred-gram baby's life may be prolonged by aggressive therapy. Sometimes the child may grow up to be normal or nearly so, but more often such therapy results in a moderately to severely disabled youngster, if it sustains life at all.

From a conceptual point of view, whether a surrogate can decide, as the President's Commission stipulates, on the best interests "from the perspective of [the] infant"[23] is questionable. Perhaps the Commission imagines a surrogate projecting the near- and far-range future of the infant and postulating from the mind-set of the infant-child-adult what he or she would desire for continued existence. But the reality is that many of the most severely compromised neonates will never develop the mental capability to consider such issues. To speak of deciding the best interests from the perspective of a never-to-be-competent infant makes questionable sense. Even more problematic is the Commission's contention that competent adults should avoid reading their own desires into imperiled children's minds: "The surrogate is obliged to try to evaluate benefits and burdens from the infant's own perspective."[24] More specifically, benefit for the infant is *not* to be determined by what "a competent decision maker" situated in the infant's condition would decide. In other words, the surrogate is to decide on the basis of what the (incompetent!) disabled infant would decide.

Even if these procedural difficulties could be overcome, a further substantive problem exists. The best-interests criterion does not specify any uniquely human qualification for assessing a moral claim to life. We can assume that almost all organisms—neonates not excepted—would decide that life was in their best interests if their "minds" could be read. The only newborn exceptions may be those whose lives are afflicted with unremitting and excruciating pain.[25] Perhaps the best-interests criterion assumes basic human qualities as givens; then the minimal conditions that constitute the human condition are important to identify, a task this position does not tackle.

The best-interests concept is helpful but incomplete. What it lacks, definitive criteria for decision making, is the focus of the next approach, personhood.

Personhood

Whereas the value-of-life position, identified in earlier chapters as physicialism, is largely a genetically based view that sees humanness as the equivalent of personhood, the personhood approach[26] is capability based. It claims that present possession of capabilities constitutes personhood, and only *person*al life has a unique claim—a moral claim—to existence in all but exceptional circumstances. The capabilities that characterize personhood are variously defined, but they all are related to advanced brain functions: self-consciousness, rationality, ability to suffer, a sense of the future, and so forth.[27] Animals other than humans possess, at least in part, these traits. The great apes, dolphins, whales, and other animals are at least quasi-persons. In the philosophizing of some ethicists, the essential value of certain mature nonhumans far exceeds the moral value of particular human beings, for example, fetuses and perhaps newborns.[28]

Although there are strong social reasons to treat newborns as personal beings, their claim to life based on personhood is weak. They possess no "moral trump card," says Earl Shelp.[29] If they are disabled—particularly mentally—their moral claim to life is weighed against competing rights of parents, siblings, and society itself and can be found wanting.

Shelp's type of thinking gets a more receptive hearing in Great Britain and Europe, where the population appears more favorably inclined toward personhood, than in the United States. However, Americans in the pre–Baby Doe era were less conservative in their professional judgments than they are today. For example in the mid-seventies a survey of United States pediatric surgeons and pediatricians were asked: "Would you acquiesce in parents' decision to refuse consent for surgery in a newborn with intestinal atresia if the infant also had (a) Down's syndrome alone, (b) Down's syndrome plus congenital heart disease, (c) anencephaly, (d) cloacal exstrophy, (e) meningomyelocele, (f) multiple limb or craniofacial malformations, (g) 13–15 trisomy, or (h) no other anomalies, e.g., normal aside from atresia?"[30]

If Down syndrome was the *only* other complication, 76.8 percent of the pediatric surgeons and 49.5 percent of the pediatricians indicated that they would acquiesce to parental decisions not to allow surgery.[31] Although *acquiesce* does not mean approval, the readiness of physicians to forgo lifesaving treatment of Down syndrome newborns as demonstrated in this survey was cited by the Department of Health and Human Services in its justification of the conservative and controversial Baby Doe regulations on treatment of imperiled newborns. (Refusal of surgery does not necessarily indicate a patient's lack of moral standing or personhood.)

Is it right to withhold lifesaving, routine surgery or even to withhold basic sustenance from an uncomplicated Down syndrome newborn? A number of lay people and pediatric specialists evidently believe so. The personhood approach to life has produced a coherent philosophy that gives a rational basis for such thinking. It is, nonetheless, inadequate for deciding the difficult cases of marginal human life.

Proximity to Personhood

No approach to ethical decision making on marginal human life, including the four sketched above, is fully adequate. Yet these positions underscore four discrete and important values: human life, parental authority, infant interests, and personal being. The value-of-life and the personhood approaches could be viewed as the most extreme. The majority of advocates in both camps, however, fail to take their positions to strict logical conclusions. As Koop's example, cited above, shows, even an ardent value-of-life advocate has difficulty being totally consistent, and personhood philosophers do not advocate open infanticide. The best-interests and parental-authority approaches are moderate positions, each emphasizing complementary aspects of the discussion—one the substantive issue of child-centered benefit and the other the procedural norm of primary decision maker. Each approach has merit, but taken by itself each is insufficient.

Of the four approaches, the personhood perspective is particularly appealing. Rather than ponder abstractions like "human" life and a child's "interests," it focuses on the specific capacities and activities of individuals that make life meaningful. It is a commonsense approach. Asked what makes life so valuable, one might answer: "I am a person of relationships and particular tastes. I can plan, act, and remember. I possess inner emotions that make me unique. I am aware of myself and of the world. I can even project myself outside of this 'self,' and think self-consciously back on what I am now doing!" If any life has intrinsic value, surely it is a *personal* life, not merely physical existence.

In a time when medical technology can sustain vegetative adult patients and disabled neonatal life, personhood's focus on uniquely personal capacities is perceptive but, finally, not adequate. Its inadequacy is particularly apparent in dealing with questions of marginal life—fetuses, disabled newborns, vegetative adults, and higher level animals such as mammals.

I now turn to the construction of a position that I suggest is more adequate—all things considered—than those just surveyed, including that of personhood. I will argue that a developing individual's right to life increases as he or she approaches the threshold of indisputably personal life, the life of the normal adult in any society. That is, the more a fetus, a newborn, or an infant approximates—or is proximate to—personhood, the greater his or her moral value and hence the greater the implicit claim to life.[32] Likewise, the further beyond the threshold of incontestably personal life an adult individual is (such as a patient with advanced Alzheimer's disease[33]), the less clear is that individual's moral status and claim to morally valuable and legally protectable life. (Similarly, once an individual, such as a normal newborn, rises above the threshold of personhood—be it understood in a moral or legal sense—the individual is as much a person as is the president of the United States. No moral lines are drawn between persons; all persons have full moral status.)

The proximate personhood approach offers three pivotal criteria for making decisions: (1) the *potentiality for* gaining or regaining personal being, (2) the *development toward* becoming a personal being or development beyond such being, and (3) the *bonding of* an individual and significant others or society at large. These criteria are, respectively, intellectual, physical, and social.

I grant the cogency of the personhood argument for the essential nature of higher-brain capacities. However, personhood, regardless of its merits, is not directly translatable into social policy because of its dire implications for marginal individuals. It offers good, commonsense insights into what is intrinsically valuable about a normal human's life but assumes that we live as normal people who are individually assessed as to our moral worth. We are a society composed, by and large, of normal people, but also we have an increasing number of individuals who are not—fetuses, disabled neonates, and severely compromised elderly patients. The proximate personhood position attempts to identify and articulate the good, commonsense reasons we employ in giving care to, for example, disabled newborns and senile patients. The personhood perspective is the foundation on which proximate personhood thinking builds. Personhood thinking is not wrong but it fails to face the challenges presented by modern medicine.

In explicating the proximate personhood position I focus primarily on human newborns. This is done more for clarity of explanation than lack of scope in application. To make the discussion more concrete, I begin by applying proximate personhood criteria to the all-too-frequent case of a baby born with Down syndrome.

Jon Will, son of columnist George F. Will, has Down syndrome. On workdays he commutes to the National Institutes of Health where he delivers mail. His retardation is not so severe, his father says, that "it interferes with life's essential joys—receiving love, returning it, and reading baseball box scores" (he has a season ticket to Baltimore Orioles' games).[34] Jon is fortunate that his retardation is not severe, as is the case with many of the 4,000 individuals born with Down syndrome each year in the U.S. Also, he may have escaped the congenital heart disease that affects so many with his disease. However, Jon will almost certainly have Alzheimer's disease within a decade or so. "After age 35, essentially 100% of patients with Down syndrome develop neuropathological changes of Alzheimer disease," writes neurologist B. T. Hyman.[35]

George Will says that a doctor told newborn Jon's parents that their first decision would be "whether or not to take Jon home." Early in this century care for Down syndrome newborns was different: their life expectancy in 1929 was nine years, whereas today some 70 percent of these newborns can expect to live beyond fifty.[36] How can use of proximate personhood criteria illumine the decision on the care of a Down syndrome newborn? The potential for truly personal life is often questionable in that the newborn could turn out to be severely retarded and hence incapable of personal existence. Of course, if only mildly retarded, the Down syndrome baby—like Jon Will—could grow to enjoy the benefits of basic self-consciousness, personal interaction, and a productive life.

For argument's sake, let us deal with a hypothetical "normal" Down syndrome newborn. Such an infant will possibly live a happy life, although not one with the intense joy—or sorrow—of the normal adult because of usually moderate retardation (average I.Q. of 50). In the judgment of the neonatologist and the parents there is a good chance for attainment of at least minimally self-conscious existence. The development toward personal life is noteworthy in that this is a physically healthy newborn who, given standard care, will likely thrive for many years except for his mental impairment. The bonding of parents with this particular newborn may be minimal. For instance, they might question whether their two-career family with two other young children can cope with a newcomer having Down syndrome.

Today, most biomedical ethicists in the United States who write on such matters contend that an uncomplicated Down syndrome newborn has sufficient moral standing to receive the same medical care given to healthy babies.[37] Professional opinion in England is otherwise, if the case of baby John Pearson, mentioned in chapter 2, is any indication. Following proximate personhood criteria, treatment of Down syndrome is mandatory if good physical health and only moderate retardation is the prognosis. This is because such a newborn has the potential for a level of mental functioning that minimally approximates that of most mature persons, and the baby's physical potential portends a body that likely will bring joy to the subject.

Proximate personhood criteria are also useful in comparing the status of human and nonhuman life. All normal newborns, admittedly, do not possess unique personal capacities, but they do *approximate* personal life. That is, human newborns approach personal being in a way in which other creatures do not. The mature ape is quite intelligent compared to other animals—and compared to the human newborn. An ape has the intelligence of a normal two-and-a-half-year-old child. However, when proximate personhood's threefold criteria for determining moral status are considered, the ape does not and should not be granted the moral status of a young child. The greater the *proximity* to personal life, the weightier is the animal's or human individual's moral status. Although the ape should have significant moral standing, the normal human newborn's is greater. The newborn's potentiality for achieving unrivaled personal capacities will be realized in only a few years, the newborn's development toward personal life is considerable at nine months, and the normal parents' bonding with their newborn is extremely significant.

The proximate personhood criteria of *potentiality, physical development, and social bonding* warrant further comment.

Potentiality

Most personhood advocates are reluctant to give moral weight to a newborn's potentiality; only the *self-conscious* individual possesses intrinsic moral stature. However, an interesting dilemma posed by certain philosophers is whether persons retain their moral standing during sleep. Our moral intuitions provide an automatic Yes. And personalists heartily agree. They recognize that there are "temporal discontinuities" in a person's life over which identity is reasonably presumed to span.[38] The topic and reasoning may appear scholastic, but the point is important: persons are preeminently valuable and, awake or asleep, are to be treated as such.

The issue here, however, is whether it is equally reasonable to recognize the unique, albeit more distant, potentiality of the infant. No direct analogy can be drawn, admittedly, between the moral status of an adult who happens to be sleeping and an infant. However, we consider the problem to illustrate just why we treat certain individuals with the highest respect.

Just as we intuitively respect the sleeping person, so we bestow love on an infant—though, strictly speaking, neither is self-conscious. The sleeping adult has the potential to be awake immediately, and the infant possesses the potential for significant personal capacity within months or a couple of years. If an intervening night's sleep does not in any way interrupt an adult's moral right to life, it seems plausible to contend that neither do the years of newborn-to-child development totally dissolve the moral value we attribute to an infant. Admittedly, the infant's moral status is not as immediate as that of the sleeping adult, but it exists. But arguments for the moral status of the infant cannot be used for the moral status of the embryo because the embryo possesses only potentiality, has developed little, and no bonding exists. It appears reasonable to presume that adults possess full personhood and that infants possess proximate personhood and make decisions based on those related moral presumptions.

A problem with recognizing potentiality is that the potential of the newborn is not new; it existed earlier in the fetus, the zygote, and even with the individual gametes. Joel Feinberg and others are correct to argue that it is a logical error to deduce actual rights from merely potential qualification for those rights. Feinberg gives an apt illustration: "In 1930, when he was six years old, Jimmy Carter did not know it, but he was a potential president of the United States. That gave him no claim *then*, not even a very weak claim, to give commands to the U.S. Army."[39]

Because of the power of such arguments, some philosophers, like Jonathan Glover, Peter Singer, and Michael Tooley,[40] equate the intrinsic morality of contraception with that of early infanticide. That is, if it is ethical to impede the conception of what would otherwise be future persons, it is equally moral to take the life of a newborn—if only the life of the newborn is taken into account—because in neither case is a person involved. R. M. Hare makes a similar point in arguing that the Golden Rule, taken simply by itself, equally proscribes abortion, contraception, and celibacy.[41] The point I would make is this: there is a limit to just how far back one can profitably take the notion of potentiality.

Mary Anne Warren also rejects the principle of potentiality. However, Warren is clear in distinguishing her rejection of any moral claim that "*merely* potential people" possess from her moral imperative to protect the interests of "actual future persons." On the one hand, she sees little moral weight in the argument that we have a duty to promote the happiness of merely possible persons such as gametes or even potential persons such as fetuses; on the other hand, she argues that actual persons—both present and future—possess a strong moral claim on us.[42]

The assertion that actual future persons possess high moral status has a direct bearing on my contention that potential for and development toward full personhood—taken together—have a direct bearing on treatment decisions for disabled newborns. Human individuals who have the potential for personal life, and who have significantly developed toward that life, are the "actual future persons" Warren views as possessing a strong moral claim to life.

Warren's actual future persons are those fetuses or newborns who will, in the normal course of development, soon be persons—and who if harmed in a prepersonhood state could suffer grievous consequences throughout the rest of their lives. She presupposes that a potential or future person—not a vegetative human body—is the subject of our thinking. Her idea of "actual future persons" is a nuanced treatment of the idea of potentiality that makes sense and is quite helpful in making difficult treatment decisions.

It is useful to distinguish the mental from the physical aspects of a disabled infant, for instance. Mental potential is of first importance because *only* this unique capacity provides a distinctly moral claim to life. Unless the severely compromised newborn possesses a mind, the most heroically salvaged body will be of no personal worth. So physical potential—a projected healthy or unhealthy body—should always be second-ary to the potential cognition of the infant. If no *personal* mental func-tioning can be projected (if, for instance, there is a prognosis of profound retardation resulting in nonawareness of existence), then the question of physical handicap is less of an issue—or perhaps no issue at all—because there is no potential or future "person."

Physical Development

The early abortion of normal fetuses, for even trivial reasons, is readily available in the U.S., but taking the life of the most disabled newborn, even for the best of reasons, is against the law. This is the case, despite the fact that neither fetus nor infant possesses so-called self-consciousness. What is the significant difference between a fetus and a newborn? Physical de-velopment. The great majority of aborted fetuses are physically under-developed, nondescript organisms less than an inch in length. But new-borns look like miniature adults.

Both Tooley and Ramsey consider the morality of abortion and in-fanticide as roughly equivalent. Ramsey states: "Since we should treat sim-ilar cases similarly, if *x* degrees of defect would justify abortion, the same *x* degrees of defect would with equal cogency justify infanticide."[43] Of course, Ramsey is opposed to both abortion and infanticide and in a stri-dent mood equates the two in order to criticize abortion. But only from a narrow perspective is abortion the moral equivalent of infanticide. In society's mind, and in the eyes of the law, whether it is a fetus or a new-born that is killed is highly significant—a distinction based primarily on the great difference in physical development.

Despite the rhetoric from liberal and conservative ethicists, physical development has some moral relevance because of parental (and societal) sentiment that escalates with fetal growth. Size itself is not of moral significance. If so, a baby elephant would have greater moral standing than a petite professor. But the physical development of the blastocyst-embryo-fetus-preterm-baby-newborn-infant is morally important in the social context because of the increasingly powerful symbol of personal life that they represent.

Passage through the birth canal surely does not represent a magic threshold of moral status or a dramatic leap in physiological development, but it does signal society's recognition—and parents' celebration!—of a significant stage of human growth. Only at birth is the baby legally registered—and cigars passed around. Whether severely disabled newborns should be registered immediately at birth is debated,[44] but the significance the state attaches to this point of development is important. Mere generic potential has reached a notable juncture in its bodily realization.

The developing fetus and the disabled newborn have heightened but not absolute value, for at times their value must be weighed against competing moral claims, such as conservation of societal resources or recognition of parental liberty. The evolving moral status of the fetus/infant presents a challenge to parental and medical decision makers, but the criterion of physical development indicates that the earlier the embryo/fetus is aborted the less morally problematic is the decision. Relevant ethical distinctions follow: better a physical barrier than a birth control pill, better a morning-after pill than a monthly abortion pill such as RU-486, better RU-486 than a ten-week abortion, better a ten-week abortion than a second-trimester abortion, better an early third-trimester abortion for an anencephalic fetus than a preterm delivery for the same condition. Similarly, if a newborn is severely disabled and a decision for nontreatment is appropriate, the earlier the decision can be made the less ethically troublesome it is.

The physical development of a newborn is particularly important in regard to the *timing* of treatment/nontreatment decisions. If a nontreatment decision is morally appropriate, the earlier the better. But it is the concept of potentiality—both mental and physical—that is crucial for the *substance* of those treatment decisions—the question of whether or not treatment may be withheld.

For instance, if a newborn is diagnosed as likely to be profoundly retarded with an I.Q. in the single digits, then nontreatment of accompanying life-threatening conditions could be morally justified. The infant could never be even a minimally aware person whose implicit interests must be considered. However, suppose that this same newborn is treated and is living as a ten-year-old with an I.Q. of five. The child contracts pneumonia or some other life-threatening disease. In this situation it is morally obligatory to treat a life-threatening condition. Because of the advanced physical development, it would be immoral to let the youngster die of conditions that might have been left untreated ten years earlier.

Treatment decisions should not require that an infant have the potential to become an Einstein or even to achieve normality. But because higher-brain capacity is the core of personal being, potential to achieve at least minimally meaningful functioning of the brain is important if treatment is to be mandatory. Likewise, because of the importance of personal embodiment, the potential for a minimally healthy and relatively painless body is also vital if treatment is to be required. In sum, if a newborn is not likely to achieve the dual goals of minimal mental capacity and minimal physical health, parents should have the freedom to choose nontreatment because their infant likely will not achieve minimal personal status.

Decision making based on minimal personhood involves at least two clear expectations for the newborn: (a) in regard to cognitive potential, the probability of being able to develop some self-awareness and to achieve interpersonal relationships, and (b) in regard to physiological potential, the reasonable anticipation of a life that the projected person would likely consider a net benefit (for instance, the anticipated pain of numerous surgeries does not outweigh the likelihood of improved health). If self-consciousness and decent physical health are probable, lifesaving treatment should be provided. But only if both these conditions are satisfied should physicians be required to give therapy, regardless of parental wishes.

Social Bonding

If we accepted the personhood criterion as the exclusive standard for determining the right to life, killing "impersonal" newborns would not be wrong. But no advocate of personhood says that infanticide is absolutely permissible. For example, Joel Feinberg advances a type of personhood philosophy, and although he does not believe that infants develop genuine capacities for personhood until their second year, he affirms that "infanticide *is* wrong" (his emphasis).[45] Infants do not have an intrinsic right to life, but for reasons of "social utility," "the common good," and "public interest" we treat them with love and care, says Feinberg. This philosopher believes that nature apparently implants in humans an instinctive tenderness toward infants that has proven to be very helpful in protecting the young from death and maintaining the population.

Feinberg is right to indicate the importance of utilitarian reasons for opposing infanticide, but this ethical argument is developed last in his essay and appears to be a secondary consideration. However, in regard to fetuses and newborns, it is anything but secondary. Parents possess powerful feelings toward their newborn child. And in unusual cases when they do not show natural parental feelings, society will take over the child's care. Society's concern is displayed in the laws we have devised to protect the social bond between persons and those individuals we might call "underdeveloped future persons."

The social bond that we feel toward marginal persons is a vital ethical consideration when deciding relevant health care issues. Related concerns exist when our subjects may never become persons (fetuses that will be aborted) or will never regain personhood (the permanently comatose). The *humanity* of the caregiver—or one who gives no care—is at stake. The brain-related capacities of the subject are important, and this is the insightful focus of the personhood perspective. However, this focus must be balanced with the social dimension that the proximate personhood approach emphasizes. The nearness of the individual to undisputed personhood is of utmost moral importance, and the nearer to such realized personal capacities, the greater the *social* bonding.

For instance, when a woman feels her fetus move at about the sixteenth week of pregnancy, it is normal for a type of physio-social bonding to form. The fetus is no longer merely an entity that can only be thought of and dreamed about. It is now a tactile reality. As the fetus grows, anticipation heightens and the woman increasingly identifies with the child-to-be within her. Yes, the potential of the human conceptus is being realized. Yes, physical development of the fetus is taking place. But at the early fetal stage of life, neither is important in and of itself. The morally vital consideration is how the woman—and by extension other persons—feels about fetuses at a particular stage in their development. (An analogy might be made to rape. The crime is not the mere act of sexual intercourse but the horrendous meaning to the woman of a forced intimate act. Likewise, the *meaning* that we attach to the developing fetus is all important—for us.)

The significance of the social bond in treatment decisions is illustrated by, for instance, a newborn with extreme short gut syndrome. Routine treatment is comfort care only. The newborn is kept comfortable with sedatives while it quite literally starves to death because of its lack of bowel. Limited success has been realized in treating some infants with total parenteral nutrition—a liquid diet given intravenously. However, with few exceptions babies thus fed die from infections or other complications within a few months or years. The financial cost and emotional price is great. Sometimes parents believe that they can care for such infants at home, and they may do so for a few frustrating weeks before the baby is returned to the hospital and allowed to die. Because of the social bonding that takes place over weeks at home, in most circumstances it is morally superior for the newborn to die earlier in the hospital rather than to go home with highly expectant parents only to return to the hospital and tragically be withdrawn from TPN in a planned, later death.

This example demonstrates that the three proximate personhood criteria are not separate ideas but interlocking realities. Considering (a) the potential for a full cognitive life but none for a body that is a net benefit to the subject, and (b) limited physical development, the third criterion of (c) social bonding suggests that the earlier the decision to forgo TPN the better. The three criteria unite in pointing toward this sad but ethically appropriate conclusion.

Treatment Categories

In light of the foregoing argument, it is helpful to identify three neonatal treatment categories.[46] The extremes of the neonatal proximate personhood spectrum are not problematic. At one end is the category of newborns who should receive *no life-saving treatment.* An anencephalic newborn typifies this class. Anencephalic infants have a brain stem with little or no higher brain and are uniformly recognized as due only custodial care. A respirator may sustain these infants for an indefinite time, but life-sustaining treatment is not indicated because of an innate medical condition that is incompatible with meaningful life.[47] Similarly, trisomy 13 and 18 infants have conditions incompatible with significant development. Pediatric professionals and bioethical writers generally agree that no specialized treatments are due the most severely imperiled newborns, but no consensus exists on the use of nutrition, respiration, and antibiotics.[48] Many of these babies could live longer if aggressive treatments were given, but "prolonging dying" (an accurate description, as opposed to prolonging life) was not deemed appropriate even by health officials of the Reagan administration.[49]

At the other end of the spectrum is a category of infants who should receive *mandatory treatment.* This class, of course, includes the great majority of babies who leave the NICU as normal or near-normal youngsters. But most important, in terms of this discussion, is the inclusion of all newborns who are reasonably expected to develop minimal capacities of personhood. A newborn with Down syndrome whose only complication is duodenal atresia would fall into the category of mandatory treatment. Also, evidence suggests that most spina bifida babies are likely to possess normal or near-normal mental capacity and therefore should receive life-saving treatment.[50]

Between newborns in the no-treatment and mandatory-treatment categories are those whose prognosis is marginal because it involves (a) considerable mental retardation (degree unknown), and/or (b) severe physical handicap. Such newborns constitute the *optional treatment* category in which parental discretion is paramount.

Consider, for example, a five-hundred-gram, premature newborn. Such infants have a significant chance of dying regardless of treatment and a likelihood of permanent damage if saved. Of similar difficulty are cases of retarded, severely imperiled infants who will have to endure a score of operations without any promise of ever gaining a near-normal existence and infants who have strong bodies but whose prognosis for brain development is so poor that it is questionable whether the child will be conscious of personal existence. A complicating feature of these difficult cases is the inability of neonatology—despite sophisticated equipment—to predict outcomes. In such cases value judgments are inevitable because failure to treat is itself a judgment.

In marginal cases treatment should be optional because of the omnipresent ambiguity. Not only is the future quality of life in question, but whether life itself can be sustained, and at what cost (emotional and financial), is unknown. Parental and societal values vary or are unclear in these cases. The medical profession, given its historical commitment to preservation of life, tends to be aggressive in treatment, and society has been well served by this stance. But if there is reasonable indication that the newborn's potential does not approximate minimal personhood, treatment should not be mandatory. Parents must possess considerable latitude. Family autonomy, a powerful corollary of personal autonomy in light of the social nature of the self, should be respected. Family autonomy, as exercised by informed and supported parents acting as surrogates, should determine treatment or nontreatment.[51] However, even appropriate parental discretion in marginal cases is bounded by society's increasing consciousness of the great cost of high-technology medicine.

A problem in many discussions of bioethical decision making is inattention to social and financial costs. Although adequate treatment of this topic is beyond the scope of this book, responsible decision making in the NICU must take note of economics.[52] Many writers recognize the need for limiting the use of expensive technology but stress that curbs should be imposed by society—not by attending physicians.[53] Physicians, it is argued, are not knowledgeable about treatment modalities' relative costs, are nonobjective because of their training and work and, most important, are treating persons with an implicit agreement to maximize the individual patient's best interests.[54] Thus, the World Medical Association's International Code of Medical Ethics states: "A doctor must practice his profession uninfluenced by motives of profit."[55] At least one bioethicist, N. G. Levinsky, advocates the principle of eschewing all consideration of cost in patient treatment.[56]

Nevertheless, in light of the maldistribution of medical expenditures in this country, some argue that using costly procedures for prolonging hopeless babies rather than helping patients whose quality of life would clearly benefit is morally indefensible.[57] However, unlike allocation decisions in Great Britain, U.S. doctors' decisions to withhold marginally helpful but expensive treatment does not necessarily mean that those funds would go for more beneficial medical care elsewhere.[58]

The present argument does not aim to solve the dilemma of allocation but to recognize its relevance to decision making about marginal individuals. In light of the nonobligatory nature of "extraordinary" treatment and the usual criteria for limiting treatment, parents especially should have considerable latitude in deciding against costly treatment for their marginal newborn. (Extraordinary care is today defined as that not offering a reasonable hope of success or that which involves excessive pain, cost, or inconvenience.[59]) Criteria for limiting treatment, according to Lo and Jonsen, is fourfold: treatment futility, treatment refusal, unacceptable quality of life, and great cost.[60] Today recognition of financial cost is imperative in any ethical analysis of expensive, high-technology medicine.[61]

Proximate Personhood and a Dominant Ethos

The proximate personhood perspective builds on the foundation of mainstream personhood thinking. This focuses on the moral centrality of *personal* experience, that is, the experience of life only available to persons. Personhood's contribution is essential, but it is too limited to decide care for the severely imperiled newborn and for the adult. What is finally accepted as a tenable policy for treatment of severely disabled new-borns must be compatible with an underlying public sentiment.[62]

The personhood position is profitably augmented by appreciation for society's dominant ethos,[63] the less tidy, but no less important public sense of rightness and wrongness. Personhood thinking illumines basic Western concepts about what makes life valuable and how decisions may be made about such life. However, the personhood perspective is far from universal, and its tenets are not a "mirror of nature," to borrow a phrase from Richard Rorty's influential *Philosophy and the Mirror of Nature*.[64] Increasingly literature, philosophy, and now theology are recognizing that they, like all other disciplines, possess feet of clay and do not give a historical grounding even to fundamental intuitions and truths.[65] In light of the conditionedness of all philosophical and social perspectives, an appreciation for—as distinguished from a capitulation to—the dominant ethos of a society is appropriate. It is the moderating addition of a basic societal ethos that sets proximate personhood thinking apart from its parent philosophy.

Attention to a societal ethos is not the equivalent of determining whether a given proposal will "play in Peoria." Such a test would be as narrow as seeking acceptance for a proposition only in a particular philosophical camp. However, given the less than absolutist nature of philosophic positions and social regulations, public perception is a weighty and ethically relevant consideration.

The issue is not a choice between good philosophy and social ethos. My contention is that a good philosophy includes sensitivity to historical and social context. We increasingly realize that all disciplines of the academy—including philosophy and ethics—are historically and socially contingent. An explicit appreciation for the social setting of a discussion is important for bioethics, particularly when policy issues are at stake. Thus, in proximate personhood thinking the dominant social ethos is candidly recognized as a component part of the perspective. Such a recognition might be labeled the principle of collective self-determination. Just as individuals possess a basic right to choose, so do societies have the right to determine their social policies.

Recognition of the importance of a dominant ethos is not unique to the concept of proximate personhood. The notion underlies tests of legitimacy in several fields that grapple with basic human values. American jurisprudence offers a prime example. Here, in areas of human conduct characterized by a plurality of considerations and viewpoints, there is a "pervasive reliance" on the notion of *reasonableness* (How would a reasonable person act?).[66] And an appeal to the notion of reasonableness is, after all, a method of invoking a society's dominant ethos.

Reasonableness, I suggest, is no substitute for the most cogent delineation of and argument for a unique social philosophy or moral idea, but it tempers an ideal so that it gains a broader hearing and possible acceptance. The proximate personhood model is proposed as a reasonable application of personhood thinking to bioethical moral decision making. The difference between a *reasonable* and an *untempered* application of personhood criteria becomes evident in discussion of a particular case. Consider the original Baby Doe. According to untempered personhood criteria it would be appropriate to conclude that the parents had the right to refuse surgery on the tracheoesophageal atresia. However, a *reasonable* application of those criteria would question such a decision. A *New York Times* editorial, for instance, held that the actions that led to Baby Doe's death were unreasonable: because Baby Doe "had been inadvertently robbed of perfection, he was deliberately robbed of life."[67] No single editorial can define reasonableness adequately but this one suggests current societal standards. Reasonableness, determined by the dominant ethos, is dynamic and it changes—but slowly, almost imperceptibly.

On the topic of newborns, it seems safe to say that the national ethos includes at least three elements: First, newborns are valuable members of the human community, as witnessed by familial behavior and governmental laws; second, newborns are generally not as highly esteemed as are older children and spouses (this is demonstrated by the differing periods of grieving and the history of tolerated infanticide);[68] and third, congenitally disabled newborns who are likely to develop into self-conscious persons with at least minimally functioning bodies that serve their interests should be medically treated.

Ethics and philosophy, in addition to law, are disciplines that are fundamentally affected by the dominant ethos. In ethics a common criterion for the acceptability of a proposed action is the test of publicity. For instance, this notion plays a key role in Sissela Bok's *Lying: Moral Choice in Public and Private Life.* The test of publicity "asks which lies, if any, would survive the appeal for justification to reasonable persons."[69] In philosophy the concept of an ideal observer serves a similar role. Roderick Firth is renowned for his development of an "ideal ethical observer," an imaginary observer of one's contemplated action who is all-knowing, dispassionate, and eminently fair.[70] Indeed, the early Christian ethic of the Golden Rule ("Do unto others as you would have them do unto you") presupposes the value of the tenets of the prevailing ethos.

As developed here, the proximate personhood model makes an explicit argument for the common belief that treatment should be provided to newborns with significant mental and physical potential. As has been argued throughout this chapter, these infants should be helped because they are increasingly near or proximate to undisputed personhood.

However, it must be acknowledged that there are beings with a higher level of cerebral functioning than newborns to whom society routinely shows less respect. I speak of certain animals. For the sake of completeness and consistency in the ethic of life being argued in this volume, it is important to deal with the animal liberation movement and its contention that animals have rights too. This is the agenda of the next chapter.

4 : Humans, Animals, and Morality

In the past a book on personhood probably would not have mentioned any life other than human. Indeed, many authors would write an exclusively human-centered book today. Ironically, this anthropocentric school of thought proudly waves the pro-life banner. But do only humans—be they embryos, newborns, adults, or comatose patients—possess valuable life? On what grounds is the sanctity of single-celled embryos greater than that of the young calf efficiently fattened at a factory farm to provide tasty veal cutlets?

The argument for recognition of animal status, at its best, is not the trendy idea that the most humanlike animals possess a right to life identical to humans. The concept is more carefully nuanced and much more basic. The argument for the moral status of animals is part of an evolving ethical consciousness that sentient beings must not continue to be viewed through a narrowly anthropomorphic lens.

A new consciousness is rising, but the inertia of human history is great and the development of new thinking is slow. The prophetic Tom Regan has proclaimed the genesis of this new consciousness in his book, *The Thee Generation: Reflections on the Coming Revolution.*[1] The present generation asks, What can I get for me? Regan sees the central question of the next generation as, What can I do for thee? The key word for the "thee" generation is community: "The human is but one life form among many, and what distinguishes us from the larger community of life is not our power to subdue but our responsibility to protect."[2] Prophetic movements are by definition contrary to established modes of thought, and the thee generation is no different. One critic is Willard Gaylin, a psychiatrist and cofounder of the Hastings Center, a premier ethics think tank in New

York. Gaylin is a mature professional who is admittedly scared at the prospects of a thee generation that has a high regard for animal life.

In his book, *Adam and Eve and Pinocchio: On Being and Becoming Human*, Gaylin writes a calculated broadside against the animal rights movement. His purpose is disclosed in the book's first sentence: "We don't much like ourselves these days." And Gaylin does his best to make us feel like superior beings. In affirming his personal affection for animals, he assures his readers that he is not against them and supports humane treatment of all creatures. Any decent human being would by definition, as an aspect of his or her humanness, be kind to animals, says Gaylin. However, he fears that the animal rights movement will "seriously undermine" our notion of the special nature of *Homo sapiens*.

Gaylin acknowledges that he is not writing as a philosopher but as a biologist and psychologist. Yet, in his concern for individual self-esteem, he does not shy away from sweeping philosophical assertions. Gaylin points longingly to the pre-Enlightenment past when humankind was singularly praised. In the Bible man and only man was created in the divine image and then told to subdue the earth and have dominion over all creation. Sophocles is quoted: "The world is full of wonderful things but none more so than man." Humans are important in life, but also in death—hence the reverence for the dead body as evidenced in the universal criticism of cannibalism.[3]

Gaylin recognizes legitimate reasons why we humans may have self-doubt: the great wars of this century, the Depression, the Holocaust, and our ecological disasters. However, he views "the dignity of man" as under attack by such modern phenomena as the animal rights movement. In criticizing animal interests it is Gaylin the psychiatrist, not the biologist, to say nothing of the philosopher, who speaks:

I acknowledge my bias. In my world, trees may have standing but animals have no "rights." In the world of morality—as in the world of politics—the animate (and inanimate) exist—valued, considered, dealt with, or destroyed, all in the service of the purposes and interests of humankind.[4]

The order of change between the chimpanzee and the human being is of such a magnitude as to represent a break, a discontinuity. We are not the next step, or even a giant leap forward. We are a parallel and independent entity; a thing unto ourselves; in a class of our own; *sui generis*. . . . The distance between man and ape is greater than the distance between ape and ameba.[5]

Of particular interest, in terms of philosophy, is Gaylin's treatment of the concept of autonomy. Until the Reformation the concept of the dignity of all humanity held sway. With the Reformation, says Gaylin, a new emphasis was placed on the believer's face-to-face relationship with God and the idea of human dignity assumed a more individual, personal character. Immanuel Kant further extended the notion of individual human worth, denoting each person as an autonomous self. He equated autonomy of person with the ability to reason. Gaylin, however, is suspicious of the elevation of autonomy for several reasons. For instance, social scientists are now attacking the concept of individual freedom and medical advances are keeping alive a growing population of nonautonomous individuals. So an emphasis on autonomy is no longer sufficient to protect the elevated niche that humans must occupy. So far Gaylin's argument is easy to follow. However, his next move is curious.

Gaylin claims that it has become "crucial" to analyze those aspects of human nature that are "beyond autonomy, that dignify and elevate our species." In the book's two major sections he explores such topics as morality, love, imagination, freedom, feelings, and romantic sexuality. One section deals with what the author says are attributes inherent in human biology and the other with attributes inherent in human potential. Gaylin delivers what he promises: eight fine chapters developing basic psychological themes—bracketed by a philosophical prologue and epilogue. However, I question whether this fulfills his desire to explicate themes that move beyond autonomy. He does move us beyond a narrow Kantian autonomy focused on the lone individual engaged in abstract reasoning. However, Gaylin offers no arguments progressing further than modern autonomy—to say nothing of moving us back to a medieval type of human dignity that uncritically generalizes about "man" and the human species. Indeed, what emerges is a very contemporary view of the individual.

In the epilogue, as in the context-setting prologue, Gaylin comes back to his larger project:

In a sense, by asking the question "What's so special about being human?" I suggest my bias: being human is indeed special. In enunciating the attributes that distinguish us from the beasts, that define our humanness, I have implicitly listed attributes of our life that must be encouraged and enhanced to maintain our status "in the image of God." Acknowledging that one of the primary aspects of our humanness is the capacity to modify ourselves, I would hold that the criterion for testing the value of change would be the degree to which the change encourages or discourages the emergence of the other noble human qualities I have analyzed in this book: a life of imagination, esthetics, and hope; autonomy; a range of feelings that includes joy, pride, guilt, and shame; romantic sexuality; work (as distinguished from labor); conscience; identification, friendship, and love.[6]

In defining humanness in this fashion, Gaylin has grandly—albeit inadvertently—substantiated a view of the human person as an autonomous, self-actualizing person. This view of persons is clearly contemporary, and very different from ancient and medieval views when "human dignity" was closely tied to natural mores and was preeminently exemplified by adult males of high rank. If modern members of the human species can even begin to approach Gaylin's ideal description of their noble traits, there is no reason for his claim that the animal rights movement erodes personal self-esteem. The modern psyche is not so fragile that an artificial gulf between all animals and humans must be postulated and celebrated.

The importance of Gaylin's volume is twofold: It shows what tough sledding is ahead for the animal liberation movement in light of the current thinking of such an urbane physician as Gaylin; second, it demonstrates how private and professional agendas can and do shape our thinking on volatile topics such as animal rights.

In this chapter I first describe the current state of the animal rights debate. I then develop my argument for a nuanced acceptance of animal liberation based on the assumption that all animals—including humans—are significantly rooted in certain natural ways of being, ways that are highly valuable to the flourishing of their own species. The less determined a species is, the greater the degree of self-awareness possible. And, as the basic point of proximate personhood indicates, the greater the degree of self-awareness or consciousness, the greater the moral claim to life. I conclude by examining the practice of xenografting—animal to human organ transplantation—in light of my proposed argument.

Contemporary Animal Rights Debate

The modern animal rights movement achieved high visibility with the publication in 1975 of Peter Singer's *Animal Liberation: A New Ethics for Our Treatment of Animals*. Singer argues in terms of bad consequences:

because sentient animals can feel pain, their suffering is morally wrong. He recognizes that each sentient species is different, and this means that dissimilar treatment may be warranted. However, all sentient creatures are due humane treatment and freedom from slaughter. Tom Regan, a fellow pioneer in the movement, takes a duty-oriented approach, arguing for the "inherent worth" of all sentient creatures because each is the "subject of a life." Arguing from different bases, both thinkers argue for vegetarianism and antivivisectionism.

Peter Singer

Peter Singer is a classical utilitarian in that he seeks the maximization of pleasure and a minimization of suffering in the world. For Singer this translates into a movement that he sees as a logical extension of the civil rights and the women's liberation movements. To the evils of racism and sexism Singer adds the evil of speciesism.

Accordingly, Singer preaches the gospel of equality of all animals. He limits his argument, however, to those that have moral significance, meaning all *sentient* creatures—animals capable, because of their neurological development, of sensing or experiencing life. Sentient animals have interests—a preference for one thing over another. An ameba or even an oyster does not qualify. "The capacity for suffering and enjoyment is *a prerequisite for having interests at all,* a condition that must be satisfied before we can speak of interests in a meaningful way."[7] Sentient animals, says Singer, are all those capable of feeling pain or sensing pleasure.

For Singer, all animals are not equally sentient, and hence they do not share identical moral standing. Thus the important concern is not *equal treatment* but *equal consideration.* "Equal consideration for different beings may lead to different treatment and different rights."[8] For example, the nature of humans is such that they have an interest in free speech and basic education, but such interests obviously do not apply to dairy cattle.

Singer is clear in stating that equal consideration does not mean equal moral worth:

A rejection of speciesism does not imply that all lives are of equal worth. While self-awareness, intelligence, the capacity for meaningful relations with others, and so on are not relevant to the question of inflicting pain—since pain is pain, whatever other capacities, beyond the capacity to feel pain, the being may have— these capacities may be relevant to the question of taking life. It is not arbitrary to hold that the life of a self-aware being, capable of abstract thought, of planning for the future, of complex acts of communication, and so on, is more valuable than the life of a being without these capacities.[9]

Tom Regan

Tom Regan is more unconventional in his claims than Singer. He approaches the topic from a duty orientation that draws upon and has much in common with a Kantian ethic—with one exception. Kant wrote of the autonomous value of rational humans, whereas Regan bestows a high Kantian dignity not only on thinking humans but on animals generally. He claims that it would be morally wrong to treat severely retarded humans as merely a means because such reasoning "would fail to acknowledge and respect the fact that they are the subjects of a life whose value is logically independent of any other being's taking an interest in it. . . . [It] is difficult at best to understand how anyone could reasonably deny that there are many, many species of animals whose members satisfy this requirement.[10] Thus a key to Regan's procedural rationale for animal rights is the marginal human argument: if society bestows high moral standing upon marginal humans, the many species whose rational capacities are equal to marginal humans should be granted elevated moral standing too.

Even more significant is Regan's claim that animals have inherent value. He repeatedly states the inherent value of humans as ends in themselves and declares that they are not to be used as mere means. Then he applies the statement directly to animals. For example:

Human beings have inherent value because, logically independently of the interest of others, each individual is the subject of a life that is better or worse for that individual. . . . Can this same line of argument be developed in the case of animals? The answer is, It can, at least in the case of those numerous species of animals whose members are, like humans, the subjects of a life that is better or worse for them, logically independently of whether they are valued by anyone else.[11]

Regan treats the idea that all subjects have inherent value as a categorical imperative: "One either has it [inherent value], or one does not. There are no in-betweens. Moreover, all those who have it, have it equally."[12]

When Singer wrote *Animal Liberation* in the mid-seventies, animal rights was a philosophically laughable topic. Years later when Regan edited an animal rights book, he stated that "Even as recently as a decade ago, not a single student in the thousands of philosophy courses offered annually in America's colleges and universities discussed the ethics of how humans treat animals."[13] A rich and diverse literature has followed in the wake of Singer and Regan's pioneering work—some of it critical and some supportive. I now turn to a summary and critical assessment of important points in an ongoing debate.

First, I look at the thought of Raymond Frey, a foremost critic of the animal liberation movement, who writes from an analytical, rationalist perspective. Second, I look at the diametrically opposed contribution of Steven Sapontzis who is critical of the high esteem that Frey explicitly gives (and even Regan and Singer implicitly give) the capacity for abstract reasoning.

Raymond Frey

Various objections can be lodged against animal liberation. For example, it is an unconventional and relatively minor moral issue, an issue that is counterintuitive to Western culture. In addition, it is a movement with radical implications for how we live our everyday lives—from the shoes on our feet to food on our tables. However, the primary objection is that the activists fight to give animals a privileged moral status that belongs only to human beings. And on this point philosopher Raymond Frey has written the most penetrating criticism of animal liberation to date, *Interests and Rights: The Case against Animals*.[14]

Frey accepts and begins with the assumption, common in animal liberation circles, that all and only beings who can have interests can have moral rights.[15] But Frey's agenda is to destroy the notion that nonhuman animals can have interests. He sets about his task by dividing interests into two subcategories, needs and desires, in regard to good health.

First, consider the sentence, "Good health contributes to John's well-being." Here "good health" is a need; good health is essential if John is to possess maximal well-being. Needs denote that which is necessary for things or individuals to function in their proper manner.

Good health is John's need, or in his interests, quite aside from whether he happens to desire it or, for that matter, even know what it is. In terms of need, what is in the interest of John—or other people or things—is quite separable from the idea of desire. So Frey talks of tractors that *need* oil for their continuing operation and Rembrandt paintings that *need* to be kept from exposure to excessive sunlight.

Second, consider the sentence "John desires good health." The very idea of desiring good health is based on the presupposition that John has an idea of what good health is. Desire denotes that which one self-consciously wants, quite aside from whether it is needed.

Whereas needs can be spoken of in relation to machines, grass lawns, or persons, desires are otherwise. Desires can only result from beliefs about something. For example, John must first have a *belief* about what personal well-being is and what good health is before he can truly desire them.

From such reasoning Frey concludes that animals cannot have morally meaningful interests. This is true because interests in the form of *needs* are too trivial, and interests in the form of *desires* are beyond animal attainment since the necessary beliefs are beyond their capacity. Beliefs require a developed self-consciousness and linguistic ability, both of which animals lack. Therefore, animals do not have interests or rights in any morally significant sense.

Frey's argument is nuanced and finally persuasive if one accepts what appears to be his underlying premise: that only the capacity for abstract reason bestows on an organism a distinctive moral status or a moral claim to existence. I analyze Frey's argument in three steps: first, a comment on his notion of interests as needs, second, a consideration of interests as desires, and finally, an analysis of his view on rationality.

Granted that tractors need oil in order to operate and that dogs (and humans) need food in order to live, does this mean that "needs" is a morally trivial category? It is true that tractors that run out of oil do not have "interests" that are violated. However, the farmer who owns the oil-depleted tractor has interests that are thereby harmed. In the case of a dog that needs food, not only the adoring master but also the dog has an interest in having his need for food met. Frey strains credulity by implicitly equating tractors with dogs, for the former possesses no sense of needing oil, and the latter acutely senses the need for food, quite aside from any human interests.

Frey's notion of interests as desires is on another plane of discussion—that of beliefs. Given the statement, "The cat believes that the ball is stuck," Frey will not allow that the cat has such a perception unless it possesses the requisite concepts, what we might call "ballness," and "stuckness." "Perception involves not only sensory detection but also comprehension by the mind."[16] Frey reasons that the cat's behavior may appear to indicate a particular belief about the ball, but because we do not know what the cat perceives, we can say nothing about the cat's beliefs. For Frey, writing in the tradition of analytic philosophy, beliefs are either true or false, and unless a subject can conceptualize the difference, it is not capable of beliefs. Hence, in another cat illustration, Frey says that he does "not see how the cat can be correctly described as believing the [shoe] laces are tied unless it can, as I do, distinguish between the beliefs that the laces are tied and that the laces are untied and regard one but not the other as true."[17]

Frey is convinced of the importance of propositions and the requisite ability to determine their truthfulness. His standard for interests and rationality is tied to syntactical formulations that must be understood as such. However, there are many practical "beliefs" that animals have about the living of their lives that need not be processed through syntactical propositions. Frey's illustration of the cat and the stuck ball is an excellent example of nonsyntactical beliefs that are the clear basis for meaningful action. Similarly, humans process much vital information without resorting to rationally processed statements. For example, if I touch a hot stove top, I spontaneously draw my fingers back on the belief that continued contact will do me further harm. However, such information is not syntactically processed, and need not be—indeed should not be—because of the urgency of the situation. Frey's "saying that beliefs are sentences clearly confuses the psychological with the linguistic," claims Steven Sapontzis.[18]

Surely human persons, beyond all animals, have the capacity to think more deeply about pain and its significance and the broader context in which it is felt. On the other hand, because pain is so immediate to an animal and presents such a potential threat to life, it may be relatively much greater to the animal than to a human person. Regardless, it is true that the ability to possess an epistemic context of understanding means that human experience is more complex and richer than animal experience. According to Sapontzis: "Acquiring a culture expands one's understanding immensely beyond the limitations of such practical understanding. However, it does not mark the advent of understanding, for the ability to recognize and solve many practical problems no more requires the elaborate machinery of language, tradition, and institutions than doing simple arithmetic requires a computer."[19]

Whereas Frey has written a key volume criticizing animal liberation, Sapontzis has attempted to broaden its base, with partial success. Sapontzis's major contribution to the discussion is his demonstration of the limits of a narrowly rational basis for our assessment of morality and for our assessment of what creatures are worthy of moral regard.

Steven Sapontzis

Sapontzis's rhetoric is that of an antirationalist. He defines the rational mode of argument (primarily that of the philosophers) as characterized by moderation, tough-mindedness, professionalism, and fact facing. He effectively demonstrates that ordinary persons are only sometimes rational and live out their lives by following emotion, hope, rhetoric, eccentricity, and intuition as well. In fact, an appropriate reaction to horrible situations such as rape or genocide is not a cool, rationally detached comment, but spontaneous revulsion!

But should not moral persons strive to be consistently rational? To the query, "Why should I be rational?" Sapontzis answers that to respond with *reasons* begs the question. One should be rational at times and at other times be emotional, hopeful, and so forth. How does one decide how to act? "It is a case of guesswork beforehand and 'Did it work?' afterward."[20] One might think that Sapontzis is merely facetious, but this is not the case. He asks, "Is there not another, more general, methodological sense of rationality, one having to do with the systematic, impartial gathering and logical use of evidence, to which we have a categorical obligation? No."[21]

Rationality, à la Kant, Rawls, and standard philosophy, is a much-hailed source of morality. However, for Sapontzis the sources of our commitments to morality are diverse. Although philosophers dispute among themselves, society has a basic sense of what constitutes moral actions. For example, an individual who thwarts a bank robbery receives commendations from society, quite aside from philosophers' quibbles about motive, accident, and so forth. One need not be a moral philosopher to do moral acts, and surely one need not be able to give an ethical rationale for one's good act for it to qualify as moral. Sapontzis thus advances what he sees as a common sense morality as opposed to Regan's deontological edifice or Singer's popular utilitarianism.

In the name of common morality Sapontzis attempts to blur the distinction between moral acts that are *agent dependent* and those that are *agent independent*. He believes that agent dependent morality is much overrated in determining the ethics of an act. For instance, a human mother instinctively risking her life to protect her children from an intruder is seen as exemplifying moral courage. Or when a child possesses a moral behavior pattern, which, thanks to good parenting, is second nature, he or she is praised as morally exemplary. Why is it then when animals, by instinct, training, or chance, perform analogous moral acts they do not have the same status as well-reared humans? Sapontzis points to feline mothers who risk their lives protecting their kittens, porpoises that have saved the lives of sailors, dogs that have pulled children from swimming pools. He cites the lifestyle of wolves as morally exemplary: wolves mate for life, show great loyalty to their pack, respect another wolf's territory, and seldom kill what they do not eat.

Is Sapontzis successful in his postrational case for animal liberation? He has made a significant contribution in demonstrating the limits of rationality as a basis for moral action. Further, he has made an impressive case for continuity and similarity between what is seen as the moral behavior of humans and the commendable behavior of some exceptional animals. Ironically, however, the form and substance of his published argument belie, at least to some extent, the valuable points he makes. His demonstration of the limits of rationality is nowhere evidenced in the type of persuasion he offers for his point of view. He presents carefully argued, cogent *reasons*—not special rhetorical appeals or emotional outbursts or viscerally based profanity at, for instance, the outrage of meat eating. Second, for all Sapontzis's arguments that the intelligence of humans does not grant them a categorical moral claim to existence beyond that of animals, the only examples he cites of animals whose behavior indicates their high moral standing are those most like humans in intelligence—dolphins, porpoises, dogs, and so forth. Thus perhaps Sapontzis's own book advocating animal liberation is a prime example of what his moral theory espouses: morality is composed as much of rhetoric as reason!

♦ ♦ ♦

An extensive literature in animal rights has developed since the mid-seventies. Although most writers on the topic are more moderate in their assertions than Gaylin, the majority of philosophers have not converted to animal liberation. The crux of the debate, in one fashion or another, is the weight one assigns to intelligence—its possession or lack thereof by the creature in question. Even Sapontzis, who convincingly argues against the relevance of rationality, illustrates his argument exclusively by citing animals of highest intelligence. Frey, one of many critics, is so dazzled by the human capacity for abstract reasoning that he claims animals do not have interests (and hence rights) because they cannot comprehend the very notion of interests. Therefore, he reasons, an animal's inclination to live is more like a tractor's *need* for oil than a human's *desire* for life.[22]

If we accept proximate personhood's notion of graduated moral status, it is understandable that the concern of animal liberationists is for animals that are most like us humans in intelligence. It is more questionable that their focus is on *our treatment of those animals*—not particularly on animals' independent well-being. That observation has led sociologist Keith Tester to argue that the movement says more about us and our need to morally define ourselves than about the animals.[23]

Thus contemporary theorists debate the status of animals, but discussion of what normative role animals should play in society is not new.

Animal Rights and Social Ethos in History

In 1386 a court of law in the Normandy town of Falsise tried and convicted a sow for biting the arms and head of a child who subsequently died. The trial followed proper procedures for a murder trial, after which the pig was dressed in human clothes and taken to the town square where it was "mangled and maimed in the head and forelegs" and hanged. The sentence was imposed by the public executioner who wore a new pair of gloves. The legal proceedings cost the town a total of ten sous and ten deniers. The event was commemorated by a fresco painted in the local church of the Holy Trinity. Although to modern sensibilities this seems a bizarre event, the Falsise pig trial was not unusual in Europe from the tenth through the nineteenth centuries.[24] Historian Edward Evans describes other incidents, including one in which Bartholomew Chassenee, a leading jurist of sixteenth-century France, established his reputation as counsel for certain rats accused of "having feloniously eaten up and wantonly destroyed the barley-crop of that province."[25] What is the explanation for such strange legal proceedings?

Evans cites more than one explanation for such trials. A general explanation is the application to nonhumans of the inexorable divine natural law of *lex talionis,* an ancient form of justice demanding eye for eye and tooth for tooth. Another and more specific explanation, as reported by Evans, is that articulated by the Jesuit priest Pere Bougeant. Bougeant, in his *Amusement Philosophique sur de Langage des Bestes,* published in Paris in 1739, disputed the Cartesian view of animals. According to Descartes, all humans—even madmen—possess immortal souls. On the other hand, all animals, regardless of their cunning or developed senses, are merely divinely created "machines" driven by organ-derived passions.[26] Bougeant, however, wrote of animals' high intelligence and keen feelings as evidence of their being possessed by billions of devils. Thus he explained a widespread Christian mistreatment of animals generally and the animal trials more specifically. He was relying on a "received ecclesiastical view": Satan's allies, the fallen angels bound for the Day of Judgment, took over the bodies of human newborns and animals while awaiting their final end. Because newborns and animals were merely the embodied souls of devils, two practices ensued: prior to baptism infants were routinely exorcised, and evil behavior by animals could result in trial and execution.[27]

The primary importance of these animal trials for us today is their dramatic illustration of the importance of the moral context, indeed the social ethos, of decisions we make about the relative value of lives. Often contemporaries do not give much thought to such issues because their presuppositions seem universal—today as well as in medieval France. But, as has been indicated in earlier chapters, our postmodern era is ever more conscious of the fact that presuppositions about value, including those dealing with animals, are omnipresent—and in need of examination. The opinion of a writer, a jurist, or an ordinary citizen regarding the life of an animal is not "value-free"—this was not the case four hundred years ago and it is not the case today.[28]

The social ethos of medieval times was, at best, anthropocentric. Humans were front and center in both the doctrine of creation and in the doctrine of immortality. All of creation was given for human ends, according to Origen, Aquinas, Luther, and Calvin.[29] Historian Keith Thomas links the theological notion of animals serving human ends to their low status and in this regard cites the popular "country house" poems of the early seventeenth century:

> The pheasant, partridge and the lark
> Flew to thy house, as to the Ark.
> The willing ox of himself came
> Home to the slaughter, with the lamb;

>And every beast did thither bring
>Himself to be an offering.[30]

Belief in the immortal soul has had a telling impact on our Western views of valuable human and animal life. As outlined by the historical survey in chapter 1, all humans—regardless of stage of development or degree of abnormality—are equally precious because of their embodiment of a soul, the entity that far transcends all mortal flesh. Given the pervasiveness of belief in the immortal soul, shared by philosopher, priest, and peasant alike, it is not difficult to understand how significant thinkers such as Thomas Aquinas might hold that we cannot logically be obligated even to be charitable to lowly animals.[31]

Not only were *Homo sapiens* held to be above the animals because of humans' immortal souls, but gradations were made among humans. Thomas Aquinas held that only man—not woman—was created in God's image.[32] Keith Thomas indicates that throughout much of the Christian tradition there was a sense that women were "near the animal state." George Fox confronted the belief among some Christians that women had "no soul, no more than a goose."[33]

However strong and widespread particular religious doctrines may be, they change—or just as important, the interpretation of them is altered. The continued belief in the immortal soul held by millions of people, for example, need not lead to denigration of animal life. Indeed, it can be a reason for enhanced valuing, as was the case for nineteenth-century Cardinal Bellarmine. The cardinal stated that he must agree with his church that animals do not have souls, but he argued that a devaluation of animal life does not logically follow. On the contrary, animals should be treated better than people because temporal existence is their only chance at life whereas wrongs done to humans can be addressed in the afterlife.[34]

Another example of fundamental change concerns the Judeo-Christian story of creation: "God said to them, 'Be fruitful and multiply, and fill the earth and subdue it; and have dominion over the fish of the sea and over the birds of the air and over every living thing that moves upon the earth'" (Genesis 1:28). The traditional Judeo-Christian interpretation of creation is thoroughly anthropomorphic. However, one revised perception of creation emphasizes the unity of life represented in this primordial myth: God places animals and humans on earth to live in mutual dependence and peace and equilibrium.[35] Seen as a call for bio-unity, the creation myth assumes its place along with other inclusive beliefs of historic religions (for instance, the Hindu belief in reincarnation).

As profound as the teachings of Moses, the Buddha, and Jesus are, their pronouncements, of course, do not answer all the challenges to belief brought by the modern era. The integrity of religious belief demands not only continuity with the past but also adaptation to new knowledge. The reinterpretation of ancient stories in light of contemporary understanding is a necessity if religion is to remain an intellectual resource for addressing present issues.

A fundamental change in our thinking about human and nonhuman lives—in both religious and secular spheres—is morally necessary and timely because of our increased knowledge about our own and other animal species.

Biologized Philosophy

Self-consciousness, both potential and realized, was the pivotal point in the discussion of proximate personhood in chapter 3. Nothing in my consideration of nonhuman animals in the present chapter lessens the seriousness of earlier contentions about the importance of intelligence. However, the central notion of personhood needs to be further developed in light of our greater biological knowledge of humans and nonhuman animals.

Mary Midgley calls for a new "biologized philosophy" of human life. As Midgley says in the first sentence of her rightfully influential *Beast and Man,* "We are not just rather like animals; we are animals."[36] It is no longer adequate for us to rely solely on Kant's philosophizing on the "pure" will or on Luther's theologizing on the "free" will. For the sake of intellectual integrity modern theorizing must at least take into account insights from schools of thought such as the behaviorism of Skinner and the sociobiology of Edward Wilson. Our recently acquired knowledge of ethnology and the human behavioral sciences is a mandatory descriptive base for contemporary, honest philosophizing and theologizing.

A central argument of this book is that normal human adults possess a unique moral status because of their possession of self-consciousness. However, it is a fundamental mistake to move from this basic conceptual point to the lived world of human beings and postulate or even assume that our brains are so much raw computer power that we can and should be able to apply to an infinite variety of chosen ends. Indeed, brain power is immense and we are continuously learning more about this organ. However, the high moral valuation we place on persons is much richer and deeper than the mere prizing of a sophisticated electrochemical computer. We highly value rational human life, at least in theory, because intelligence is directed toward laudable ends. For example, medical science is valued because its aim ideally is the well-being of persons, not their misery. Pursuit of human misery would be the height of irrationality, the more so as it is "intelligently" carried out.

Further, the great majority of humans agree on much more than the proposition that survival is rational. For that reason great novelists provide us with penetrating insights into ourselves by highly nuanced accounts of characters' lives, implicitly promoting some behaviors as better than others and inevitably inviting deep soul searching about what is appropriate action.[37] The very use of words such as *inhumane* and *irrational* suggests at least a general consensus about certain ends and not others.

Midgley speaks of rationality as having two aspects, cleverness and integration. Cleverness means the ability to perform sophisticated, abstract processing of information and decision making. Her notion of integration is especially significant: "having a character, acting as a whole, having a firm and effective priority system."[38] By utilizing the psychological term integration she is explicitly and purposefully arguing that rationality is an aspect of a being with certain basic characteristics. And the most fundamental of those ends and even the means of achieving them are not freely chosen by individuals—even very clever ones—as much as they are received by us humans as a part of our existence. Science is beginning to recognize that just as physical traits are a part of genetic inheritance, so certain fundamental psychological and social patterns are passed on as well.

This line of argument has a long history. It goes back at least as far as the fathers of Western philosophy—Socrates, Plato, and Aristotle. These thinkers discussed the notions of form and matter, form dealing with thought and matter referring to things. For Plato the essence of life existed in a transcendent realm of reality uncontaminated by earthly matter. The eternal forms (of thought) were pure; their terrestrial (and hence material) counterparts were inferior. For Plato, matter was irrational, evil, the negation of the real, and finally absurd. On the other hand, Aristotle, the first biologist-philosopher, prized matter, viewing it as potency—material with the ability to become something in particular. Rationality was not merely a speculative enterprise; it concerned life's palpable existence. Aristotle believed he could ascertain the given telos of every form of life from studying its behavior. This biologist-philosopher was rigid and literal, but there is considerable value in this biological perspective, even if we must now update his prescient early thinking.

A modern development of the "natural" philosophizing pioneered by Aristotle is the comprehensive thinking of Alfred North Whitehead. Whitehead's "process philosophy" is a helpful system of thought that portrays contemporary scientific views of life within in a conceptual whole, a metaphysics. His task was grand: to account for every element of experience in "a system of ideas which bring aesthetic, moral and religious interests into relation with those concepts of the world which have their origin in natural science."[39] Process thought is based on the assumption that becoming is more central than being, transition and activity are more characteristic of life than are permanence and substance. Such presuppositions are not opposed to science, per se, but are contrary to the narrowly defined science of the past that tended to define reality according to atomistic and mechanistic assumptions as found in the traditional concepts of physics and chemistry.

For Whitehead all that exists is comprised of "moments of experience." Each of these moments is both an "actual occasion," denoting its temporality, and each is an "actual entity," suggesting its integration. Each moment is distinguished by its own inner reality and by its being integrally related to past moments of experience—its own and more distantly to others'.

Process philosophy parts company with medieval philosophy, which viewed nature as a *kingdom,* governed by a sovereign Lord who created separate material and spiritual substances. Transitory matter was categorically subordinate to the immortal soul, and all matter served human souls whose goal in this life was to prepare for the next. Process thought, as with modern science, views nature as a *community* of interdependent beings. The most complex human experiences are not discontinuous with thoroughly natural, material processes. A thoroughgoing mind/body dualism, though basic to traditional scientific thinking, finds little support in modern science.

In process philosophy there are no dualisms. Organisms vary greatly in the complexity and richness of their experience, but all that exists is on a continuum. All matter possesses a "physical pole" and a "mental pole" in Whitehead's aesthetic-philosophical model, and hence material life is continuous, from a common rock to the human brain. The atoms that comprise a stone are theoretically open to self-determination, but the physical pole so dominates that the change is almost nil. At the other end of the continuum, there is the human brain that can be explained according to neural processes, and such an explanation is merely parallel to the phenomena of mind and self-consciousness. At the higher levels of being, actually new events and entities can easily come into being.

Ian Barbour, accepting and building on the basic insights of process philosophy, underscores the importance of the notion of a hierarchy of complexity in organisms. He has his quibbles with Whitehead, such as his suggestion of the possibility of novelty in rocks (since it is so vanishingly small). But any disagreement is minor compared to Barbour's agreement on the mutual interdependence of life and emergent novelty. The subjectivity made possible by an organism's mental pole is limited in a mosquito but great in an adult human. Therefore, to attach greater moral value to normal adult humans comports with what is found in nature, according to process thought.[40]

This brief discussion of natural philosophy demonstrates that our historical consciousness will not allow us to accept either Plato's ideal forms or Aristotle's pure biology. Whitehead's process philosophy is appealing because he posits an overarching form that makes sense of today's scientific knowledge, quite aside from whether one accepts all Whiteheadian particulars. We now know that Plato and Aristotle—and Whitehead—constructed systems of thought that are open for revision or rejection as our knowledge base expands and as ideas change. Finally, our world view is the integration of our evolving knowledge of life and the paradigms that form and filter that knowledge. In light of contemporary views it seems counterintuitive to deny that human experience has strong parallels to the biological experience of animal life.[41]

Human and animal life are definitely on a continuum and this fact has direct implications for our discussion of proximate personhood. We must face the realization that those capacities that indisputably give most humans a rightful claim to life are shared by at least some animals.

Feeling and Thinking

Consider the common honey bees. These social creatures, indeed all social insects, are driven primarily if not solely by instinct. Midgley speaks of "closed instinct" as that instinct in which desire and technique go together. Bees, for example, desire to communicate to other bees the presence of a distant nectar source, and so they dance a particular pattern. Their desire and their technique for achieving that end are both instinctual. The bee has no capacity for considering other methods of communicating the vital information. Persons have other options for fulfilling desires, and these are discussed below. But first let us consider the proposition that persons also follow instinct.

In some basic ways it seems that we humans behave instinctively just as do nonhumans. As I write this the South Los Angeles riots have just ceased and again the video images of Rodney G. King being beaten by LAPD officers are fresh in mind. When King was commanded to lie flat on the pavement, he was repeatedly beaten by police batons and instinctively assumed a defensive neonatal position. Another instance of such behavior is the "maternal instinct" to protect children, found not only in human mothers but also in many social animals.

At a higher level of functioning, however, humans are governed much more by socialization than by instinct. We are now aware of how thoroughly we humans are social creatures. For example, the famous story of the "wolf boy" illustrates the degree to which persons' behavior is sociologically determined. To a significant degree we become who we are because of our interactions with other persons. Martin Buber's anthropology is based on his fundamental insight that the human reality is not centered in or reducible to either of two relating subjects (in Buber's words, the *I* and the *Thou*); rather, it is found in the "between" dimension of the two persons in genuine meeting. Regardless of how clever a person may be, his or her basic system of integrated priorities—whatever they may be—are not devised in a social vacuum but are formed in reaction to or in action toward others. It appears that sociality is natural to humans, just as it is to many other advanced animals.

Often instinctive actions, feelings between persons, and subjective meanings are relegated to the affective dimension of consciousness that is opposed to the dimension of *ratio*. This widespread and unfortunate dualism is contrary to what a biologized ethic portrays. Particular basic patterns for the living of life are passed on to us through both our genes and our society. Life preferences may be modified by clever individuals, but they are not created *ex nihilo*. And recognition of this fact does not stifle human creativity. On the contrary, it makes it possible. It is just because one has a basic sense of identity, established and reinforced both genetically and socially, that one can apply creative powers to unique ends. A person who has no centered self typically is so obsessed with basic survival issues that only minimal attention for creative efforts is available.

It could be argued that some creative individuals have been estranged from their societies. For instance, Friedrich Nietzsche carved out a creative philosophical perspective while writing for a decade in solitude, culminating in a mental breakdown and finishing his life in an asylum. The life of Jesus of Nazareth was such that his idiosyncratic views brought him to the cross. The lives and deaths of these two prophets could be seen as illustrations of social misfits. But this would be a great oversimplification. Nietzsche and Jesus, I would argue, expounded and deepened basic ideas resident within their communities—personal mastery and social love, respectively. These two men are profoundly within the Western tradition, even if some of their pronouncements are not to be taken literally. They only appear to be at society's edges because they tugged their societies toward radically different and neglected ends, which they made dramatically more explicit.

My basic point is that feelings and intuitions of what life is about and how it should be lived are complementary to and not opposed to reason. The capacity to reason is merely a tool of the brain to organize its more primitive and basic affective dimensions. This capacity is minimal in insects; it is great in normal adult humans. However, the end or ends of that abstract organizational skill are not sui generis. The ends one chooses for one's life come from biology, in-depth interaction among persons, and life experience in general. Such a view of life is processive and dynamic, as opposed to traditional views of life as comprised of unchanging essences.

Because of our increasing biological knowledge, the gap between human individuals and animals is becoming less distinct. Among the implications of proximate personhood is the realization that animals such as the African apes are at least quasi-persons.

Common Animal Sentiments

The common honeybee has closed instincts. It has no option but to dance in a particular pattern to tell others its rudimentary message. However, the more complex the animal, the more options are available for meeting common desires. But the increased number of options leaves more possibility for error—failure to meet basic needs. So that the basic life goals of the higher species are met, those species' desire for certain ends— say the rearing of offspring—must be even stronger than in those animals with closed instincts, contends Midgley: "Mammals could not improve on the automatic brood-tending of bees merely by being more intelligent about what benefits infants. They have to want to benefit them. And they must want it more, not less, than bees, because they are so much freer, and could easily desert their infants if they had a mind to, which is the sort of thing that could simply never occur to a bee."[42]

Human persons, of course, are extremely clever and could conceivably choose to live their lives in any one of many diverse patterns. But the diversity of lifestyle that the mind can conceive must not mute the similarities between human persons and other animals at a more basic, affective level of our lives—the level where we love, copulate, rear our offspring, and communicate friendship.

Lorenz cites the case of ganders:

A gander may have affairs of long duration, regularly meeting a female other than his wife in a "secret" place and copulating with her. However, she is his partner only in copulation; he never accompanies her when she is walking and he never gives even the slightest hint of a triumph ceremony in her presence. In this respect he remains absolutely faithful to his wife. Nor does he guard the strange female's nest; should she happen to be successful in acquiring a nest site and in rearing a family, she must do so unaided by the gander.[43]

A less titillating example of nonhuman animal behavior, which has uncanny resemblance to that of humans, concerns the conduct of what Lorenz describes as a low-ranking female jackdaw after becoming the mate of the troop leader:

She knew within forty-eight hours exactly what she could allow herself, and I am sorry to say that she made the fullest use of it. She did not stop at gestures of self importance, as High-rankers of long standing nearly always do. No—she always had an active and malicious plan of attack ready at hand. In short, she conducted herself with the utmost vulgarity.

You think I humanize the animal? . . . What we are wont to call "human weakness" is, in reality, nearly always a pre-human factor and one which we have in common with the higher animals. Believe, me, I am not mistakenly assigning human properties to animals; on the contrary, I am showing you what an enormous animal inheritance remains in man, to this day.[44]

Midgley contends, in light of such evidence, that we humans live according to certain natural patterns, such as marriage and family life, maternal instinct, and special behavioral differences in acting toward males and females. These patterns of life are indicative of inherited ways of human life that are innate. And although they may be modified somewhat, we "can no more get rid of them than we can grow wings and tusks."[45] One basic gesture is the outstretched hand, a symbol of friendship. This gesture is shared across cultures and also with the apes. Midgley contends that such gestures have immense implications for higher animals (including humans) that dwarfs their apparent triteness: "To be disposed to make the gestures, you must also be capable of the emotions. . . . These gestures bring us all back to the same group of behavior patterns for our deepest exchanges. Anyone who thinks this a boring restraint should reflect that, without it, we should have no chance of reciprocation at all."[46] Certain core and common sentiments that humans share with other animals is the substratum upon which our civilized life is built.

Higher Animals' Otherness

Animals are like us, but they have their own lives quite apart from our own. Iris Murdoch had this fact impressed upon her: "I am looking out of my window in anxious and resentful state of mind, brooding perhaps on some damage done to my prestige. Then suddenly I observe a hovering kestrel. In a moment everything is altered. The brooding self with its hurt vanity has disappeared. There is nothing now but kestrel. And when I return to thinking of the other matter it seems less important."[47]

The worlds of insects, birds, and mammals have their lives quite apart from us and our troubles and joys. When we take the time for reflection, we encounter the radical otherness of a system of existence that came into being and will persist apart from us—in some cases only exist apart from us. The ecology movement is helping us to appreciate the value of all of nature, but our purpose here is to contend for the relative importance of higher animals having their own life projects that are valuable to themselves.

Taking its lead from Plato, Western civilization claimed intellect as the distinguishing feature of our own species. It surely is our intellectual powers that set most of us apart. However, to move from that fact to the argument that therefore only we possess a unique claim to existence is a distinct moral judgment that happens to be a non sequitur. We have earlier established that many mammals have considerable intelligence—in addition to other abilities, such as superior strength, speed, agility, sight, sense of smell, and so forth. Unlike General George Custer, we must not decide the moral value of Indians—or any other beings—merely on the basis of being able to kill many more of them than they of him. By analogy, would it be appropriate for dolphins to evaluate whether we humans qualify as "swimmers," given our relative lack of proficiency in this area?[48] Midgley uses another analogy: "There is no question of keeping the chimps out of the castle. They and many other animals have always been inside, and only our conceit and prejudice have stopped us from seeing them. They are all over the ground floor, which is still a central area of our life as well as theirs."[49]

On what basis do we decide that it is intelligence alone that should determine our unique moral claim to life? Accurate taxonomy does not necessarily translate directly into just moral norms. Must the criteria for a moral claim to life be narrowly construed? Why should the moral claim to life not rest, rather, upon excellences having to do with our whole natures, perhaps a sense of meaningful sociality?[50] It is true that nonhuman creatures may have their own life projects that are quite other to us. However, to argue that their claim to life is based on their "otherness" is questionable. As Keith Tester reminds us, "It is society, it is 'the idea of humanity in our own person' that says animals should be respected because they cannot be known. But exactly that conclusion does make animals known; they are classified as the unclassifiable."[51] So, finally, the contention that apes have a claim to existence cannot be based on the fact that some philosophers have built a case for their "otherness" that demands respect. The claim gains its moral weight from the fact that we see, study, and know how other animals experience pain and joy in ways analogous to our experience but, admittedly, not with the self-reflective depths of meaning that we attach to our own experiences. Nature's myriad species allow no magic line to be drawn above which all animals possess a moral claim to existence. Rather, as was argued in chapter 3, the more closely that an animal approximates undisputed personhood such as most adult humans' possess, the greater the moral claim to life and its various goods.

But just why ought persons—those individuals I have described as possessing self-consciousness—be given a moral status denied to other beings? This is the timeworn question of the naturalistic fallacy, the so-called "is/ought" problem. What is there about any characteristics observed in nature, including human nature, that leads to the conclusion that something ought to be? Or, more to the point, why should a "person" (defined in terms of the nonmoral capacity for self-consciousness) be accorded maximal moral status? How does one move from the "is" of "that's a person" to the "ought" of "we should accord moral rights to persons"?[52]

A strict logical sequence from *is* to *ought* does not exist, but I do think there can be reasonable and unreasonable correlations. The reasonableness of various data and arguments throughout this volume might be summed up thus: pragmatically, resources cannot be equally expended on respecting the lives of all species, so some lines delineating moral status need to be drawn; philosophically, the greater the richness of experience available to an entity (as illustrated by one's capacity to even contemplate the idea of an experience), the greater the moral status; and theologically, a belief that the Mystery of the universe—called by whatever inadequate name—intended persons to be marked by high moral status. And, in humility, I think we must admit that it is likely no happenstance that we persons have devised the scheme by which we end up with highest moral status.

Humans and Privilege

Humans have and should continue to hold a privileged position in the hierarchy of beings. This is so at least because of the truism that out of the ten million species of organisms known to exist, not all can be given equal moral weight. And human persons hold a privileged position because of their possession of the highest degree of self-consciousness and richness of experience.

Chimps are of relatively high intelligence. They can, for instance, use concepts via American Sign Language. "Formal tests in which color slides of new objects are displayed to ASL-using chimpanzees show that tree, to them, as to us, refers to a class of trees and treelike plants rather than to any specific tree."[53] Their ASL use is not as clear as that of human adults who have acquired ASL as their first language, but their signing is intelligible. In addition, some trained chimps have transmitted words from one generation to another with human aid. Researchers report that one chimp learned some fifty word-signs from his adolescent and adult chimp companions.[54] However, chimps still do not come close to mature humans in intellect. In fact, the syntactical abilities of the most advanced chimp are quite primitive (by human standards) and are surpassed by a three year old. Chimps have the syntactical abilities of a normal two-and-a-half-year-old human child. By the time a child is five he or she can produce an almost infinite variety of sentences. Some animal liberationists would minimize the difference between chimps and humans by citing the fact that chimps have a genetic composition that is over 99 percent similar to the human species, closer than are some rabbit species to other rabbits.[55] But this fact cannot camouflage the significant cerebral difference between humans and other animals.

The basis for the gap rests in the related capacities of reasoning and language use, as manifest especially in self-consciousness. The brains of chimps and all other higher mammals—including humans—are distinguished by their larger relative size—especially that of the neocortex. The neocortex aids in the perception and interpretation of sensory data, the performance of complex motor skills, and the integration of senses with thought and action. Humans have larger brains than other mammals, with much larger frontal regions of the neocortex. The human prefrontal cortex is twice as large as that of a comparable ape brain.[56] Another significant difference between humans and apes is that the human neocortex is involved with the voluntary control of speech.[57]

Human persons are far ahead of other animals in raw intelligence. This has immense implications for the degree of self-awareness that is possible and the resulting ability of humans to determine the contours of their lives. Associated with a high degree of self-awareness or consciousness are the notions of memory, anticipation, and the vesting of prior events and coming events with a significance that directly impinges on the human person's present life. For example, the capacity to recall one's childhood and be able to assess its strengths and weaknesses is a significant aid in an adult's ability to be a mature, adjusted self. Similarly, for a middle-aged person to contemplate retirement on an adequate pension brings a sense of comfort that is not available to the brightest chimp because no non-human animal is capable of such contemplation.

The well-being of a person is significantly affected by factors beyond gratification of immediate needs such as food, shelter, sex, and so forth.

This fact has far-reaching implications for why it is important to place a high premium on the life of a human fetus or a newborn—quite aside from that young human's intrinsic moral worth or lack thereof. Thoroughgoing personhood thinkers, as described in chapter 3, attach minimal value to the fetus or newborn for one basic reason: these nascent humans do not possess the capacity for reasoning or self-consciousness. Therefore, Tooley, for example, concludes that it is intrinsically moral to kill infants up until three months of age, a time at which significant brain development has occurred.[58] Tooley's reasoning is coherent, given his individualistic premise: he looks at merely the individual human or animal in question and makes a moral judgment. However, as I have argued, humans in particular are social beings and the richness of our lives is achieved within a broad context of past, present, and future. Neonates are valuable little humans at least because of the mere fact that we persons attach great value to them. In part we do so instinctively, just as do many other animals. Just try to separate a bear cub from its mother! Typically the socially higher level animals have a strong brood-tending instinct. But despite knowing that we share a maternal instinct with other animals, still we *choose* to bestow great value on newborn humans. We know that within a very short time, misfortune excluded, our newborn will become a person in his or her own right. Therefore we appropriately "impute"[59] the status of personhood to the baby—irrespective of that baby's capacities, which are mostly potential.

Use of Humans and Other Animals

In his book, *The War of the Worlds,* H. G. Wells portrays super-intelligent Martians as enormous heads on mechanical trolleys who are intent on annihilating the human race without attempting to understand it. They are merely exercising the obvious right, according to Wells, that we have long exercised over "the cow and the cucumber." It is axiomatic for many people that every member of the human species, without exception, is categorically more sacred than all nonhuman forms of life. Adherents of the great Eastern religions have long believed in the sanctity of animal life, and now a growing idea in the West—for generally different reasons—is that higher animal life possesses intrinsic value.

The place where the conflict between animal moral status and public behavior is most blatant is the dinner table. Vast numbers of animals are slaughtered each year in the United States for food. If sentient animals do possess moral status, as I argue, how great must that status be to outweigh the value of Americans' taste satisfaction? Increasingly, vegetable-based meat substitutes are appearing in the grocery stories. The use of meat for food is morally suspect in a country of abundant fruits, grains, and vegetables. Vegetarianism makes for a superior diet on several grounds—morality, ecology, and health.

No member of the over 750,000 animal species is on the same moral plane with the normal adult human. This conclusion is implicit in the argument for proximate personhood presented here. Because of our capacity for a significantly more complex and rich existence, human lives are morally superior in value to all other organisms. However, this contention does not translate into the denial of existence to lower animals. It primarily acknowledges the strong claim to life and other goods possessed by uncontested persons. But every life, regardless of how lowly, has a prima facie claim to existence that can only be overcome by some good reason. And good reasons are provided by three human societal needs that animals have legitimately filled or continue to fill: the need for food, vital organs, and medical research subjects.

One reason for the sacrifice of lower life may be to allow the existence of disproportionately higher life. Thus, Native Americans could ethically justify their hunting of game in order to avoid starvation. But the United States is a far different country today, and the moral case for game hunting must be made on different grounds. Once one grants the moral status of animals, the case for vegetarianism in countries such as the United States is easily made. However, as it is unlikely that America or the world will soon convert to vegetarianism, at least ethically progressive countries should continue to make the raising, treatment, and slaughter of stock a relatively more humane practice.

Perhaps the most direct way in which the sacrifice of animals contributes to human welfare is the transplantation of body parts and organs. Is it ethically appropriate to procure primate hearts and livers for transplantation to humans with fatal organ failure? More specifically, is it moral to sacrifice an ape in order that a hypoplastic left heart syndrome newborn might live? If the question is considered as an individual instance, provided certain conditions are met, I believe that the answer is yes. By "individual instance" I mean, for example, a case of a baby that is otherwise healthy and on the brink of death who could be saved by the transplant of an ape's heart. Necessary conditions would include a solid medico-scientific basis for success, the choice of a primate that is single, and the emotionally and physically painless killing of the ape.

However, to justify an individual instance of sacrificing a baboon to save a dying human is not to justify the routine practice. This distinction is common in ethical decision making: a contrast is set up between moral decisions made on the basis of individual action-based assessment and on the basis of general rule-based assessment of what morally ought to be done in a particular situation. A concrete example is active euthanasia. Many would say that a physician was justified in helping a particular patient to die who was suffering intractable pain but would not be in favor of legalizing active euthanasia. By analogy, then, it is one matter to justify a particular xenograft operation done as a last resort but quite another to raise hundreds or thousands of apes to be systematically sacrificed for transplants. The two matters have much in common, of course, but they must be conceptually distinguished.

A less ethically objectionable approach to xenografts is to do research on bridging the immunological barrier between less advanced animals—such as sheep—so they could be used as organ sources. More will be said on this below. However, morally superior to using either class of animals is to produce artificial organs, which, of course, do not involve the sacrifice of any other being. Following the logic of proximate personhood, the use of mechanical devices to satisfy the need for substitute human organs is morally superior to the sacrifice of any animal for xenografts. Further, if mechanical devices are not available, the use of animals of lower-brain development is morally superior to the use of animals possessing some degree of self-awareness.

Animals as medical research subjects are less controversial than animals as organ sources, but the practice is much more pervasive. A circumscribed use of animals in medical research is appropriate for at least two reasons. First, we use humans in research and therefore it would be unusual to ban nonhuman animals, and second, nonhuman animals have less of a moral claim to life than do normal adult humans.

Hundreds of thousands of people in this country participate as subjects in medical research. All research involving human subjects that is federally funded is mandated to go through an institutional review board, a peer-review process that exists at all research hospitals in this country. One of the most important aspects of the research plan or protocol is the informed consent form that each research participant must sign. The form must give an overview of the research and its risks and benefits and be read by each participant before that individual signs it. Although questions are raised by critics as to whether lay people, particularly ones who are ill, can give a genuine "informed consent," the process is a giant step forward in curbing abuse.

One controversial area of research using human subjects concerns children. It was the topic of a classic debate in bioethics between Richard McCormick and the late Paul Ramsey. Ramsey held that because children are minors and therefore incompetent to assess risks and benefits, they should never be used in medical research protocols. On the other hand, McCormick argued that because children are a part of the human community, they can rightfully be expected to bear a share of the burden of societal advance in medicine. McCormick advocated that children could be used if the research was of considerable benefit and involved no discernible risks, notable pain, or notable inconvenience.[60] If consenting human adults and nonconsenting human children can be used as research subjects, it follows that some use of animals in research should be allowed. We all, animals included, benefit from the discovery of penicillin and antibiotics, and all stand to benefit from new drugs.

Another reason to allow research on animals is that they have a weaker claim to existence than do human persons. Their lives only approximate the richness and complexity of human existence. But although all non-human animals are of a lesser order than normal adult humans, even routine laboratory animals such as the common white rat are sentient creatures and should be viewed as such. The rat often outsmarts the human householder who uses a mouse trap to attain an animal-free attic: the rat pack leader recalls an unpleasant encounter with a similar wood-wire contraption baited with cheese and, despite what appears to be a convenient meal, tells his companions to pass it up—and they do. Who says that this rat and his mouse relatives have lives that are morally irrelevant? Furthermore, because of their particularly high mental abilities, animals such as primates, whales, and dolphins should not be used in experiments that cause more than moderate pain and suffering. My point, however, is not to dictate rules for appropriate animal use but to join those who are calling for a conceptual revolution in our thinking about animals and moral status. In medical research this would require that each proposed project be ethically justified by weighing the potential benefit against the likely pain caused to the experimental animals. Further, the research should be conducted, in so far as possible, to ensure the animal's ability to live its life according to its own nature and be shielded from suffering to the greatest extent possible.[61]

A heightened consciousness about the value of nonhuman animals calls for changes in scientific and governmental policy. For example, much more can be done to reduce the use of animals in research by substitution of computer models. The federal government should pass legislation that mandates a statement of moral justification for the use of any animals in biomedical research posing more than a minimal threat to the well-being or life of the animal subjects. And more cities should pass regulations requiring the spaying and neutering of pets to control their population growth and avoid the necessity of killing unwanted pets.

Xenografts as a Case Study

I return to the topic of xenografts because of continued interest in the procedure and because of the related issue of a growing shortage of transplantable organs. In June 1992 physicians at the University of Pittsburgh in Pennsylvania successfully transplanted a baboon liver to a man dying of liver failure. The thirty-five-year-old patient had Hepatitis B, which can destroy a human liver; physicians thought that a baboon liver might not be susceptible. If the xenograft had not been performed the patient could have died because of the shortage of available human organs. As of February 1992 there were 25,574 people on a national list waiting for kidneys, hearts, livers, lungs, and pancreases. More than two thousand waiting patients die each year because of organ shortage.[62]

Many moral and scientific questions surround the practice of xenografting. If research in xenografting is morally permissible, should we restrict ourselves to animals below the primate level? Or is some use of apes morally appropriate? If research proves successful, would use of apes on a massive scale be ethically permissible? Would use of primates be an unmitigated good? Could xenografting be the magic answer to our severe organ shortage?

Although the procedure presents major ethical questions, xenografts may be a *qualified* good, though not the ideal answer to shortage of human organs. A more morally licit option, from a proximate personhood perspective, is use of organs from individuals who are unalterably beyond consciousness.

Consider an imaginary transplant case involving three needy organ recipients.[63] Each possible recipient needs a different organ—a heart, a kidney, or a liver. According to matching procedures, two organs can best be supplied by one of the potential recipients to benefit the other two. In other words, for two to be saved, one must die. If no one is sacrificed, all three will die. Just suppose that the three donor-recipients are an *adult human,* an *infant human,* and a *mature baboon.* From whom should the organs come? Whose life is *least* valuable?

Of course, the baboon's. Not the adult because she is a fully self-aware person whose value to herself and others is immense. Neither the infant because he has the potential to become a fully functioning person, although he has just recently emerged into society. At present the baboon has more self-awareness and personal capacity than the infant, but its level of awareness does not match that which the infant will have in a few short years—to say nothing of the rich web of familial relationships of which the infant is already a part.

But use your imagination a bit more. What if the child was a third-trimester fetus requiring a prenatal transplant for survival. What if the only available donor was Koko, the great "talking" ape of *National Geographic* fame? What if the adult needing a transplant was not "thirtysomething" but an elderly patient who had been in a persistent vegetative state for fifteen years?

Such questions, I believe, indicate our need for an inclusive ethic—not one of human life only, as vital as that is, but of animal life more generally. Such an ethic does not claim that "all creatures great and small" are of equal value. Rather, I am arguing for an ethic that recognizes a hierarchy of moral status or value dependent on an animal's capacity for something approaching self-consciousness, which itself is the basis for richness of experience. Let me be quite concrete: a human anencephalic infant is not capable of the significant life experience that a Koko possesses and is therefore a more morally appropriate organ source. (Admittedly, these two individual lives are here considered quite apart from current social sentiment and regulations, and any socially responsible policy, of course, must take such factors into account.)

Medical science is forcing us to make distinctions never before necessary. Formerly if one were not a reasonably well functioning human being, life would soon be over due to natural causes. But we have ushered in the era of Nancy Cruzan, of resuscitated anencephalics, of artificially fed and hydrated patients in persistent vegetative states. This medical landscape is the context in which we must consider the ethics of xenografts. The ethics of xenografting involve at least three discrete but related issues.

Xenografts and Human Good

First, xenografts promise to be an undisputed good for humanity. Xenograft, literally, means transplant of alien tissue. In this basic sense xenografts are widespread and highly beneficial. Surgeons routinely depend on sheep intestine for surgical sutures, cow tendons, and bones and heart valves from pigs for replacement parts.

Even the xenografting of major organs is not new. From the early 1900s primarily kidney transplants from various animals, including rabbits, pigs, lambs, and nonhuman primates, were attempted. Although organ function in some of these transplants is noted in the literature, no patient having received a xenografted organ survived beyond a few days.[64] By the late 1950s the immunologic nature of the rejection of transplanted organs had been established and there was a resurgence of interest in xenografts. In the following decade several clinical programs in renal transplantation were begun.[65]

Pioneering work in modern xenografts, using immunosuppressive therapy and baboon and chimpanzee organs, was performed by Keith Reemtsma and Thomas Starzl in the 1960s. Most grafts failed within a two-month period, although one patient receiving a chimpanzee kidney survived for nine months.[66]

The evidence to date suggests that cross-species transplantation of major organs has not been successful. The major hurdle is hyperacute rejection. This is manifested by a rapid increase of the arterial resistance and cessation of blood flow within the organ. Although much about this phenomenon is not known, the triggering mechanism is believed to be preformed natural antibodies fighting a variety of tissue antigens. If xenografts are to be successful, some form of therapy is needed that can remove circulating antibodies from the recipient's serum. Although some researchers believe xenografts may be utilized as bridge devices until allografts can be found, long-term xenograft organ replacement is not an option at present. However, several researchers believe that success is only a matter of time.[67] Xenograft transplantation appears to be more a question of *when* than *if,* and the medical possibility of xenografts promises a significant increase in organ availability.

Xenografts Are Not Ideal

A significant number of lives could be saved if vital human organs were in virtually limitless supply. Since this is not the case, medical researchers logically are looking to animals. But could and should animals be the source of limitless organs for human use? There is something revolting in the idea of raising primates for calculated death. The issue of baboon farms and gorilla feeding lots where these animals—so genetically similar to us—are corralled for sacrifice is a morally charged subject.

Animals' lives are valuable. This is especially the case with many primates because of their advanced mental capacities. Koko, for instance, a gorilla studied intensively by specialists at a foundation in northern California, made national news a few years ago. She knows five hundred words in sign language and recognizes five hundred more. She named her pet kitten "All Ball," and when the kitten was killed by an automobile, she mourned until she was given another.[68]

Ethicists and philosophers vary in their recognition of animals' moral status. Some insist that all sentient animals, including humans, dogs, cats, and so forth, have a considerable interest in continuing to live.[69] To fail to recognize the claim to life of nonhuman species is to be guilty of what Singer has termed "speciesism":

a prejudice or attitude of bias toward the interests of members of one's own species and against those of members of other species. It should be obvious that the fundamental objections to racism and sexism made by Thomas Jefferson and Sojourner Truth apply equally to speciesism. If possessing a higher degree of intelligence does not entitle one human to use another for his own ends, how can it entitle humans to exploit nonhumans for the same purpose?[70]

Singer and other leading animal liberationists do not conclude that recognizing the evil of speciesism means that the life of white mice and the lives of readers of this book are of equal value. Nevertheless, they reject the traditional Western notion that most animal sacrifices are justified if performed for human ends. Surely, there are trade-off cases in which the taking of even a primate's life may be justified to save the life of a human person. But "hard cases" do not mean that the animal involved has no rights any more than the practice of rescuing women and children before men from a sinking ship means that men have no—or diminished—rights.

Whereas society sees a woman or child as equally deserving of life as a man, it is unclear on whether very intelligent animals and merely vegetating humans possess an equal claim to life. Kushner and Belliotti address this latter issue in arguing for a "cognitive capacity principle" in determining what "animal" may morally be sacrificed for the good of another. For example, if we would be willing to sacrifice a chimpanzee in organ procurement for a specified human good, we should be willing to take the life of a human of similar capacity for self-awareness in order to procure an equal good.[71]

Arthur Caplan holds that nonhuman animal life is a relative good. It would be wrong to breed and kill animals systematically to get organs for human transplantation unless such organs could not be secured in any other manner. In such cases he does not see any other option than to use animals.[72]

There is a considerable lack of coherence and consistency in how we treat animals. In 1989 the international community spent over a million dollars to save two whales in an Alaskan ice hole. But while the whole world lamented the potential loss of these two whales, at least three times that number were being slaughtered for their blubber on the open sea, with only Greenpeace and a few other groups appearing to care.

Although some may question the use of higher-level animals as organ sources, our general society cannot easily forbid the use of xenografts as long as we engage in wholesale slaughter of animals for our dinner tables. America, leading the world in slaughter of animals, annually kills and eats over three billion chickens and hundreds of millions of cows and other livestock.[73] By comparison, the sacrifice of hundreds, even thousands of baboons so that many humans might live seems conventionally logical.

Xenograft researcher Eric Rose and his associates at Columbia-Presbyterian Medical Center in New York City are sensitive to the problematic use of higher primates. Rose reports that the basic hurdle to wide usage of animals as organ sources is the hyperacute humoral immune response—a response that increases as the species involved in the xenografts are more disparate. However, because of ethical concerns about the use of higher primates, Rose and his associates turned their focus to the problems of organ rejection associated with cross-species transplantation to humans from sheep and goats.[74]

Transplantation and Self-Absent Individuals

The use of lower animals as organ sources is problematic. "Self-absent" individuals have been suggested as a solution. Self-absent individuals are those, such as anencephalic infants and permanent coma patients, who are legally alive but will never attain, or regain, self-consciousness. In such individuals the capacities of the higher brain—which are the bases for all that is distinctively human—are absent and will remain so. Such individuals will never be selves; in fact, even the slightest rationality is forever beyond them.

However, at the present time the reliability of diagnostic tests for permanent coma and persistent vegetative state patients is doubtful.[75] Consequently, until diagnostic tests are more precise, the argument I now pursue is more one of principle than a recipe for current practice.

That anencephalic newborns and permanent coma patients are legally alive is beyond dispute. To use such individuals as organ sources would require changing regulations from a whole to a higher-brain criterion for the determination of death. One could marshal considerable historical support for a change in the law. Criteria for determining death have often changed. For example, 250 years ago the professional standard for determining death was when putrefaction had begun. This measure was deemed necessary by physicians and laity alike because of too many incidents of exhumed graves with coffin lids scarred by claw marks. In the succeeding decades better diagnostic skills such as the use of smelling salts and clinical tests were developed for accurately determining death.[76] Diagnostic measures for ascertaining cessation of respiratory and cardiac function have improved over time, with determination of brain death being only the latest method. Although the simmering debate over whether higher-brain cessation should be the standard for legal death is an important discussion, it is not the main issue here.

The present argument is more modest: individuals who have devolved to the status of permanently self-absent humans should have the legal right of organ donation. Just as people's rights over their own medical care can continue after their competence is lost, so individuals should have the right, if desired, to specify organ donation under conditions of permanent self-absence.

Competent individuals should be able to write into their Durable Power of Attorney for Health Care directives a stipulation that if the subject truly enters a condition of permanent loss of higher-brain function, vital organs would be available for donation. Of course, if basic organs such as the heart or liver were procured, death to the organism would result. But ideally the individual would be legally dead already, having opted for a higher brain definition of death (see chapter 6). Vital organ procurement is ethically justified on the basis of drastic and permanent decline of moral status—a loss that in the previously competent person's judgment is tantamount to death.

Consider an analogy. In 1986 the American Medical Association ruled that it is ethical for physicians to terminate artificial nutrition and hydration in cases of permanently comatose patients. The result of such withdrawal of treatment, naturally, is the death of the patient. And this withholding of life support is done for the benefit of the loved ones or society—not for a patient who is beyond being benefited. If artificial life support may be withdrawn from a comatose patient at others' request, that *same* patient—permanently comatose *and* on a ventilator—should be able to decide for organ donation. In terms of euthanasia, the voluntary death would be triggered by organ donation but it would be the patient's underlying deterioration that "caused" the death, just as in nonvoluntary death, triggered by withdrawal of artificial life support, it is the underlying condition that is listed as the cause of death.[77]

Permanent loss of self-consciousness is the crucial line between life that possesses full moral standing and life that is without that status. The autonomic functions of circulation and respiration controlled by the brain stem suffice to constitute legal life, but the moral status of such individuals is a question of escalating importance in society.

The President's commission on bioethics identified the problem of vitalism in arguing for the importance of integrative neurological functioning as opposed to the morally negligible presence of some neurological cellular activity.[78] Currently, transplant surgeons must not mistake reflexive bodily movements for those of a conscious nature. Occasionally declared organ donors who have been competently determined to be brain dead continue to have bodily movement on the operating table before vital organs are procured. Confidence in the neurologist's determination of loss of meaningful brain function, not cessation of bodily movement, is what allows the surgeon to follow out the donor's desires.

My basic argument from this analogy is that if a certain class of patients, such as those in a persistent vegetative state, are allowed to die through withdrawal of nutrition, then similarly situated patients should be able to serve as organ sources. If there are good organs that would merely deteriorate from lack of nutrition and soon be useless and then buried, why prohibit a patient from predetermining that those organs should be a gift of life to others? A patient should have the right to decide for organ donation should he or she become self-absent. Making such an option available would recognize voluntary discretion over an important religious/philosophical issue, do great good without harming the interests of anyone, and help protect the lives of the many primates whose lives would be sacrificed if xenografting is the only immediate option as a source for organs.

5 ❖ The Moral Status
❖ of Anencephalic Infants

Transplantation of neonatal organs now saves scores of fatally ill newborns and the possibility for saving more is on the horizon as techniques and medications are perfected. Over six hundred infants afflicted by hypoplastic left-heart syndrome are born annually in the United States,[1] with cardiac transplantation as a leading possibility for treatment. Liver transplant is the only hope for four to eight hundred children with liver failure.[2] Another four to five hundred children suffer from end-stage renal disease, and dialysis regimens could be stopped if transplantable kidneys could be procured.[3] Each year in this country hundreds of other infants are born with fatal immunologic and endocrine deficiencies, and their only hope is transplant of various tissues.

However, an unfortunate paradox exists: as neonatal transplant science advances, the already acute shortage of small organs will likely grow worse unless new sources are identified. Currently, most organs come from infants who suffer traumatic deliveries, are victims of child abuse, or are involved in automobile accidents. Improved survival statistics can be expected in these areas. Currently, there are 40,000 infant deaths per year in the United States, with approximately 1 out of 100 due to brain death. Therefore a maximum of four hundred brain deaths may be declared each year.[4] Primates are a potential, though socially controversial and morally questionable, source of organs, and this possibility is still being researched. At present anencephalic newborns—described in chapter 4 as belonging to the category of self-absent individuals—are being considered as a source for neonatal organs. In this chapter I describe anencephaly and sketch the differing views on and approaches to the use of anencephalic infants as organ sources. I also report on a survey of knowledgeable clinicians and ethicists regarding the moral status of anencephalic infants and construct an ethical rationale for limited use of anencephalic infants as organ sources.

Anencephalic Infants and Transplantation

Anencephalic infants are fatally impaired. Most of both cerebral hemispheres are missing, and there is little if any brain function above the brain stem. These infants' foreheads are absent and they possess a mass of abnormally developed brain tissue covered by a membrane capping their shortened heads. The eyeballs bulge from defective sockets, and the ears are usually malformed.

Although anencephalic infants do not have higher-brain functions, their brain stems allow for some typical newborn activity. Most important, circulatory and respiratory functions are performed naturally. Crying and swallowing occur. Some infants with anencephaly may have the mobility of a four-month-old fetus. These infants respond to vestibular stimuli and some to sound. Reflexes are usually strong, particularly their response to painful stimuli. The grasp reflex is easily initiated.[5] Such infants are not dead according to currently accepted standards—common law or the relatively recent state laws reflecting the Uniform Determination of Death Act, the former using cardio-pulmonary criteria and the latter including whole-brain death.

Although most anencephalic infants are stillborn, 25 to 45 percent are live births, resulting in an estimated 1500 still births and 1000 live births each year in the United States. Approximately 40 percent of those born alive survive at least twenty-four hours. Of these survivors, one out of three will be living at the end of the third day and 5 percent will live to at least seven days.[6] Rarely have anencephalic infants lived to several months. Possibly these infants could live longer, but aggressive treatment is routinely withheld. Standard treatment is "nursing care only" because the condition is incompatible with a life of any self-consciousness and an early death is inevitable. Although birth rates of anencephalic infants vary widely according to ethnicity and perhaps other factors, the birth rate in the United States is $1/1850$.[7] If a small percentage of these infants could be utilized as organ sources, a significant supply of neonatal organs would become available. Theoretically, a single anencephalic infant with healthy thoracic and abdominal organs could supply vital organs to save the lives of two other infants (one needing a heart and another a liver) and enhance the lives of several others (needing kidneys, corneas, and various transplantable tissues).

Taking organs from anencephalic infants following death determined by cardiovascular criteria is not new. The practice is almost as old as organ transplantation itself, dating back to the early 1960s.[8] Medical literature reports at least twenty-three renal transplants from anencephalic infants, with a success rate varying according to clinician and age of patients.[9] There is reason to believe that considerably more renal transplants may have been done than those reported. Particularly in a country like Japan, transplants from anencephalic infants are a likelihood. Although Japanese physicians report only one case of kidney procurement from an anencephalic infant in English medical literature, one native research group concludes that "because of the need for cadaver kidney transplants in children, we will continue to use anencephalic neonates as donors despite the potential technical complications."[10] In Germany there was one case of procuring a vital organ from an anencephalic newborn. This provoked a private Roman Catholic organization in Munster to bring a suit involving murder, but to no avail. Although it was reported in a medical journal, based on this case, that the West German government had ruled that anencephalic newborns are "dead," thus allowing immediate organ procurement, this statement is not accurate.[11]

Reliable clinical data on the quality of organs and tissues from anencephalic infants are not yet available, but early indications suggest optimism. Surgeons from the Children's Hospital in Cincinnati who have had the greatest success with kidney transplantation, have found that the organs are only three quarters the size of normal kidneys but assume normal weight rapidly after transplantation. Further, they report a 50 percent success rate in their kidney transplants, with one patient functioning well nine and a half years after transplantation.[12]

Although organ procurement from anencephalic infants is not new, widespread public interest is a recent phenomenon. It began in 1987 with the first successful heart transplant from an anencephalic newborn— Canadian Baby Gabrielle's heart saved the life of baby Paul Holc, a newborn afflicted with hypoplastic left-heart syndrome. Within a month Paul was released from Loma Linda University Medical Center. Public interest was rekindled in 1992 when Laura Campo and Justin Pearson, thirty-one-year-old parents of two children and residents of Florida, gave birth to an anencephalic daughter, Theresa Ann Campo Pearson. Because of prenatal tests, the parents knew of their daughter's fatal disease. After the birth they went public in a case that became a national news story, decrying the fact that they could not legally donate vital organs from their dying daughter so that another infant might live. Their baby died on March 30, 1992. Public fascination with the human interest side of the anencephalic dilemma inspired the made-for-TV movie, *Heart of a Child,* produced by NBC and shown at prime time, May 9, 1994. The movie dramatized the baby Paul Holc case.

Why the widespread public interest? First, the successful transplant of Baby Paul and the subsequent hope of procuring organs from the anencephalic Baby Theresa Ann dramatized the possibility of routine procurement of organs from anencephalic infants. Second, cardiac transplant is more dramatic than renal transplant, the primary type of transplant previously reported.[13] Although renal dialysis is available to sustain life when no transplantable kidneys are available, without a heart transplant Baby Paul would most likely have died, and in the Baby Theresa case the issue was vital organs.

Four Models for Use of Anencephalic Infants as Organ Sources

Since the 1987 transplant of a heart into Baby Paul, four distinct approaches to using anencephalic infants as organ sources have emerged. The first model to be proposed was based on the idea of "cooling" the anencephalic infant. The proponents of this option acknowledged that cooling the body would have two effects, one good and one debatable. Cooling would preserve vital organs for transplant by preventing warm ischemia, a major risk to organ viability. But a side effect, which the researchers argued was justifiable, would be the possible hastening of death by cerebral swelling.

The authors of this proposal recognized that practitioners of cooling could be cited for active euthanasia. Their response: "We think it unreasonable to construe legal and ethical doctrines against direct, active killing so broadly as to prohibit organ preservation in such cases and believe that reasonable people would agree with such a conclusion."[14]

A second model involves procurement of organs as soon as possible, with maximal life support provided in the interim. No regard need be given to brain activity because of "brain absence," a phrase describing the condition of anencephalics, coined by a transplant surgeon, that is colorful but wrong in that these newborns have brain stems and often some loose midbrain tissues.[15] According to this model, because anencephalic newborns possess only a brain stem and will never have a cerebrum or neocortex, meaningful brain function is impossible. The idea that anencephalic infants do not qualify as protectable human life has a considerable following in America. But various proposals based on brain absence are sitting on the shelves of teaching hospitals. Their authors realize that individuals and institutions implementing such protocols would be open to charges of murder, given current laws.[16]

The third model advocates using ventilators for selected anencephalic newborns to sustain organ viability while brain death occurs. The Loma Linda University Medical Center developed a protocol that specifies that a ventilator be used for a maximum of seven days; if the anencephalic subjects are not brain dead by that deadline, normal death is allowed to occur without prospect for organ procurement.[17] After brain death is medically determined by pediatric neurologists, procurement of organs from the dead body can legally proceed.

Twelve newborns were entered into the protocol, and only two infants met brain-death criteria at the end of seven days. The protocol was suspended. Mechanical ventilation not only sustained the viability of transplantable organs but apparently sustained brain stem activity as well.[18]

A fourth approach was developed by a medical task force on anencephaly: the anencephalic newborn is given routine care until a cardiac arrest occurs. There is no attempt at resuscitation and the organs are immediately removed. In the report of the task force, nine anencephalic infants—seven in North America—from whom organ procurement was attempted fit this category. Only one transplant was successful.[19]

A Moratorium on the Use of Anencephalic Organ Sources?

Considerable debate ensued when physicians at Loma Linda University Medical Center successfully transplanted a heart from anencephalic Baby Gabrielle to baby Paul Holc. At least one prominent pediatrician called for a moratorium on organ procurement from anencephalic infants until further medical data are available, greater social and professional debate is heard, and a consensus develops.[20] Further discussion has continued in the medical literature. The Medline data bank lists 239 articles on anencephaly from January 1988 through January 1991—some on strictly medical aspects but many focusing on social, ethical, and legal concerns.

The American Medical Association, through its Council on Ethical and Judicial Affairs, issued a December 1988 report on anencephalic infants as organ donors. In reaffirming and expanding a statement the council had issued six months earlier, it stated: "As in other circumstances involving organ donation, it is not unethical to provide anencephalic infants with ventilator assistance and other medical therapies that are necessary to sustain organ perfusion and viability until such time as a determination of death can be made in accordance with accepted medical standards. The organs of an anencephalic donor may be retrieved only after such a determination of death is made."[21]

In June 1994 the council significantly modified its position on the use of anencephalic infants as organ sources. The council ruled that it is unnecessary for the anencephalic newborn to meet standard brain-death criteria before organs may be procured ethically. If the diagnosis is certain and if parents have indicated in writing their desires for organ procurement, "it is ethically permissible to consider the anencephalic as a potential organ donor, although still alive under the current definition of death." The explanation given is that "use of the anencephalic infant as a live donor is a limited exception to the general standard because of the fact that the infant has never experienced, and will never experience, consciousness."[22]

The American Medical Association's House of Delegates, in December 1995, instructed the council to suspend its 1994 policy on the use of anencephalic newborns. In part the approved suspension states: "While the Council believes that its initial report and opinion were well-reasoned discussions of an important ethical issue, the Council also recognizes that its conclusions cannot be implemented until greater understanding of consciousness in anencephaly is achieved."[23] The earlier opinions ignited a virtual fire-storm of political opposition among certain religious groups as well as many physicians, with at least one neurologist arguing that rudimentary consciousness may be possible in anencephalic newborns.

In the discussion that has taken place over the last few years, there have been no new calls for moratoria, but two pleas for continued experimentation with anencephalic infants have been voiced.

First, Ronald Cranford, a University of Minnesota neurologist, who served as a leading member of the Medical Task Force on Anencephaly, calls for the continued use of anencephalic infants as organ sources if certain guidelines are followed:

- The transplantation center is open about its practices and protocol.
- The center has well-formulated polices and protocols that include a listing of all major alternatives to the procedure.
- Interested parties, including affected health care providers and the family, are informed of all alternatives and outcomes.
- The center is willing to systematically collect its data and experience and is committed to dissemination of the information as quickly as possible in the medical community and beyond.
- The center is large enough to assure that sufficient numbers of anencephalic infants will be referred over a reasonable period of time.
- A multidisciplinary, broad-based ethics committee with community representatives is actively involved in formulating the protocols and policies and in monitoring the process.[24]

Second, the Canadian Paediatric Society and an Ontario teaching hospital have taken a leading role in furthering discussion and use of anencephalic infants as organ sources.

Guidelines for the use of organs from anencephalic infants in transplant programs were issued in 1990 by the Canadian Paediatric Society.[25] The Society views anencephalic newborns as potentially useful organ donors after whole-brain death—unmodified in any way—is determined. The direct and immediate use of anencephalic infants (before whole-brain death is determined) is explicitly rejected on basically utilitarian grounds. Key recommendations are:

- Maintenance care only until brain death has been declared, then use of aggressive care (such as mechanical ventilation) to prolong organ viability for a finite period to be determined by each center.
- Review by the medical institution's research and ethics committees, and preferably by external consultants as well.
- Full disclosure to the families of donors and recipients of the investigative nature of the program and the likelihood that the number of anencephalic newborns who become successful donors "will be very small."

- Evaluation of the protocol's outcome in regard to the anencephalic sources, the recipients, and their respective families.
- No aggressive life support in "anticipation" of brain death.
- Provision of separate teams to manage potential recipients and donors.
- Need for basic research to determine and prevent hypoxia and ischemia from affecting the viability and functioning of organs before and after transplantation.

A protocol at the Children's Hospital of Western Ontario (Victoria Hospital) for the use of anencephalic infants as organ sources was closed in December 1988 due to controversy. Four infants were entered into the protocol, with two involved in successful organ transplantation (one being Baby Gabrielle).[26]

The Western Ontario hospital's protocol, revised in light of the Canadian Paediatric Society's guidelines and further reflection, was given full approval by that hospital's review board for research in January 1991. The reopening of the protocol was planned for June 1991 but then postponed. The core of the protocol is unchanged. When auscultatory asystole or cardiac arrest occurs, mechanical ventilation and other specialized treatment may be utilized for up to seven days after birth or until brain death—whichever occurs first.

Of particular interest to the Western Ontario researchers are three issues: first, the timing of brain death following cardiac arrest; second, the viability of the organs that may be procured; third, whether the protocol leads to distress of the health care team and lessens respect for human life. The Children's/Victoria Hospital protocol is giving special attention to the third point. The principal investigator has developed an approach that was endorsed by the University of Western Ontario's health sciences review board for research involving human subjects.

According to Dr. T. C. Frewen, director of the Children's Hospital's pediatric critical care unit, he and his colleagues believe that a reliable brain-death determination can be made through use of apnea testing and clinical criteria. Although testing for brain death in newborns is not as reliable as it is for older children, the researchers are confident that because of lack of cerebral development the determination of brain death in anencephalic infants is even more sure than with normal newborns.[27]

Divided Opinion on Anencephalic Infants as Organ Sources

Knowledgeable physicians and bioethicists continue to be divided over the ethics of using anencephalic infants as organ sources and argue whether the legal status of anencephalic newborns should ever be changed.

Even if anencephalic newborns could be utilized as organ sources, at best a relatively few hundred other infants needing transplant organs would be saved each year.[28] However, the treatment of anencephalic infants raises questions far beyond mere organ transplantation:

- What gives a human moral standing, so that he or she has a unique moral status?
- In determining protectable human life, what are the respective roles of medical, legal, and social considerations?
- Does every legally alive human individual possess an equal claim to medical resources and continued life?
- What role should cerebral life/death play in determining which individuals deserve common protection?

These questions exist against the backdrop of a burgeoning medical technology that can sustain human life far beyond what most observers would consider meaningful or functional.

In 1990 I conducted a survey of clinicians and bioethicists to determine their views on the procurement of transplant organs from anencephalic newborns. A total of 119 people were surveyed. Eighty-three (70 percent) completed the questionnaire.

The names of the people surveyed came from two rosters: people who wrote or served as consultants to the Medical Task Force on Anencephaly report,[29] and attendees at the 1990 Annual Bioethics Retreat, Lutzen, Minnesota.[30] The former group is predominantly physicians, the latter mostly doctors of philosophy. Of those responding to the survey, forty-six (55 percent) were M.D.s, twenty-five (30 percent) Ph.D.s, eight J.D.s, and four did not have medical or doctoral degrees. Any individual possessing an M.D. is listed as a physician regardless of the possession of other degrees; two individuals categorized as Ph.D.s also held J.D.s. (The small number of attorneys participating makes percentage figures of dubious value and hence percentages of J.D.s answering questions is not given.)

The percentages given are the percentages of M.D.s and Ph.D.s completing the question. Respondents could check more than one answer if desired.

Survey on Anencephalic Infants, Organ Use, and Death

1. Of the physicians, 82 percent stated that the medical institutions with which they are associated have had some discussion of use of anencephalic infants as organ sources. Of the medical institutions represented, 75 percent are teaching hospitals. Of the physicians, 37 percent said that discussion at some level continues on this topic, and 30 percent said that if legal difficulties were removed, some discussion—or greater debate—of this topic would be likely at their respective institutions.

2. If the law allowed for the use of anencephalic infants as organ sources *before* the brain stem irreversibly ceased functioning, what would be the respondents' personal positions on the *morality* of such use?

   - Use of anencephalic infants as organ sources is intrinsically moral: M.D.s, 57 percent; Ph.D.s, 72 percent
   - Use of anencephalic infants as organ sources is intrinsically immoral: M.D.s, 13 percent; Ph.D.s, 6 percent
   - Other (room for comments was provided): M.D.s, 30 percent; Ph.D.s, 22 percent

   Of those writing comments, most elaborated on their answers to the first of the three options listed above. Typical comments included: "It is also intrinsically humanitarian"; it "would depend on parent's desires—not intrinsically immoral"; "such use would be morally permissible." Two respondents commented on the immorality of such a change in law: "Wrong for consequentialist reasons"; "use faces a stiff burden of moral justification."

3. The use of anencephalic infants as organ sources before the brain stem irreversibly ceases functioning

   - should remain illegal: M.D.s, 37 percent; Ph.D.s, 30 percent
   - should be made legal: M.D.s, 52 percent; Ph.D.s, 70 percent
   - other: M.D.s, 10 percent; Ph.D.s, 0 percent

Four respondents who chose the "should remain illegal" added a comment. Three said such organ donation should remain illegal "at this time"; one held that although it is intrinsically moral, "there are pragmatic reasons for keeping it illegal." Of the four choosing the "should be made legal" option and adding comments, two spoke of the need for restrictions. Five people chose the third option, giving a variety of comments.

4. If the law on anencephalic infants were altered, what form of alteration is personally preferable?

   - A change from whole-brain death to cerebral-brain death (for all individuals—not only anencephalics): M.D.s, 32 percent; Ph.D.s, 37 percent
   - Making the diagnosis of anencephaly an exception to whole-brain death standards (that is, anencephaly = death): M.D.s, 49 percent; Ph.D.s, 32 percent
   - Other: M.D.s, 24 percent; Ph.D.s, 32 percent

   Seventeen people choose option three, with six writing "none" or its equivalent, indicating a strong preference for no change in the law. Other comments ranged from "it should be a medical decision," to "anencephaly consistent with death if parents agree." Two respondents chose the second option but stated a preference for the third option when cerebral death can be reliably diagnosed.

5. Of the 56 percent of respondents who stated that use of anencephalic infants as organ sources should be made legal,

   - 38 percent thought that a cerebral death standard should apply to all qualifying subjects—not just anencephalic infants.
   - 13 percent thought that anencephalic newborns should be an exception to the whole-brain death standard. The other portion of the 56 percent—nearly half—stated various views.

6. How, if at all, does the "slippery slope" argument (the idea that relaxation of a fixed moral position will lead to recognizably wrong practices) affect thinking on this topic?

   - For me personally, this argument has little or no relevance here: M.D.s, 63 percent; Ph.D.s, 58 percent

- For me, this argument has considerable relevance: M.D.s, 22 percent; Ph.D.s, 21 percent
- For society, I believe this argument has little or no relevance here: M.D.s, 26 percent; Ph.D.s, 16 percent
- For society, I believe this argument has considerable relevance: M.D.s, 54 percent; Ph.D.s, 53 percent

7. If current law on brain death (that is, whole-brain death) is appropriate for society, what are personally convincing reasons for this position?

    - The current law on brain death is morally right and good: M.D.s, 37 percent; Ph.D.s—5 percent
    - The current law on brain death can be medically validated with a high degree of accuracy: M.D.s, 63 percent; Ph.D.s, 68 percent
    - The current law on brain death reflects a "natural position on the subject," that is, a position more or less self-evident to most rational observers: M.D.s, 42 percent; Ph.D.s, 26 percent
    - No convincing reasons exist: M.D.s, 5 percent; Ph.D.s, 11 percent
    - Other: M.D.s, 14 percent; Ph.D.s, 5 percent

    Nine people marked "other" and wrote widely varying responses.

8. Respondents were asked regarding their own attitudes about the whole-brain death standard.

    - It is a firm standard that should be upheld indefinitely: M.D.s, 39 percent; Ph.D.s, 26 percent
    - It is a standard that should serve until . . . (space was provided for completion of the sentence): M.D.s, 59 percent; Ph.D.s, 74 percent Twenty-five of the respondents chose the second option and also completed the sentence. The majority of the responses fall under two categories: eight respondents essentially said that the whole-brain standard should hold until, as one of them wrote, "a higher brain standard can be diagnosed with a high degree of medical certainty." Six respondents said that the whole-brain standard should remain until, as one wrote, "society is convinced that death begins with the cessation of cerebral activity" or some variation of this theme. Other comments varied widely.

9. Respondents were queried regarding their personal philosophies of death:

- Irreversible loss of total brain functioning: M.D.s, 38 percent; Ph.D.s, 38 percent
- Irreversible loss of or absence of cerebral functioning: M.D.s, 51 percent; Ph.D.s, 60 percent
- Other: M.D.s, 16 percent; Ph.D.s, 5 percent

10. Conservative and liberal responses. At least four of the possible questionnaire answers could be seen as indicating a "conservative" position on the use of anencephalic infants as organ sources:

   a. Such use before whole-brain death should remain illegal.
   b. Such use is intrinsically immoral.
   c. The whole-brain death standard should be upheld indefinitely.
   d. My personal philosophy of death is based on the irreversible loss of total brain function.

Twenty-two percent of the M.D.s and 25 percent of the Ph.D.s picked at least three out of the above four options.

At least four of the possible answers in the questionnaire could be interpreted as "liberal" responses:

   a. Use of anencephalic infants as organ sources before whole-brain death should be made legal.
   b. Use of anencephalic infants as organ sources before whole-brain death, if legal, would be intrinsically moral.
   c. The whole-brain death standard should only stand until certain conditions are met.
   d. Human death truly occurs when there is irreversible loss or absence of cerebral functioning.

Forty-eight percent of the M.D.s and 70 percent of the Ph.D.s picked at least three out of the four answers above.

Ethical Issues

There are a variety of issues in the continuing discussion over the use of anencephalic infants as organ sources. These include: the quality of organs,[31] the likelihood of a diminished anencephalic infant pool,[32] the effect of controversial transplants on the national transplant program,[33] and the possible exploitation of women.[34]

However, there are three basic categories of response to this question: (a) philosophical acceptance—personal openness to and belief that society should now discuss policies allowing use of anencephalic infants as organ sources; (b) social reticence—personal openness to such use but opposition to ethical and legal changes at this time for social reasons; (c) philosophical opposition—personal opposition to such use as intrinsically wrong and hence unacceptable for society.

Philosophical Acceptance of Anencephalic Infants as Possible Organ Sources

A majority of the survey respondents appears to be in this category. For example, nearly half of the M.D. respondents and over two-thirds of the Ph.D. respondents chose three out of four "liberal" answers in the survey. Over half of the M.D.s and nearly three-quarters of the Ph.D.s stated that they personally viewed the use of anencephalic infants as organ sources as "intrinsically moral." Only one in ten respondents saw such use as intrinsically immoral. Not surprisingly, over half of the respondents described their personal philosophy of death as characterized by irreversible loss of or absence of cerebral functioning. What then is a "convincing reason" for maintaining the whole-brain death standard, which is current law? In answer to this survey question, two-thirds of the respondents replied that a high degree of accuracy can be attained in determining loss of functioning of the whole brain.

Is society ready to accept anencephalic infants as organ sources? The respondents are not so sure. Although six out of ten say that the "slippery slope" argument has little or no personal relevance here, nearly that many think that society may perceive a slipping from solid moral ground if anencephalic newborns are used as organ sources.[35] The vital social dimension to this issue is recognized by medical professionals. Bioethicists and physicians who are at all open to using anencephalic infants as organ sources frequently end their articles on this topic with a call for societal debate.[36]

Reticence to Seek a Change in Law for Social Reasons

Some of the survey respondents view the direct use of anencephalic infants as "intrinsically moral," but this admission does not necessarily lead to advocacy of a change in the law. One of these respondents, a leading bioethicist, commented: "But there may be decisive extrinsic moral factors." The most troublesome moral issue for this respondent was the threat that use of these controversial organ sources may pose for the nation's established organ donation program. Further, this bioethicist views the slippery slope argument as having considerable relevance for both himself and for society. Thus for various reasons he states his hope that the whole-brain death standard holds indefinitely.[37]

Roger W. Evans, now at the Mayo Clinic, Rochester, Minnesota, may or may not believe in the morality of using anencephalic infants as organ donors, but he is clearly opposed to such use. He contends that if it is authorized, the increase in supply of infant hearts would be marginal. More important, such use "could easily jeopardize current organ-procurement efforts. Despite claims to the contrary, the American public is not ready or willing to equate anencephaly with death."[38]

Perhaps a number of the survey respondents also have social reasons for not wanting to see anencephalic infants used as organ sources. At least this is a likely explanation for one set of contrasting data from the survey: only one in ten respondents believes that the direct use of anencephalic infants is intrinsically immoral, but more than three times that many believe that direct use should remain illegal.

Philosophical Opposition to Use of Anencephalic Infants as Possible Organ Sources

One in four respondents chose at least three out of the four answers in the survey that could reasonably be labeled "conservative." Thus a substantial block of the respondents believe that the direct use of anencephalic infants should remain illegal, with a hard core—one out of ten professionals surveyed—viewing the direct use as intrinsically immoral. The survey was not intended to probe undergirding philosophies of life, but a substantial pro-life philosophy exists that supports the view that the direct use of anencephalic infants is intrinsically immoral.

Jesuit theologian William E. May has articulated an exemplary statement on the intrinsic worth of all human life—a position similar to that of philosopher Peter Byrne outlined in chapter 1. (The number of respondents who would subscribe to the conservative physicalist view of human life is unknown.) May argues that all humans are "beings of moral worth" precisely because of their membership in the human species. All humans are "valuable, precious, irreplaceable" and as such possess "inalienable rights . . . that demand legal protection by society." The basis for this high claim is that "something is rooted in their being human beings." This "something" is defined as spirit or soul, a principle of "immateriality." This species endowment allows most humans to become "minded beings," but, regardless, it transfers equivalent moral standing to all humans, "including neonates, infants, raving maniacs and fetuses"—and presumably anencephalic infants.[39]

Protestant theologian Gilbert Meilaender and UCLA pediatric neurologist Alan Shewmon, who joined May in a pro-life manifesto,[40] write specifically about the value of anencephalic infants. Meilaender emphasizes the importance of human embodiment, bodily human form—regardless of the presence or absence of higher-brain capacities. Thus he opposes any lengthening of anencephalic newborns' lives or any medical intervention whatever intended to aid transplantation.[41] Meilaender criticizes the dualism of those who would divide mind from body: "We can know people—of all ranges of cognitive capacity—only as they are embodied; there is no other 'person' for whom we might care. Such care is not useless if it 'only' preserves bodily life but does not restore cognitive capacities. If this view is characterized as an objectionable 'speciesism,' I can only reply that at least it is not one more way by which the strong and gifted in our world rid themselves of the weak."[42]

Shewmon, writing in the *Journal of the American Medical Association,* argues that the phenomenon of neuroplasticity could in principle allow the anencephalic newborn to possess more complex integrative activity than expected. "Thus, it neither logically nor physiologically follows that anencephalic infants by definition . . . can neither feel nor experience pain."[43] Regardless of what philosophies of life are held by people in the category of philosophical opposition, there are able advocates of this viewpoint in the medical literature. The survey results suggest that those who hold to a conservative position on the direct use of anencephalic infants are not in the majority. But they can demonstrate a coherent philosophy to support their position.

Given the advanced medical technology that makes possible thousands of organ transplants each year in America, the problem of organ scarcity will not be solved in the foreseeable future. This suggests that the discussion of anencephalic infants—and other controversial potential organ sources—is in its initial stages. Regardless, medical progress is forcing us to be much more clear and explicit in explaining why humans such as anencephalic newborns can or cannot be used as organ sources.

Anencephalic Infants as Organ Sources: An Ethical Rationale

In the next chapter I take up the issue of whether the law should be changed to allow direct, immediate organ procurement from anencephalic newborns—procurement of vital organs that, of course, would result in their death. However, I now put forward a rationale for the use of anencephalic infants within current law—a rationale that supports protocols such as those formerly used at Loma Linda and contemplated for use in Ontario.

I begin the present argument with the presupposition that current statutes on brain death are legally binding. That is, organs may only be procured from humans who have been certified as dead. However, this only sets the ground rules for consideration of three salient issues facing those who regard dead anencephalic newborns as legitimate organ sources: first, the ethical issue of using one human as a means for maximizing the good of another; second, the medical topic of determination of brain death; and third, the social question of anencephalic infant research.

A commonplace in Western society for centuries, if not millennia, has been a high valuation of individual human life.[44] Persons are ends in their own right and are not to be used as means to advance even the noblest of others' ends. Things, not people, are to be used as mere means. This idea was most persuasively articulated by Immanuel Kant in the second form of his categorical imperative: "Act so that you treat humanity, whether in your own person or in that of another, always as an end and never as a means only."[45]

Does putting anencephalic infants on ventilators, as has been done at both the Loma Linda and Ontario hospitals, involve using these newborns as only a means (not as a means only, but admittedly as a means primarily)?[46] The basis of the present ethical argument supporting dead anencephalic infants as organ donors rests, admittedly, upon a certain "use" of their minimal, fleeting life. Certain liberties are taken and appropriately may be taken—but surely are not mandatory—with such human beings.

An instructive comparison may be drawn from how we care for patients who are permanently unconscious. Such patients have been kept alive for years, even decades.[47] However, society increasingly recognizes the futility for all concerned in such a procedure. Accordingly, the American Medical Association's ethical and judicial council ruled in 1986 that the withdrawal of artificial life support—specifically denoting nutrition and hydration—is "not unethical."[48] Such treatment, or nontreatment, is permissible because of the vegetative state of human life into which the patient has irreversibly passed.

Similarly, the anencephalic newborn—at the other end of life's spectrum—regretfully possesses only a minimal degree of uniquely human existence, given the absolute lack of potential for possessing consciousness and the likelihood of imminent death. Accordingly, standard treatment for anencephalic newborns is only nursing care. These babies are fed and kept warm, but no specialized treatment is given to prevent early deaths.

A contemporary way to state the ethical rationale for providing this minimal care involves the notion of the infant's best interests.[49] In the case of anencephalic newborns, their "best interests" are not served through aggressive therapy, and therefore it may be forgone. However, as John Arras has insightfully indicated, the best-interests criterion for decision making is limited. He takes it to its logical conclusion by citing a worst-case example: a profoundly retarded, nonambulatory, deaf and blind newborn who will spend years in the corner of a neonatal intensive care unit. Best-interests criteria would logically lead to aggressive treatment because such an infant has never known a better life and presumably would desire to live. If the retarded newborn *could* think and speak, according to Arras, the infant's likely response would be: I'm fed, changed and occasionally cuddled, and although life doesn't hold much I'll play out the meager hand I've been dealt.[50]

Helpful as a best-interests standard may be in most cases, in instances such as profound mental handicap and anencephaly, it begs the question of the basis for decision making. We might imagine that an anencephalic newborn, as a live being, possesses a "pro-life" sentiment like that projected for the profoundly retarded infant. But for an anencephalic infant the analogous answer is even more questionable: no personal best interests can be projected. Use of the language of best interests overextends the concept and only underscores the marginality of such human beings. It is this marginality and the total inability to remedy it that justifies medicine's tradition of mere custodial care.

As has been stated, the proposed use of a ventilator to sustain an anencephalic infant until death and subsequent organ procurement is based on the underlying condition of these newborns that has long been cited as the reason for the withholding of treatment. This condition makes the application of best-interests criteria dubious and strains the present helpfulness of the ends/means distinction. Both best-interests and ends/means models of decision making presuppose subjects who possess at least minimal capacities or potential capacities for distinctly human life, and these are missing in anencephalic infants. This is not to argue that they may be used as a "means only," for these are *human* newborns. As such they must be treated with a certain dignity that, even if not warranted intrinsically, is demanded by the humanity of parents, caregivers, and society.

A Kantian-based ends/means criticism of any use of anencephalic infants as organ donors is widespread,[51] but what Kant meant by persons as ends is debatable. W. D. Ross contends that Kant did not mean persons qua persons but rather persons as actual or potential possessors of "good will." If persons were genuinely self-subsistent ends, Kant's interpretation of "treating men as ends" as the positive "advancement of humanity" would be meaningless. Although Ross laments Kant's ambiguity, he substantively agrees with his position as he interprets it: good will, not particular individuals, possesses absolute value.[52]

Kantian scholar Patrick A. E. Hutchings takes strong exception to elevating good will over concrete persons. He makes his point with a practical illustration: If X is standing by an uncongenial colleague on a wharf, it would be wrong for X to push the colleague into the water regardless of the latter's good will or lack thereof; the colleague is a rational being who deserves respect as an end in himself. According to Hutchings, rational being—not human life qua human life—is valuable as an end, a view in accord with the high priority Kant places on autonomous reason and the immediate context of Kant's statement on treating persons as ends.[53]

The point of this brief excursion into Kantian analysis is not to solve a dispute among specialists but to indicate the state of scholarly discussion on Kant's ends/means aphorism. Regardless of the interpretation of Kant's categorical imperative, it appears that he did not have nonself-aware humans in mind. Therefore, to apply Kant's standard to anencephalic infants is, at best, beyond his writings.

Kant's dictum has a powerful hold on popular thought, however,[54] and it appropriately comes to mind in discussion of anencephalic organ procurement. But his powerful maxim must not become omnipotent. It is important but, ultimately, a myth—in the best sense of the term.[55] It is an ideal that supports our sense of exalted human worth and individual rights, but it has practical limitations. High valuation of individual life is weighty, but if we are more enamored of symbolic rather than actual personal life, the Kantian doctrine of infinite worth has surpassed its usefulness. The duty-oriented absolutism of Kantian thought has done much to foster individual well-being, but this emphasis needs to be balanced with the compelling utilitarian claims of a great number who would suffer from a thoroughgoing Kantian ethic.

An ethical justification for ventilator use with anencephalic newborns may take either a duty-oriented (such as a Kantian) or a utilitarian position. In a duty-oriented approach, the weighing of potentially competing obligations is helpful. The prima facie duties that may be important in this case are: respect for the vulnerable life of the anencephalic infant, concern for saving the life of a potential organ recipient, attention to the wishes of the anencephalic newborn's family, and regard for relevant legal statutes. All these concerns are important, but in terms of the proposed ventilator use, attention to the family's wishes and compliance with the law are overriding duties, with the latter taking precedence if a choice must be made. (I do not see this as an appropriate case for civil disobedience.) Most commentators would view respect for the anencephalic infant and concern for the potential recipient as relevant duties and hold that the recipient should be saved if this does not violate respect for the life of the organ source. I believe that the duty to save a potential recipient's life can and does meet that requirement in the context of ventilator use.

A sound utilitarian approach views these obligations in the context of the need to make a decision that will realize, or is intended to realize, the greatest possible good. The saving of human life is a laudable good to which medicine is dedicated. If potentially hundreds of infants needing vital transplant organs could be saved without displacing or violating equally valuable individual or societal goods, they should be saved. The good of procuring a significant number of needed vital organs from anencephalic infants can be realized without, on balance, harming other important goods. Societal welfare is thus maximized. This is true because the proposed use of a ventilator with anencephalic infants is attentive to the aforementioned obligations, compatible with medical precedents for using some marginal human beings for the good of others, and is accompanied by certain ethical safeguards.

Medical Precedent

Usually patients are treated in a manner solely conducive to the subject's—and not others'—best interests. However, there are recognized exceptions that have at least a loosely analogous relationship to limited ventilator use with anencephalic infants.

Dying Organ Donor

A leading transplant center devised a protocol that gives optimal care to the patient while viable life can be sustained, but shifts emphasis from prolongation of life to maintenance of organ vitality at an appropriate point in the organ donor's dying process.[56]

Pregnant Patients Approaching Death

On more than one occasion women far along in their pregnancies have suffered traumatic accidents and while still alive have been placed on and/or kept on ventilators for the sake of their fetuses. Typically, the women are subsequently determined to be dead, but their vital bodily functions are maintained by artificial life support so that the fetuses develop to the point of viability, at which time a Cesarean section is performed.[57]

Dying Neonates

Not infrequently an imminently dying baby is vigorously sustained by neonatal intensive care unit personnel for the sake of relatives who are traveling from a distance for a single chance to see and hold the child.

The contemplated use of a ventilator and perhaps medications to sustain the vitality of an anencephalic newborn's organs while the baby dies is in the spirit of these examples of nonroutine treatment of patients. Further, these analogies suggest that *the issue finally is not the diagnosis of anencephaly in and of itself but the immediacy and inevitability of the death of a permanently unconscious subject.*

Determination of Brain Death

Whereas the ends/means dilemma is the most troublesome ethical issue, the determination of brain death has emerged as the salient medical issue. As described above, the Loma Linda protocol for organ prolongation in anencephalic infants specifies a seven-day limit on ventilator use while brain death is determined and organ quality is ascertained. A basic issue is whether brain death can be medically determined early enough to allow healthy, oxygenated organs to be procured from the newly dead anencephalic infant.

Shewmon contends that "It is highly unlikely that these (anencephalic) babies will meet the current legal and medical criteria of death while on respirators."[58] This declaration could be interpreted in at least two different ways. First, it could be argued that anencephalic newborns attached to ventilators will not die within a reasonable time limit. Significantly, Loma Linda's protocol committee shelved its work for several months because of questions about whether a ventilator-supported anencephalic newborn could with any likelihood be predicted to die within a reasonably short time. The fact that Baby Gabrielle became brain dead after two days of being ventilator supported was an important indication that ventilators may not unduly prolong the dying process. On the other hand, ten out of twelve anencephalic newborns that were entered into Loma Linda's experimental protocol did not meet brain death criteria within a seven-day period.[59]

A second issue raised by Shewmon is whether determination of brain death in artificially sustained anencephalic infants is possible. I believe that such a determination can be made based on many of the currently accepted criteria for determining brain death in children.[60] No body of data now exists on determination of brain death in anencephalic infants because the need for determination is only recent and very little empirical knowledge exists, not because of technical or conceptual difficulties.

Research on Anencephalic Infants

The humanitarian intent of parents who offer their anencephalic babies as potential organ sources[61] and of physicians and medical centers that engage in transplantation is commendable. However, because of the increasingly severe shortage of transplantable neonatal organs, the need for basic knowledge of anencephalic newborns is great.

There are still few data on their death—the cause, the effect of ventilator use, and the reliability of early determination of brain death. Nor are we knowledgeable about the quality of their organs and their effect on attending health care personnel.

Although physicians and ethicists at some teaching hospitals have recognized the need for thorough research on anencephalic newborns as organ sources, the idea of doing human research on the weakest of the weak carries little intrinsic appeal. For such research to be acceptable, two issues must be addressed: first, the pure versus applied nature of the research, and second, its moral and regulatory permissibility.

At this time I do not see any need for pure research on anencephalic infants totally apart from a humanitarian protocol. Good data on organ quality can be gained by procedures such as diagnostic ultrasound, blood sampling for arterial blood gases, chemistry profiles, hematologic studics, and urinalyses. Study of the visceral and neurological function may also be necessary.

The question of whether children should ever be the subjects of human research has been hotly debated. However, responsible research can and ought to be done with children. Further, in very limited circumstances, when the good of other children is intended, they may be subjects of research even when they may gain no personal benefit. This position has been previously defended by Richard McCormick, who views the child as a most valuable individual in a larger social context for which we all are morally responsible:

When a particular experiment would involve no discernible risks, no notable pain, no notable inconvenience, and yet hold promise of considerable benefit, should not the child be constructed to wish this in the same way we presume he chooses his own life, because he *ought* to? I believe so. He *ought* to want this not because it is in any way for his own medical good, but because it is not in any realistic way to his harm, and represents a potentially great benefit for others. He *ought* to want these benefits for others.[62]

The Department of Health and Human Services appears to have sided with this utilitarian view. In 1983 the Department published its current regulations for the protection of human subjects in the Code of Federal Regulations. These govern "all research involving human subjects conducted by the Department . . . or funded in whole or in part by a Department grant, contract, cooperative agreement or fellowship." Two parts of the Protections for Children section are of direct relevance:

The Department of Health and Human Services "will conduct or fund research in which the IRB (Institutional Review Board) finds that more than minimal risk to children is presented by an intervention or procedure that does not hold out the prospect of direct benefit for the individual subject . . . only if the IRB finds that: (a) The risk represents a minor increase over minimal risk; (b) The intervention or procedure presents experiences to subjects that are reasonably commensurate with those inherent in their actual or expected medical . . . situations; (c) The intervention or procedure is likely to yield generalizable knowledge about the subjects' disorder or condition which is of vital importance for the understanding or amelioration of the subjects' disorder or condition; and (d) Adequate provisions are made for soliciting assent of children and permission of their parents or guardians as set forth in #46.408."[63] (Section 408 obviates the need for child consent in cases such as the one under consideration.)

The federal regulations for the protection of human subjects also permit research on children "that does not hold out the prospect of direct benefit for the individual subject" under certain conditions.[64]

Because the Department of Health and Human Services Protections for Children are a recognized national standard, they are important for any contemplated research involving anencephalic infants. There are at least three key criteria in the published regulations: the risk to subjects is only a minor increase over minimal risk; the research is reasonable and of vital importance for understanding or ameliorating a serious problem affecting the health of children; and informed consent is obtained.

A research protocol for anencephalic newborns based on ventilator use can meet the spirit and the letter of these regulations. First, a minor increase to minimal risk is most difficult to define. But if risk refers to life threatening, the ventilator is no threat and may prolong life. If risk refers to additional pain, steps should be taken to see that any pain caused by ventilator use is indeed only minimally beyond that which normally dying anencephalic infants may suffer.

Second, designing a humane protocol is of great importance if medical science is to better understand—though not now prevent or ameliorate—anencephaly. The generalized knowledge to be gained is great. Clearly current research on anencephalic infants would be done primarily to benefit other children. Third, only fully informed parents—both mother and father when possible—will suffice. In light of the experimental nature of this procedure, only freely volunteering parents are acceptable.

The use of a ventilator with anencephalic newborns, finally, may be ill-considered in light of Loma Linda's experience. Physicians in Canada are yet to give this basic approach further attention. Regardless of whether a ventilator-dependent procedure for organ procurement from anencephalic newborns is successful, I have argued that this approach is an ethically and medically appropriate step within the law toward meeting a severe shortage of neonatal organs. However, a significant moral and legal question is whether it is or should be necessary to go to great lengths in justifying an elaborate protocol utilizing whole-brain death in anencephalic infants. A significant number of leading physicians and bioethicists are philosophically open to a change in current law that would allow organ procurement from anencephalic infants immediately after birth—quite aside from the technicalities of determining brain death. It is this ethical and legal topic to which I now turn in the next chapter.

6 : Anencephalic Infants and the Law

Baby K [Stephanie Keene] was born in October 1992 in Fairfax Hospital in Falls Church, Virginia. The fetus was diagnosed as anencephalic, but the woman continued her pregnancy despite recommendations from her pediatrician and a neonatologist. At birth the baby had difficulty breathing, and a ventilator was begun. Within a few days physicians began urging the mother to give permission for ceasing the ventilation, but she declined. A hospital ethics committee recommendation was also refused. Within six weeks Baby K was no longer ventilator dependent, and the mother agreed to have the baby transferred to a nursing facility with the stipulation that her baby could return if respiratory support became necessary. Baby K was returned to the hospital at least three times because of breathing difficulties.

Fairfax Hospital went to court claiming that it must not be forced to render "inappropriate" care. The mother's position was that "all human life has value, including her anencephalic daughter's life." The mother "has a firm Christian faith . . . [and] believes that God will work a miracle."[1] The trial judge ruled in July 1993 that the mother had the legal right to acquire life-saving treatment for her infant. Under the Emergency Treatment Act, enacted by Congress to prevent "patient dumping," treatment must be provided until the patient is medically stabilized. The hospital conceded that respiratory distress was an emergency condition, but it argued that such treatment was "futile" and "inhumane." The judge disagreed, further stating that both the Rehabilitation Act and the Americans with Disabilities Act also prohibited discrimination against Baby K based on her anencephaly. On February 10, 1994, the U.S. Court of Appeals, in a two-to-one ruling, affirmed the earlier judgment of the trial court. The majority opinion held that the language of the Emergency Treatment Act was unambiguous and had been interpreted correctly. The Court sympathized with the hospital's interest in appropriate treatment but said that the U.S. Congress was the appropriate branch of government to "redress the policy concerns."[2]

The Baby K case is an exception, and this infant is likely the longest surviving anencephalic in history, living for two and a half years until the spring of 1995. Much more typical is the Campo-Pearson situation.

Laura Campo and Justin Pearson, parents of two children and residing in Coral Springs, Florida, discovered during prenatal tests that their female fetus had anencephaly. Because of the critical need for pediatric organs, the parents decided to continue the pregnancy so that they could donate their newborn's organs for transplantation. Their 1992 case made headlines because they openly complained that organ donation, the single joy that might emerge from their personal tragedy, was illegal and ostensibly immoral. Circuit Court Judge Estella Moriarty in Fort Lauderdale ruled that the parents could not donate their daughter's vital organs prior to her death: "I can't authorize someone to take your baby's life, however short, however unsatisfactory, to save another child. Death is a fact, not an opinion."[3] The parents appealed in vain to the Fourth District Court of Appeals and the state Supreme Court rejected a petition to conduct an emergency hearing.

The Campo-Pearson situation was almost identical to that of the earlier case of Gail and Greg Marell of San Francisco. "I question the 'ethics' of a system that allows the life of a child, who can't possibly live, to be prolonged, when at the same time it could allow another child, who might survive, a chance at life," asserted Gail Marell.[4]

Many people sympathize with couples such as the Campo-Pearsons and the Marells—and with all parents of babies with fatal organ failure. However, the issue is not whether the plight of anencephalic infants or of babies needing transplanted organs is tragic but whether concrete steps should be taken to make vital organ donation from the one to the other a legal possibility. In this chapter I address this issue and contend that, because of differences in Americans' views of an individual's moral status, parents should be legally able to opt for organ donation from their anencephalic newborns. I assess the pros and cons of changing the law to allow this and then argue that parents should be able to choose among three circumscribed options for determining the death of their anencephalic newborn—cardio-respiratory, whole-brain, or higher-brain death.

Legal and Ethical Issues

The present legal status of anencephalic babies appears to be straightforward. All babies born alive are considered citizens and receive Constitutional protection. Deliberately taking an anencephalic infant's life would lay one open to possible homicide charges. Anencephalic newborns have no "higher" brain, but their brain stem functions are intact, and hence they possess spontaneous respiration and circulation. They are not dead under current whole-brain definitions. They have good reflexes and are not dissimilar to well babies in many primitive respects.

Ethically, the issue is anything but straightforward and bristles with questions: Would society's general good be served by organ transplantation from anencephalic infants? Assuming that the transplantation is medically sound, would it be defensible civil disobedience to sustain an infant by procuring an organ from an anencephalic source? In what sense would killing to procure organs be a harm to the anencephalic newborn?

These issues are valid and initially can be subsumed under a very practical and more narrowly focused question: Is it ethically appropriate to so alter existing laws that procuring organs from breathing anencephalic infants would become legal?

In February 1986 a California state senator, Milton Marks, introduced Senate Bill 2018, which called for amending the state's Uniform Determination of Death Act (UDDA) to include a clause stating that "an individual born with the condition of anencephaly is dead." Marks later modified the bill, proposing that a state health advisory board examine the issue of severely disabled newborns and make recommendations regarding their treatment, the feasibility of infant organ transplants, and the acceptability of anencephalic infants as donors with attention to the UDDA and possible "necessary changes."[5] The logic of declaring anencephalic newborns to be brain dead is questionable unless the brain stem is not seen as part of the brain, but the larger issue is whether UDDA-based statutes and homicide laws should be amended to allow for organ procurement from anencephalic infants. Andrea Scott, an attorney who believes that they should be so amended, has put forward a concrete proposal:

An anencephalic infant whose organs are to be used for transplantation may be declared dead at birth, whether delivered pre-term or full term as a result of spontaneous labor or Cesarean section, if the following conditions are met:

A. Prenatal Diagnosis of Anencephaly
   1. Prenatal diagnosis of anencephaly must be confirmed to a reasonable medical certainty by no less than three types of diagnostic testing, including but not limited to sonography, alphafetoprotein testing, and roentgenography.
   2. Prenatal testing must be performed by no less than three qualified physicians including but not limited to an ultrasonographer, a perinatologist,

and a geneticist. All physicians performing such testing must be free from any involvement with any transplantation efforts and potential organ recipients.

B. Neonatal Diagnosis of Anencephaly
Neonatal diagnosis of anencephaly must be confirmed to a reasonable medical certainty by no less than three qualified physicians, including but not limited to a neonatologist, a neurologist, and a geneticist. All physicians making the diagnosis must be free from any involvement with transplantation efforts and potential organ recipients.

C. Consent
Written informed consent, reflecting a reasonable comprehension of the meaning and consequences of donation of the body of an anencephalic infant for organ donation, must be obtained from the parents of any anencephalic infant whose organs are to be used for transplantation.[6]

To legalize declaring a spontaneously breathing human individual "dead" would be a serious development. An action that achieves the same effect in this case is advocated by the American Medical Association's Council on Ethical and Judicial Affairs in a 1994 opinion (now suspended): make anencephalics an exception to the whole-brain definition of death.[7] A redefinition of death or making anencephalics an exception to the current definition requires even wider public discussion than has taken place. I turn to significant arguments on both sides of the debate, beginning with three arguments in favor of current law that prohibits procurement of organs from liveborn anencephalic newborns.

The Case against Direct Organ Procurement

Definition of Death

Anencephalic infants are not dead according to the currently accepted criteria of common law or the relatively new UDDA, the former using cardiopulmonary tests and the latter including whole-brain death as an alternative standard. The autonomic nervous system that controls respiratory and circulatory functions is intact in liveborn anencephalic newborns. Further, they possess a primitive mobility and respond to light and painful stimuli. Some have elongated, drooping ears, an upturned face, and various other deformities and have traditionally been called monstrosities in the medical profession.[8] Other anencephalic newborns appear nearly normal except for the absence of the upper head—often covered with a knit cap in the hospital. In sum, anencephalic newborns share so much in common with other newborns that the current laws on determination of death should continue to apply to *all* newborns.

Gerald Winslow argues that it is absurd to declare spontaneously breathing anencephalic infants "dead." Saying that society is not ready for a redefinition of legally protectable human life, Winslow shows a strong affinity for current practices and laws on death, despite his concession that an anencephalic infant lacks intrinsic moral value: "We should admit, for the sake of clarity, that a *life*, even without intrinsic value, is not [the] same as a corpse. Better yet, we should admit that what is really at stake is the *evaluation* of a life. We should ask ourselves if we are prepared to take any life, however pitiful, to save another life, however promising."[9]

Continuity of Law

Because defining death is such an important issue, an enduring, clear, and enforceable regulation is mandatory. This is true for at least two reasons: First, individual patients need to be protected against any possibility of premature decisions on their deaths. Hans Jonas, in the late 1960s debate over organ transplants, argued for the "primary inviolability" of the individual patient and for "mandatory respect for invasion-proof selfhood." On the issue of defining death he contended: "Since we do not know the borderline between life and death, nothing less than the maximum definition of death will do—brain death plus heart death plus any other indication that may be pertinent—before final violence is allowed to be done."[10]

Second, society is best served by a public policy that unambiguously states its settled convictions on important matters. After much study and consultation with medical authorities, philosophers, theologians, and others, the President's Commission for the Study of Ethical Problems in Medicine and Biomedical and Behavioral Research settled on a self-confessed "conservative" brain death definition. The commission consciously rejected a neocortex-related definition and chose a whole-brain standard because the latter expressed "the understanding of death that enjoys near universal acceptance in our society." The commission further explained: "On a matter so fundamental to a society's sense of itself—touching deeply held personal and religious beliefs—and so final for the individuals involved, one should desire much greater consensus than now exists before taking the major step of radically revising the concept of death."[11]

Good law embodies and carefully articulates society's deepest sense of right behavior. Further, good law defines basic functional boundaries that give life its public meaning and within which life is enriched and flourishes. Many of the taboos of primitive communities are now appropriately rejected as superstitions, but early taboos promoted vital social integration. Today, a reasonably derived consensus on regulations concerning life and death is essential to us if our social fabric is to remain strong.

Admittedly, giving priority to social stability limits individual autonomy. However, the well-being of society rightly takes precedence over individual hardship cases. Law written on the basis of hard cases is poor law. In certain difficult circumstances ethical reality may demand civil disobedience. But for compelling social reasons, the law that prompts an act of civil disobedience may be a generally good law. Such is the argument in support of laws against aiding and abetting suicide. On the other hand, some object that such laws place an undue burden upon the terminally ill who suffer unbearably and desire aid in ending their lives. But finally, regardless of individual circumstances, rights and needs of autonomous individuals are bounded by the collective good.

Slippery Slope

Declaring anencephalic newborns to be functionally dead may initiate a slide down the "slippery slope." Paul Ramsey, cited earlier as a conservative Christian thinker, advances this argument against what he sees as the related practices of abortion and infanticide: "Since we should treat similar cases similarly, if x degree of defect would justify abortion, the same x degrees of defect would with equal cogency justify infanticide."[12] Ramsey made his mark on bioethics by taking strong, principled stands—not consequentialist positions as suggested by his "x degrees" reasoning. However, another bioethicist, James F. Childress, explicitly advances a "rule-consequentialist" argument against altering current law to allow for parental donation of organs from their anencephalic offspring.

Childress advances two related reasons why allowing direct procurement (that is, procurement of vital organs immediately after birth and before heart failure) from anencephalic infants could initiate a slippery slope. First, he points to the "conceptual difficulties" facing those who would see anencephalic infants as an exception to current law. Surely the law could be tightly written, but the logic that allows for donation from anencephalic newborns could—and some would argue should—conceptually include other patients. The moral principle of universalizability (treating similar cases in a similar way) or the legal doctrine of precedent could be cited as justification for going beyond anencephalic infants as donors.

Second, Childress describes the "psychological, cultural, and social context" of exceptions to established rules. He envisions how relatives of dying or "just seriously ill" patients may feel compelled to help other patients needing transplant organs. But these noble motives are insufficient: "Neither therapy for parents of anencephalic newborns nor therapy for other children in need of organs is a sufficient justification either for changing the current standards of death or for creating a special exception for anencephalic newborns."[13]

Significantly, Childress does not argue for the innate moral value of anencephalic infants (although he does speak of the disrespect and indignities sometimes inflicted on an anencephalic infant that breach "fundamental moral considerations"). His bottom line is clearly result oriented:

From a consequentialist standpoint, there are good reasons to worry that tampering with the legal rules regarding death (to accommodate the use of living anencephalic newborns as sources or organs) will threaten the whole system of organ procurement and donation, which, as recent experience indicates, already is fragile. Distrust and mistrust appear to be major reasons for nondonation, and alteration of the legal rules, with the conceptual problems noted, could increase the negative attitudes that currently limit donations.[14]

The Case for Direct Organ Procurement

Although the reasoning summarized above is powerful, at least three arguments can be made in favor of excluding anencephalic infants from the current definition of death or altering that definition.

Best Interests

Conservatives and liberals alike agree that the best interests of anencephalic newborns are not served by sustaining them with the intensive care given routinely to most other severely ill infants. Hence, they receive custodial care only. Given the condition of anencephalic newborns, it is questionable whether the concept of best interests is applicable. Society may see its own interests served by providing minimal care for anencephalic babies, but this should not be confused with the infant's best interests. The

President's Commission on bioethics views the best-interests test as the primary standard for deciding treatment or nontreatment for highly compromised neonates. But because anencephalic newborns do not possess any higher brain they do not have the rational potential that the best-interests standard necessarily presupposes. (Of course, because of the loose way that "best interest" is used, one can linguistically speak of the best interest of all flora and fauna, but the more removed the subject is from conscious, interest-capable life, the more strained the usage.) Thus the best-interests criterion for decision making, it can be argued, does not apply to this class of newborns and is itself no ban on direct organ procurement from anencephalic newborns. The American Medical Association appeared to implicitly agree with this assessment in its 1994 opinion that direct organ procurement is ethical. The AMA's reasoning was based on the anencephalic newborn's lack of consciousness—"their lack of a functioning cerebrum permanently forecloses the possibility of consciousness. . . . the infant has never experienced, and will never experience, consciousness."[15]

Life Sustaining

It would be wrong, of course, to use organs from anencephalic infants for transplantation if the organs serve their host's interests. But they do not, and the organs might sustain other infants' lives. Although the interests of the primary patient are most important, when these are no longer served, or never existed, the ulterior use of the host's organs assumes major importance. Many babies with severe congenital heart defects will die unless a source of suitable hearts is found, and it appears today that anencephalic newborns are one of very few sources. Further, a number of parents of anencephalic newborns desperately desire that at least some good for another sick baby might come from their own personal tragedy. If immediate, post-delivery procurement of organs from anencephalic newborns is the only viable option for transplants, such a procedure should be legitimate after the newborn is pronounced dead.

Apt Laws

Governmental laws provide the moral framework upon which a people's social fabric is stretched. To maintain this role, laws need modification as conditions change. As medical technology sustains increasingly marginal life, society must reevaluate laws designed to safeguard life in regard to affected newborns. Laws written to further personal well-being are ill served if used to protect merely biological human life, which is now known to be absent of any personal potential.

The ability of physicians to certify death has evolved during the past two centuries, and the law has changed accordingly. In the eighteenth century macabre incidents of "corpses" reviving during funerals led to widespread distrust of physicians, who were limited to such diagnostic techniques as checking for fixed pupils and feeling for pulse. By the mid-nineteenth century, with the invention of the stethoscope, medical science came to a consensus that cessation of circulation and respiration constituted death. This criterion was reflected in common law as recorded by *Black's Law Dictionary* up through the 1968 edition. During the 1960s life-sustaining technology had so developed that precise criteria were needed to know when to replace appropriate care for the living with respectful handling of the dead. This compelling need led to the landmark Harvard criteria[16] on brain death, a series of tests so reliable that no individual has met the criteria and later regained brain function. From these the President's Commission developed the widely accepted Uniform Determination of Death Act. It merely states that one of two criteria must be met for death to be certified: (1) cessation of circulatory and respiratory functions, and (2) irreversible cessation of all brain functions, including those of the brain stem.

Although the UDDA incorporated the Harvard committee's definition of death as related to the whole brain, it refined the criteria for measuring it. The Harvard/UDDA criteria go significantly beyond the traditional circulatory- and respiratory-related definition of death. Early physicians who merely listened for a heartbeat did not perceive themselves as committed to a neurological-integrating-capacity concept of life, the basis of the whole-brain death standard.[17] A further step needs to be taken today.[18]

There are far-reaching implications in the American Medical Association judicial council's 1986 determination that it is ethically permissible for all treatment—including IV nutrition—to be withdrawn from the permanently comatose. That families of such patients may choose to let loved ones starve—a startling notion in the mid-eighties, although the language used by the AMA was discreet and caused little disturbance—possesses a clear meaning: patients such as those in permanent comas are individuals whose moral status is so diminished that appropriate surrogates are within their moral right to let them die. This reasoning suggests that those same comatose individuals should be able to donate their organs if they had registered such in an advance directive. The judicial council's 1994 opinion was that anencephalic newborns should be immediately available upon birth as organ sources. The 1986 and the 1994 opinions are different in that they concern passive and active euthanasia, respectively. But they are identical in their respect for a recognized surrogate's decision about the permanently unconscious patient and ethically licit ending of a physical existence that could be sustained temporarily.

Laws defining human life and death are designed to serve conscious citizens—not to aid and support the permanently unconscious. Precisely because of the advances in medical technology, it is possible to sustain not one but hundreds of Baby Ks and thousands of Karen Ann Quinlans. But our technology is testing our ethics and it has surely outpaced our laws. It is time to realize that when there is no personal life, the individual is dead.

Which Ethical Rationale Is Right?

Whether an argument in favor of direct organ procurement or one opposed is more persuasive depends on exactly what question is being asked. Is it one of *individual* or *societal* ethics? If the question concerns individual ethics and is limited to intrinsic worth, the argument for direct procurement appears to be commendable.

Imagine, for example, that a pediatric heart surgeon skilled in transplantation is on a small Pacific island with two dying babies—an anencephalic newborn and a hypoplastic left-heart infant. The latter will die within hours unless the anencephalic baby's heart is immediately transplanted. The physician's decision has no implications beyond the island. Many would agree that the transplant operation is not only morally permissible but obligatory.

But, of course, transplant surgeons do not live on isolated islands. An ethics that focuses on the individual is vital, but an ethics that fails to take broad societal sensibilities into account is inadequate. Society is increasingly pluralistic, and this plurality must be respected for the good of all. This does not require an ethics of the lowest common denominator, but it does indicate the need to proceed openly and deliberately in areas of moral controversy.

Another facet of the dilemma is technological. Modern medicine's ability to sustain life forces us to confront the difference between the treatment of merely genetically human individuals and the treatment of individuals who possess or are capable of attaining/regaining self-consciousness. If society moves toward defining individuals in terms of self-consciousness, direct organ procurement from anencephalic infants may be realized. But society today is clearly a composite of views. Some people hold passionately to physicalism's genetically based notion of humans, others contend for personalism's higher-brain-based definition of human value, and most of us are intuitively drawn toward features of both.

Three Options

Considering the diversity of opinions, what is society to decide about anencephalic newborns as organ sources? In light of the pros and cons just cited, there appear to be two alternatives. However, both have their drawbacks, and I suggest a third option.

In the first option, society could affirm the *legal status quo,* viewing the topic as too controversial for change at present. Relatively few anencephalic infants are live births each year (about one thousand in the U.S.) and fewer yet are potential organ sources. Yes, scores of parents of anencephalic newborns will feel that the status quo definitions are ill-made, and perhaps hundreds of other infants will go without vital, often life-saving organs. However, it would be argued that it is better to maintain a uniform brain death standard, especially since the dying process is not fully understood by science or society at large as yet.

Second, society could *change the law* on brain death. Cardio-respiratory death and now brain death statutes have served us well through the years. But today medical science has catapulted us into a new era that demands updated laws to carry out the intent of traditional law. Definitions of death were never meant to bestow on anencephalic newborns a moral status equal to that of normal newborns. Society now needs to alter the law (a) to make anencephalic infants exceptions to the standard definition of brain death or (b) to change the definition from *whole-* to *higher-*brain death.

A common problem with legislating either the status quo or the change option is that parents of strongly opposing views would be coerced by a position at odds with their beliefs. Therefore, I suggest a third option, one that takes into account the need for change but also recognizes our uncertainty over the moral status of individuals such as anencephalic newborns.

We should allow parents to choose among *circumscribed options.*[19] Precisely because society is so divided over the moral status of anencephalic infants, parents should be able to choose among three definitions of death for their anencephalic newborn: (a) cardio-respiratory death (the law until the 1970s when brain death standards began to be adopted by states), (b) whole-brain death, or (c) higher-brain death. Who would choose which options? For example, some orthodox Jews may opt for cardio-respiratory death. Most parents would likely accept society's current definition of death, whole-brain death, as applicable to their newborn. Other parents, those who view higher brain functioning as that which bestows moral status, would choose higher-brain death and thereby make direct organ donation possible. (Although the focus of this chapter is on newborns and their death, there is no good reason against extending the three options for defining death to competent adults, and any new public policy in this area should be inclusive.)

The circumscribed options approach requires certain restrictions because parental autonomy is not and should never be absolute. The essential parameters of this third alternative concern present and potential cerebral functioning: Only anencephalic or other newborns and permanently unconscious patients that are equally and absolutely devoid of the possibility of cerebral life are candidates. In other words, no infant, child, or adult that has *any* possibility of attaining higher-brain function could be defined as dead. Although only persons have full moral status, current lack of personhood *does not* necessarily define death under the third option. Only if the permanently comatose condition is medically incontestable does the patient qualify as dead. In light of considered professional and general lay opinion, the standards of cardio-respiratory death, whole-brain death, and higher-brain death qualify as reasonable options for declaring death.

There are several reasons supporting this third alternative:

- Parents already make vital decisions about their offspring when they consider abortion—within legal limits. If making such a decision in regard to healthy fetuses is permissible, it should be permissible for parents of higher-brain-absent newborns to consider their tragic infants to be legally dead.

- The basis for deciding the use or non-use of an anencephalic new-born's organs is rooted in "deep" philosophy, that is, religion.[20] The transplant dilemma has been created by modern medical science, and in this uncharted territory a certain morality will hold sway, even if by default. It is proper in this land of civil and religious liberty to allow parents to make decisions within reasonable limits.
- There are hundreds of infants who are ill or dying and potentially could be benefited. Consider only the need for neonatal hearts. Each year in the United States several hundred infants are born afflicted with hypoplastic left-heart syndrome, a universally fatal condition until late successes in infant heart surgery and particularly in neonatal heart transplantation.

Finally, a decision to donate the organs of one's anencephalic newborn—or of another permanently unconscious family member—is a most personal decision arrived at through deeply conflicted emotions. There is mounting evidence that many parents want great good for another couple and their baby to come from their own personal trauma. Nothing can take away the despair of the parents of an anencephalic newborn, but neonatal transplantation now makes possible a partial win-win situation out of what has always been a total lose-lose tragedy. Allowing parents to choose among circumscribed options may appear too permissive. But in reality modern medicine is forcing an increasingly heterogeneous society to go back to its various fundamental views of life and death. In fact medical progress has long compelled society to refine its definitions of life and death.

A Historical Perspective on Definitions of Death

Throughout Western history, definitions of death have closely followed society's views about cessation of vital functions. The ancients agreed that temporal death occurred the moment heartbeat and breathing stopped. Because Hippocratic medicine prohibited medical treatment of the terminally ill, physicians withdrew before the loss of circulatory and respiratory functioning, and actual acknowledgment of death was a nonmedical act.[21]

The idea that death occurred with the cessation of heartbeat and breathing was challenged by the eighteenth-century discovery of various resuscitative techniques (such as electric shock, smelling salts, chest thumping, and artificial breathing). The new societal—and medical— consensus was that only putrefaction provided certain proof of death. By the mid-nineteenth century, the need to await bodily decay to ensure death yielded to tests of coldness, relaxed sphincters, and unblinking eyes, and to use of the newly invented stethoscope and ophthalmoscope. Earlier societal fears of premature burial yielded to broad acceptance of medical expertise in the determination of death.[22]

By the mid-twentieth century, resuscitative techniques and long-term sustenance of permanently comatose patients had so advanced that physicians were dissatisfied with traditional definitions of death. In 1957 the International Congress of Anesthesiologists sought the advice of Pope Pius XII, who left the definition of death to physicians but declared that no "extraordinary" means need be used to maintain patients seen as medically hopeless.[23] A decade later a Harvard medical school ad hoc committee advocated the adoption of brain criteria to determine death. This was endorsed by a presidential commission and adopted by all the states. Widespread acceptance of brain criteria occurred because of modern medicine's ability to sustain vital organs long after the cessation of brain functioning, the emotional and financial costs of sustaining such patients, and the growing need for transplantable organs to sustain other patients' lives.[24]

As modern medicine approaches the next century, a further development is needed—not a new national or universal definition of death but a recognition of society's religious and philosophical diversity on what constitutes life and death.

Many laypersons and medical professionals are ready to accept a refinement in the brain-based definition of death. This chapter has focused on anencephalic newborns and their parents, and the parents appear to favor strongly the allowance of organ donation. The Campo-Pearson and Marell stories are typical; more than fifty similarly situated families contacted Loma Linda University Medical Center in the months after baby Paul Holc's successful transplantation.

Because of the innate condition of anencephalic infants (and other permanently unconscious patients), the issue is finally not the person of these infants themselves so much as it is our own sensibilities. This point appears to be granted in a relatively recent article that is otherwise highly critical of the use of anencephalic infants as organ sources. The authors, in drawing an analogy between anencephalic infants and permanently comatose persons, state that "inaccuracies in the declaration of brain death make no difference whatsoever from the point of view of dying, comatose patients themselves. The importance lies rather with the larger impact on society of establishing a tolerance toward sloppiness in either the conceptualization or implementation of standards for determining death."[25]

Sloppy conceptualization is uniformly bad; what is needed is reconceptualization. That is what the Marells implicitly called for. Because of their daughter's anencephalic condition, her life was not of great intrinsic value, but it could be used to sustain another infant, and the parents desperately desired to make the donation.

Would it be right to anesthetize a newborn infant such as the Marell baby (for the caregivers' sake more than the infant's) and then allow transplant physicians to procure organs to sustain other lives? Because the Marells knew that their infant would not survive very long—she lived three hours—they were outraged that such a procedure was not a legal option. Some critics will point to the common reflexive actions that anencephalic infants share with normal babies (such as yawning and crying) and argue that this similarity militates against flexible definitions of death and hence the possibility of immediate organ procurement. However, regarding reflexive movement, analogous and contrary arguments can be made about brain-dead patients who receive paralyzing agents to calm twitching on the operating table as procurement of organs is performed.

The idea of a legally dead human body still capable of some physical movement—albeit reflexive and hence nonvoluntary—causes uneasiness for good reason. From a purely emotional point of view, the idea of organ procurement from such a human body is distasteful. Why cannot physicians wait until all nerve cells die and the body is still? In one sense this would be more humane, but in another it is cruel. Such a wait would preclude all transplantation of lifesaving organs. The moral point is not that taking organs from warm bodies is an unmitigated good; it is that forbidding parents, who see their anencephalic newborn as dead, to make organ donations violates their deepest personal values and results in hundreds of needless deaths. The fact that a brain-dead body of today is quite unlike a putrefying dead body of the eighteenth century has not eroded our respect for persons. Indeed, respect has been heightened, for organ transplantation is an acknowledgment that the uniqueness of persons is not in thoracic organs—lungs, livers, or even the hearts—but in the embodied and functioning mind.

♦ ♦ ♦

The Spanish writer José Ortega y Gasset holds that "the person portrayed and the portrait are two entirely different things." He is right. We have been grappling with the concept of moral status, but despite the thousands of words that I have dappled on canvas, the portrait pales before a real, live person. That person defies mere intellectual explanation, as carefully as one may try to lay it out. And the reason that each of us resists capture is our possession of self-consciousness—the mysterious personal essence that resides in a three-pound brain but probes the universe for knowledge and meaning.

The central point of this book is that the capacity for consciousness of self is the distinctive characteristic that gives high moral standing. Probably few would argue about the great importance of the human mind. But after that recognition, the issues become complicated by a variety of beliefs. Conflicting beliefs about humans exist for at least two reasons: embodiment and culture. Consciousness is not a pure, naked commodity that exists in a vacuum. Because our consciousness totally resides in our bodies we have bestowed on them a high esthetic, if not moral, standing. The body as flesh is not an end in itself. Because the person is so highly valued, even after death an individual's body is treated with a certain respect and ritually dealt with.

The problem of the connection between body and consciousness is complicated by the different beliefs of different cultures. And even in a single culture, traditional ideas about the body and its importance may be retained for emotional reasons, despite our understanding that those old ideas are factually outdated. For instance, in commenting on the Baby Fae transplantation involving a baboon heart, a leading bioethicist appeared on national television and said that the operation made him feel "queasy." Of course, in biblical times both Jews and Christians spoke of the heart as the seat of intellectual processes, and our contemporary celebration of Valentine's Day is not based on a view of the heart as an efficient pump. So, for psychological, sociological, and religious reasons we possess the ideas we do about human consciousness and our bodies. I have developed the physicalist and personalist camps at some length, but these are only two ways of perceiving human consciousness and the body as they have developed in the Western world.

The physicalist approach to valuing life is simple in that it allows for a clear, biological demarcation between types of beings: all human life is of highest moral value, whether the life is a single-celled zygote or an aged individual who exists in a persistent vegetative state. Personalism, on the other hand, is capacity based and equates moral status with possession of self-consciousness.

Beyond both is proximate personhood, a more complex concept. It suggests a commonsense approach to establishing moral status, reasoning that the more closely an individual life approximates that of an undisputed person, such as a reader of this page, the greater is that individual's moral status. This approach is not advocated as a neat, cookbook answer to difficult specific cases. Rather it is a philosophical perspective that makes moral sense of the life we find in a myriad species and the human life we know so well as a process of growth and decay. Proximate personhood comports with our contemporary view of life as evolutionary and processive—not static. But it is also traditional in its commitment to the universal idea that something unique beyond mere physical existence bestows sacredness—be it the Hebrew ruach (spirit) or the Greek pneuma (spirit) or psuche (soul).

Ancient empirical knowledge of life in general and of human life in particular was minimal compared to today. And it is our enhanced knowledge, made possible by modern research in the biomedical sciences, that has driven my reconsideration of traditional ethical understandings of life.

Contemporary research shows that some nonhuman animals possess a significant degree of self-awareness. What should we do with the knowledge that a chimpanzee shares 99 percent of our genes and, as an adult, possesses the I.Q. of a two-and-a-half-year-old human child? What do we make of the fact that wolves mate for life, show great loyalty to their pack, respect another wolf's territory, and seldom kill what they do not eat? Increasingly scientific observation suggests that other species—such as dolphins—have a distinctive and "other" personal and social order of life that is enjoyed by them. However, we have no reason to believe that even the most highly intelligent nonhuman animals possess our capacity to sense the richness—and tragedy—of life.

But, while we know that some animals approach the threshold of human self-consciousness, we also know that some humans are totally without consciousness and will never attain or regain this capacity. Modern medicine can sustain such humans. But do anencephalic infants or PVS patients possess moral status? On what basis are such judgments to be made?

Questions about the moral status of nonhuman animal life and about noncognitive human life are but more precise formulations of the title of this book, *What Is a Person?* The standard of proximate personhood is advanced in the hope that it corresponds to the considered moral intuitions of many in today's informed citizenry.

Notes

Introduction

1. Ronald Dworkin, *Life's Dominion: An Argument about Abortion, Euthanasia, and Individual Freedom* (New York: Vintage Books, 1994), x.

Chapter 1: Modern Bioethics and Religious Roots

1. See Winston L. King, "Religion," *The Encyclopedia of Religion,* 16 vols. (New York: Macmillan, 1987), 12:286.

2. "Besides quickening greatly our benevolent affections, [Christianity] definitely and dogmatically asserted the sinfulness of all destruction of human life as a matter of amusement, or of simple convenience, and thereby formed a new standard higher than any which then existed in the world"; and "That which appealed so powerfully to the compassion of the early and medieval Christians, in the fate of the murdered infants, was not that they died, but that they commonly died unbaptized" (W. E. H. Lecky, *History of European Morals from Augustus to Charlemagne,* 2 vols., 11th ed. [London: Longmans, Green and Co., 1869], 2:21–22, 25).

3. Barry A. Kosmin and Seymour P. Lachman, *One Nation under God: Religion in Contemporary American Society* (New York: Harmony Books, 1993), 1. Also see Princeton Religion Research Center, "Downtrends in Denominational Preferences Level Off," *Emerging Trends* 9 (Feb. 1987): 1–2.

4. See, for instance, Isaac Newton, *Observations upon the Prophecies of Daniel and the Apocalypse of St. John* (London: J. Darby and T. Browne, 1733), and *Mathematical Principles of Natural Philosophy,* trans. Andrew Motte (Berkeley: University of California Press, 1960).

5. Neither model is offered as a complete account of historical individuals or movements that are used in developing the paradigms. They are mere typologies constructed to highlight broad, different approaches to the topic of human worth. There are certainly elements missing from the models that could weaken—or perhaps strengthen—them. The physicalist and personalist models are structures of historical philosophy. They are meant to be heuristic constructs to illustrate my

contention that competing views of the human person have underlying philosophical/religious roots. These constructed models, I suggest, illumine contemporary discussion of our Nancy Cruzans and similarly situated individuals.

6. Kosmin and Lachman, *One Nation under God*, 2.

7. Max Weber, *The Protestant Ethic and the Spirit of Capitalism*, trans. Talcott Parsons (New York: Charles Scribner's Sons, 1958), 182.

8. James M. Gustafson, "Theology Confronts Technology and the Life Sciences," *Commonweal* 105 (16 June 1978): 386.

9. Ibid., 388.

10. Quoted in ibid., 386.

11. Paul Ramsey, "Introduction," in *Infanticide and the Handicapped Newborn*, ed. Dennis J. Horan and Melinda Delahoyde (Provo: Brigham Young University Press, 1982), xv.

12. Hans Jonas, "Technology, Ethics, and Biogenetic Art: Observations on the New Role of Man as Creator," *Communio* 12 (Spring 1985): 92–107.

13. Daniel Callahan, "On Feeding the Dying," *Hastings Center Report* 13 (Oct. 1983): 22.

14. Daniel Callahan, *What Kind of Life: The Limits of Medical Progress* (New York: Simon and Schuster, 1990), 234–35.

15. See, for instance, Richard Rorty, *Philosophy and the Mirror of Nature* (Princeton: Princeton University Press, 1979).

16. John Cobb Jr., "Does Theology Make a Contribution to Bioethics?," in *Theology and Bioethics*, ed. Earl E. Shelp (Dordreche: D. Reidel, 1985), 303–7. Several of the ideas expressed in this section are from Cobb.

17. Aristotle criticizes Plato's notion of the good in *Nicomachean Ethics* 1.6.

18. See Charles Curran, *Transition and Tradition in Moral Theology* (Notre Dame: University of Notre Dame Press, 1979), 32.

19. Peter Byrne, "The Moral Status of the Embryo: The Relevance of the Animation Tradition in the Light of Contemporary Philosophy," *Nederlands Theologisch Tijdschrift* 41 (Apr. 1987): 143.

20. Ibid.

21. This comes from the opening sentences of Kant's 1784 essay "What Is Enlightenment?" See Immanuel Kant, *Perpetual Peace and Other Essays on Politics, History, and Morals*, trans. Ted Humphrey (Indianapolis: Hackett, 1987), 41.

22. Walter Muelder, "Personalism," in *The Westminster Dictionary of Christian Ethics*, ed. James F. Childress and John Macquarrie (Philadelphia: Westminster Press, 1986), 469.

23. Quoted by Paul Deats, "Introduction to Boston Personalism," in *The Boston Personalist Tradition in Philosophy, Social Ethics, and Theology*, ed. Paul Deats and Carol Robb (Macon: Mercer University Press, 1986), 5. See Muelder, "Personalism," 470, for a catalog of personalist ideas.

24. Frank Hugh Foster, *A Genetic History of New England Theology* (Chicago: University of Chicago Press, 1907), 29.

25. Ibid.

26. Arminius was engaged in lifelong theological controversy. Soon after being appointed as theology professor at Leyden University, one of the chief institutions of learning in Europe, he was charged with Pelagianism—a charge that he successfully refuted. He was steadily supported by the university curators but continued be to controversial because of his liberal views. Arminius's ideas had considerable influence on the formation of modern European theology, at least indirect influence on English religious thinking, and direct impact on Wesleyan Methodism—both in England and in America. Gerald O. McCulloh, "The Influence of Arminius on American Theology," in *Man's Faith and Freedom: The Theological Influence of Jacobus Arminius,* ed. McCulloh (New York: Abingdon Press, 1962), 64–87, is excellent on the Arminius-Methodist connection.

27. Ibid., 79.

28. Ibid., 75.

29. Ibid., 73.

30. Ibid.

31. Such thinkers as Alfred N. Whitehead and Charles Hartshorne are labeled "panpsychistic idealists" by John H. Lavely. Whitehead, for example, views reality as a hierarchy of psychic beings determined by the degree of consciousness possessed. This is an extension beyond personal idealism that focuses on the consciousness of the person and the divine but does not in principle rule out the possibility that there are degrees of consciousness possessed by other "monads." See Lavely, "Personalism," *The Encyclopedia of Philosophy,* 8 vols. (New York: Macmillan, 1972), 6:107–10.

32. Charles Hartshorne, "Concerning Abortion: An Attempt at a Rational View," *The Christian Century* 98 (21 Jan. 1981): 42–45.

Chapter 2: Vying Models

1. In this chapter the terms physicalism and personalism are used to identify opposing views of *personhood,* a category of beings who possess full moral standing. The terms "human-aliveness" view of personhood and "self-consciousness" view of personhood might be more accurate. However, such labeling would achieve philosophical precision at the price of considerable awkwardness. I use personhood, like its cognate person, to denote a class of individuals who possess full moral standing. (This is not necessarily the definition used by others.)

2. Mary Meehan, "The Bishops and the Politics of Abortion," *Commonweal* 111 (23 Mar. 1984): 169–73.

3. Ruth Macklin, "Personhood in the Bioethics Literature," *Milbank Memorial Fund Quarterly: Health and Society* 61 (Winter 1983): 35–57.

4. Mary Ann Warren lists five criteria: "1. Consciousness (of objects and events external and/or internal to the being), and in particular the capacity to feel pain; 2. Reasoning (the *developed* capacity to solve new and relatively complex problems); 3. Self-motivated activity (activity which is relatively independent of either genetic or direct external control); 4. The capacity to communicate, by

whatever means, messages of an indefinite variety of types, that is, not just with an indefinite number of possible contents, but on indefinitely many possible topics; 5. The presence of self-concepts, and self-awareness, either individual or racial, or both" ("On the Moral and Legal Status of Abortion," in *Contemporary Issues in Bioethics,* 2d ed., ed. Tom L. Beauchamp and LeRoy Walters [Belmont, Calif.: Wadsworth, 1982], 256).

5. Albert R. Jonsen and Stephen Toulmin, *The Abuse of Casuistry: A History of Moral Reasoning* (Berkeley: University of California Press, 1988), 18–19.

6. There are good reasons to use the term *person,* including its cognates personalism and personhood, to designate an important approach to the issues I address. For example, *The Encyclopedia of Philosophy* includes a major article entitled "Personalism" (Lavely, 6:107–10) as well as one on "Persons" (Arthur C. Danto, 6:110–14) and "Personal Identity" (Terence Penlhum, 6:95–107)—all using *person* in the normative fashion advocated in this book. *Merriam Webster's Collegiate Dictionary,* 10th ed., defines person, in part, as "the personality of a human being: SELF." But it defines the noun *human* as merely designating the species.

7. Dworkin's thesis in *Life's Dominion* is that almost all of society—conservatives and liberals alike—accepts the idea that all human life regardless of its stage of development is intrinsically valuable, even sacred. Such a view is a religious view, he contends. And because it is held by indisputable persons, the doctrine of religious freedom granted by the First Amendment guarantees citizens the right to decide momentous questions involving the "intrinsic, cosmic importance of human life" as individuals (217). Society itself must not legislate such issues. This position is furthered by Dworkin's contention that fetal life, as opposed to adult lives, is developmentally incapable of possessing interests or rights, regardless of the rhetoric of many in the pro-life camp. Although Dworkin's essay deals with some of the key issues discussed here, its agenda is quite different. Dworkin *conflates* societal views on the high value of all human life in order to proceed to the even higher value of religious freedom for undisputed persons to decide such "religious" questions as abortion and euthanasia. However, I *analyze* contending societal views of human life in order to clarify the different philosophical or religious bases that underlie the differences. Dworkin and I agree that the fetus, for example, is developmentally incapable of possessing interests or rights.

8. Daniel E. Dennett, *Consciousness Explained* (Boston: Little, Brown and Co., 1991); Owen Flanagan, *Consciousness Reconsidered* (Cambridge: MIT Press, 1992); Colin McGinn, *The Problem of Consciousness: Essays towards a Resolution* (Oxford: Basil Blackwell, 1992); William Seager, *Metaphysics of Consciousness* (London: Routledge, 1991); John Searle, *The Rediscovery of Mind* (Cambridge: MIT Press, 1992).

9. Dennett, *Consciousness Explained,* 21.

10. David F. Kelly, *The Emergence of Roman Catholic Medical Ethics in North America* (Lewiston, N.Y.: Edwin Mellon Press, 1982).

11. William E. May, "What Makes a Human Being to Be a Being of Moral Worth?" *The Thomist* 40 (July 1976): 416–43. Page numbers given in the text refer to this article.

12. Benedict M. Ashley, "Ethical Decisions: Why 'Exceptionless Norms'?," *Health Progress* 66 (Apr. 1985): 50–53, 66.

13. Ibid., 53.

14. Ibid., 66.

15. For example, *The Declaration on Religious Freedom*, ed. John Courtney Murray (New York: Macmillan, 1966), begins by acknowledging, "A sense of the dignity of the human person has been impressing itself more and more deeply on the consciousness of contemporary man."

16. Charles Curran, *Catholic Moral Theology in Dialogue* (Notre Dame, Ind.: Fides, 1972), 164.

17. Ibid., 168–69.

18. Joseph Bernardin, "Call for a Consistent Ethic of Life," *Origins* 13 (29 Dec. 1983): 491–94.

19. Joseph Bernardin, "Enlarging the Dialogue on a Consistent Ethic of Life," *Origins* 13 (5 Apr. 1984): 705–9; "Health Care and the Consistent Ethic of Life," *Origins* 15 (6 June 1985): 36–40.

20. Bernardin, "Call for a Consistent Ethic of Life," 491.

21. See, for instance, Meehan, "Bishops and the Politics of Abortion."

22. Joseph Bernardin, "Medical Humanism: Pragmatic or Personalist?" *Health Progress* 66 (Apr. 1985): 46–49. Page numbers given in the text refer to this article.

23. Ibid., 49.

24. See, for instance, Peter Singer, *Animal Liberation: A New Ethics for Our Treatment of Animals* (New York: Avon Books, 1975).

25. Bernardin, "Medical Humanism," 48–49. Page numbers in the text refer to this article.

26. Ellen Goodman, "Request to Die Has No Single Answer," *Birmingham Post-Herald*, 11 Feb. 1984, p. 4A.

27. J. Stephen Cleghorn has written a sociological analysis of Bernardin's "Seamless Garment" ethic and concludes that church leaders must not assume widespread public agreement on or understanding of the notion of sacredness of life. The public, Cleghorn claims, separates "personal choice" issues from "defense of society" issues. Religion has influence on the former, but many people view the latter as the realm of the state, and they keep choice and defense issues quite separate in their thinking ("Respect for Life: Research Notes on Cardinal Bernardin's 'Seamless Garment,'" *Review of Religious Research* 28 [Dec. 1986]: 129–41).

28. See a full account of this case in Helga Kuhse and Peter Singer, *Should the Baby Live? The Problem of Handicapped Infants* (Oxford: Oxford University Press, 1985), 1–11.

29. Raanan Gillon, "Conclusion: The Arthur Case Revisited," *British Medical Journal* 292 (1986): 543–45.

30. See, for instance, Kuhse and Singer, *Should the Baby Live?*; Earl E. Shelp, *Born to Die? Deciding the Fate of Critically Ill Newborns* (New York: Free Press, 1986); H. Tristram Engelhardt, *The Foundations of Bioethics* (New York: Oxford University Press, 1986); Michael Tooley, *Abortion and Infanticide* (Oxford: Clarendon Press, 1983); "The Problem of Personhood: Biomedical, Social, Legal, and Policy Views," special issue of *Milbank Memorial Fund Quarterly: Health and Society* 61 (1983); Carol A. Tauer, "Personhood and Human Embryos and Fetuses," *Journal of Medicine and Philosophy* 10 (1985): 253–66. Early exponents of personhood criteria were Joseph Fletcher, *Humanhood: Essays in Biomedical Ethics* (New York: Prometheus Books, 1979) and Richard A. McCormick, "To Save or Let Die," *Journal of the American Medical Association* 229 (1974): 172–76. For an analysis of five perspectives on making decisions regarding handicapped newborns (value of life, parental authority, best interests, personhood, and proximate personhood), see James W. Walters, "Approaches to Ethical Decision Making in the Neonatal Intensive Care Unit," *American Journal of Diseases of Children* 142 (1988): 825–30.

31. Michael Tooley, "Abortion and Infanticide," *Philosophy and Public Affairs* 2 (Fall 1972): 44, 48, 55.

32. Tooley, *Abortion and Infanticide,* 349.

33. See Engelhardt, *Foundations of Bioethics,* 116–19.

34. Ibid., 105.

35. Ibid., 106–10.

36. Ibid., 115.

37. Ibid., 119.

38. Ibid., 120.

39. Ibid., 123.

40. Ibid., 11.

41. Ibid., 116.

42. Ibid., 120, 216 (emphasis added).

43. R. M. Hare, *The Language of Morals* (Oxford: Clarendon, 1952) (emphasis added).

44. Engelhardt, *Foundations of Bioethics,* 12, 22.

45. Paul L. Lehmann, *Ethics in a Christian Context* (New York: Harper and Row, 1963).

46. "By law, paramedics are required to try to resuscitate patients. . . . But this month marks the start of a new policy in Orange County that allows dying patients to reject emergency measures and permits paramedics to heed their wishes" (*Los Angeles Times,* 29 July 1991, pp. A3, A20).

47. Surely, in light of the context of this statement, the Supreme Court meant life with significant if not full moral status.

48. Walter Ullmann, *The Individual and Society in the Middle Ages* (Baltimore: Johns Hopkins University Press, 1966), 36–37.

49. Quoted in Steven Lukes, *Individualism* (New York: Harper and Row, 1973), 3.

50. Immanuel Kant, *The Moral Law: Groundwork of the Metaphysic of Morals,* ed. and trans. H. J. Paton (New York: Barnes and Noble, 1967), 95.

51. Willy De Craemer, "A Cross-Cultural Perspective on Personhood," *Milbank Memorial Fund Quarterly: Health and Society* 61 (1983): 19–34.

52. For example, an individual "is what he is in so far as he is a member of this community, and the new materials out of which this particular individual is born would not be a self but for his relationship to others in the community of which he is a part" (George Herbert Mead, *Mind, Self, and Society,* ed. Charles W. Morris [Chicago: University of Chicago Press, 1974], 200).

53. Renee C. Fox and David P. Willis, "Personhood, Medicine, and American Society," *Milbank Memorial Fund Quarterly: Health and Society* 61 (1983): 127–47.

54. Robert N. Bellah, Richard Madsen, William M. Sullivan, Ann Swidler, and Steven M. Tipton, *Habits of the Heart: Individualism and Commitment in American Life* (Berkeley: University of California Press, 1985), 83.

55. Sherman Block, "Army of Occupation Won't Work" (editorial), *Los Angeles Times,* 18 Dec. 1990, p. M7.

56. Viktor E. Frankl, *Man's Search for Meaning* (New York: Pocket Books, 1976), 164.

57. "Man Does Not Live by Reason Alone" (interview with Leszek Kolakowski), *New Perspectives Quarterly* 8 (Spring 1991): 16–23.

58. Clifford Geertz, *The Interpretation of Cultures* (New York: Basic Books, 1973), 122.

59. In particular, see ibid.

60. Jeffrey Stout, *Ethics after Babel: The Languages of Morals and Their Discontents* (Boston: Beacon Press, 1988), 109–15.

61. See, for instance, Richard Rorty, *Philosophy and the Mirror of Nature* (Princeton: Princeton University Press, 1979).

62. Alasdair MacIntyre, *After Virtue* (Notre Dame: University of Notre Dame Press, 1981); *Whose Justice? Which Rationality?* (Notre Dame: University of Notre Dame Press, 1988).

63. Martin Buber, *Between Man and Man* (New York: Macmillan, 1975), 203.

64. *I and Thou,* trans. Ronald Gregor Smith (New York: Charles Scribner's Sons, 1958).

65. Buber, *Between Man and Man,* 203.

66. James M. Gustafson, *Ethics from a Theocentric Perspective,* 2 vols. (Chicago: University of Chicago Press, 1981), 1:119.

67. Ibid., 1:201.

68. Quoted in Stout, *Ethics after Babel,* 181.

69. Ibid., 181–82.

70. Salman Rushdie, "Is Nothing Sacred?," *New Perspectives Quarterly* 8 (Spring 1991): 14.

71. See Thomas H. Murray, "Why Solutions Continue to Elude Us," *Social Science and Medicine* 20 (1985): 1103–7.

72. Jonathan Bennett, "The Conscience of Huckleberry Finn," *Philosophy* 49 (1974): 123, 134.

73. J. B. Schneewind, "Moral Knowledge and Moral Principles," in *Revisions,* ed. Stanley Hauerwas and Alasdair MacIntyre (Notre Dame: University of Notre Dame Press, 1983), 118–19.

74. Sidney Callahan, "The Role of Emotion in Ethical Decisionmaking," *Hastings Center Report* 18 (June–July 1988): 10.

Chapter 3: Proximate Personhood

1. For instance in the Baby Boy Houle case a court mandated treatment for a catastrophically ill baby who died the day after the order; in the well-known Baby Doe and Baby Jane Doe cases the courts allowed nontreatment. Baby Doe, born in Indiana in 1982 with treatable abnormalities of the esophagus and trachea, died during court proceedings wthout receiving necessary nutrition and hydration. For additional difficult court cases see Robert Weir, *Selective Non-Treatment of Handicapped Newborns* (New York: Oxford University Press, 1984), 93–98.

2. The value-of-life position is analogous to that of humanhood and physicalism (see chapters 1 and 2).

3. C. Everett Koop, "The Handicapped Child and His Family," *The Linacre Quarterly* 48 (Feb. 1981): 23.

4. "American Academy of Pediatrics Joint Policy Statement: Principles of Treatment of Disabled Infants," *Pediatrics* 73 (Apr. 1984): 559–60.

5. Leslie A. Fiedler comments on surviving Thalidomide babies who have matured: "Not one of them, at any rate, was willing to confess that he would have wished himself dead" ("Tyranny of the Normal," in *Which Babies Shall Live? Humanistic Dimensions of the Care of Imperiled Newborns,* ed. Thomas H. Murray and Arthur L. Caplan [Clifton, N.J.: Humana Press, 1985], 153).

6. Ramsey, "Introduction," xv.

7. Kuhse and Singer, *Should the Baby Live?,* 91–94. In regard to euthanasia the authors argue that present concern for the individual infant's well-being is generically different from the Nazis's concern for developing a racially pure *Volk.*

8. Robert A. Burt, "Authorizing Death for Anomalous Newborns," in *Genetics and the Law III,* ed. Aubrey Milunsky and George J. Annas (New York: Plenum Press, 1985), 263. Compare Robert A. Burt, "The Ideal of Community in the World of the President's Commission," *Cardozo Law Review* 6 (Fall 1984): 207–8.

9. Great Britain's Chief Rabbi Immanuel Jakobovits speaks of the infinite value of every human life: "Since infinity is, by definition, indivisible, it follows that every fraction of life, however small, remains equally infinite so that it makes morally no difference whether one shortens life by seventy years or by only a few hours" (quoted in Kuhse and Singer, *Should the Baby Live?,* 19).

10. "Child Abuse and Neglect Prevention Treatment Program" (final action), *Federal Register* 50 (15 Apr. 1985): 14878–88.

11. See the transcript of the proceedings before the U.S. District Court for the District of Columbia, *American Academy of Pediatrics et al. v. Margaret M. Heckler, Secretary, Department of Health and Human Services, Washington, D.C.,* Civil Action no. 83–0774, 21 Mar. 1983, 421–25.

12. "Child Abuse and Neglect Prevention Treatment Program."

13. *Laws 6.*

14. Both Shelp, *Born to Die?*, 27–41, and Weir, *Selective Non-Treatment of Handicapped Newborns,* 3–28, have good abbreviated histories of infanticide; Shelp emphasizes evolving parental attitudes toward children.

15. After detailing the introduction into Western thought, through Christianity, of the sanctity of life principle, Kuhse and Singer conclude: "In a pluralistic society which accepts the separation of Church and State, laws cannot be defended by showing that they are in accordance with the beliefs of one particular religion" (*Should the Baby Live?*, 117).

16. President's Commission for the Study of Ethical Problems in Medicine and Biomedical and Behavioral Research, *Deciding to Forego Life-Sustaining Treatment* (Washington, D.C.: U.S. Government Printing Office, 1983), 212.

17. "Although a 1982 Presidential Commission suggested a model of shared decision making between physician and patient, case law has since chosen patient (or surrogate) directed care as the legal standard" (Frank I. Clark, "Intensive Care Treatment Decisions: The Roots of Our Confusion," *Pediatrics* 94 [July 1994]: 98–101).

18. James F. Childress, "Protecting Handicapped Newborns: Who's in Charge and Who Pays?," in *Genetics and the Law III,* ed. Milunsky and Annas, 273.

19. See Weir, *Selective Non-Treatment of Handicapped Newborns,* 236.

20. Norman Fost, "Ethical Issues in the Treatment of Critically Ill Newborns," *Pediatric Annals* 10 (Oct. 1981): 21.

21. "Permanent handicaps justify a decision not to provide life-sustaining treatment only when they are so severe that continued existence would not be a net benefit to the infant" (President's Commission, *Deciding to Forego Life-Sustaining Treatment,* 218).

22. The idea that certain medical conditions render individuals' lives "incompatible with personal life" does not mean that those lives cannot be sustained at an elemental level, given society's advanced medical technology. Anencephalic Baby K, born in Virginia in 1992, was given aggressive treatment (rather than the standard comfort care) and died in 1995. George J. Annas says that Baby K "may be the longest-lived anencephalic infant in medical history" ("Asking the Courts to Set the Standard of Emergency Care: The Case of Baby K," *New England Journal of Medicine* 330 [26 May 1994]: 1542–45).

23. President's Commission, *Deciding to Forego Life-Sustaining Treatment,* 219n.78.

24. Ibid., 219.

25. Nancy K. Rhoden and John D. Arras, "Withholding Treatment from Baby Doe: From Discrimination to Child Abuse," *Milbank Memorial Fund Quarterly:*

Health and Society 63 (1985): 34–35. These authors explore the problems created by the best interests approach. Also see John D. Arras, "Toward an Ethic of Ambiguity," *Hastings Center Report* 14 (Apr. 1984): 25–33.

26. Personalism, as delineated in chapter 2, is here called "personhood"—as is common in most discussions of these topics.

27. According to Engelhardt, "Persons strictly . . . are moral agents, rational, able to choose freely according to a rational plan of life, and are possessed of a notion of blameworthiness and praiseworthiness. Persons strictly are protected by the moralities of mutual respect and of beneficence" (*Foundations of Bioethics*, 145). See also Kuhse and Singer, *Should the Baby Live?*, 132–34.

28. Members of some species "would be quasi-persons, and their destruction therefore wrong to a greater or lesser degree. Finally, normal adult members of some species—such as, perhaps, chimpanzees, whales, and dolphins—might be persons, so that their destruction would be comparable to the destruction of normal adult human beings" (Tooley, *Abortion and Infanticide*, 412).

29. Earle E. Shelp, *Born to Die? Deciding the Fate of Critically Ill Newborns* (New York: Free Press, 1986), 164.

30. Anthony Shaw, Judson G. Randolph, and Barbara Manard, "Ethical Issues in Pediatric Surgery: A National Survey of Pediatricians and Pediatric Surgeons," *Pediatrics* 60 (Oct. 1977): 588–99.

31. Ibid.

32. Edward A. Langerak, "Abortion: Listening to the Middle," *Hastings Center Report* 9 (1979): 24–28, argues from the principle of potentiality as supplemented by the notion of societal sensibilities. One salient difference in the conceptual framework of his piece and the argument here is that Langerak argues that potentiality—evidently from conception on—bestows on the human subject an "inherent" claim to life.

33. Alzheimer's disease is a progressive neurological disorder that results in complete cognitive loss. The development of numerous senile plaques and neurofibrillary tangles in the brain can occur before symptoms are apparent. Five symptoms are predictive of dementia severity in Alzheimer's disease patients: the tendency to produce meaningless sentences, poor reading comprehension, inappropriate conversations, failure to recognize humor, and failure to complete sentences. See Kathryn A. Bayles and Cheryl K. Tomoeda, "Caregiver Report of Prevalence and Appearance Order of Linguistic Symptoms in Alzheimer's Patients," *The Gerontologist* 31 (Apr. 1991): 210; Marilyn S. Albert, "Parallels between Down Syndrome Dementia and Alzheimer's Disease," in *Down Syndrome and Alzheimer Disease*, ed. Lynn Hadel and Charles J. Epstein (New York: Wiley-Liss, 1992), 77–102.

34. George F. Will, "Jon Will's Aptitudes," *Newsweek* 121 (3 May 1993): 70.

35. B. T. Hyman, "Down Syndrome and Alzheimer Disease," in *Down Syndrome and Alzheimer Disease*, ed. Hadel and Epstein, 124. Also see President Bill Clinton's Proclamation CC11, National Down Syndrome Awareness Month, *Weekly Compilation of Presidential Documents* 20 (10 Oct. 1993): 2073 (2).

36. Hyman, "Down Syndrome and Alzheimer Disease," 124.

37. See, for example, Childress, "Protecting Handicapped Newborns," 277.

38. See, for example, Engelhardt, *Foundations of Bioethics,* 122.

39. Joel Feinberg, *Freedom and Fulfillment: Philosophical Essays* (Princeton: Princeton University Press, 1992), 51.

40. Jonathan Glover, *Causing Death and Saving Lives* (Harmondsworth, U.K.: Penguin, 1977); Peter Singer, "Killing Humans and Killing Animals," *Inquiry* 22 (1979): 145–56; Tooley, "Abortion and Infanticide," 37–65; Tooley, *Abortion and Infanticide.*

41. R. M. Hare, "Abortion and the Golden Rule," *Philosophy and Public Affairs* 5 (1975): 201–22. In fairness to Hare, it must be pointed out that after he acknowledges the many legitimate factors that must be weighed against the prima facie duty to increase the number of happy people on earth, he comes close to the position he initially seems to be opposing.

42. Mary Ann Warren, "On the Moral and Legal Status of Abortion," in *Contemporary Issues in Bioethics,* ed. Tom L. Beauchamp and LeRoy Walters, 2d ed. (Belmont, Calif.: Wadsworth Publishing Co., 1982), 250–60.

43. Paul Ramsey, *Ethics at the Edges of Life* (New Haven: Yale University Press, 1978), 190.

44. See Kuhse and Singer, *Should the Baby Live?,* 195.

45. Feinberg, *Freedom and Fulfillment,* 52.

46. I am indebted to Robert Weir for the idea that categories of treatment depend on the severity of disability. See Weir, *Selective Non-Treatment of Handicapped Newborns,* 211–15.

47. See James W. Walters and Stephen Ashwal, "Organ Prolongation in Anencephalic Infants: Ethical and Medical Issues," *Hastings Center Report* 18 (1988): 19–27.

48. See, for instance, Weir, *Selective Non-Treatment of Handicapped Newborns,* 235; Shaw et al., "Ethical Issues in Pediatric Surgery," 588–99; and Betty Wolder Levin, "Consensus and Controversy in the Treatment of Catastrophically Ill Newborns: Report of a Survey," in *Which Babies Shall Live?,* ed. Murray and Caplan, 169–212.

49. Department of Health and Human Services, Office of Human Development Services, "Baby Doe Regulations," *Federal Register* 45 (10 Dec. 1984): 48161.

50. Working Group on Current Medical/Ethical Problems in the Northern Health Region, "The Prognosis for Babies with Meningomyelocele and High Lumbar Paraplegia at Birth," *Lancet* 2, no. 8462 (2 Nov. 1985): 996–97.

51. The right of legitimate surrogates—usually families—to make decisions to withdraw life-sustaining treatment from incompetent adult patients is gaining recognition. The *Barber, Conroy,* and *Bouvia* cases, three landmark cases from the early 1980s, cases are evidence that the courts are beginning to recognize that adults with marginal lives have the right to end a miserable existence. In particular, this right should not be denied to marginal newborns. The decision to end a miserable, even painful, life is a wrenching experience for a self-aware adult

because of the rich, mixed emotions of a lifetime. However, if the catastrophically ill newborn is our major concern, we must realize that the baby suffers no mental agony and need not endure physical pain.

52. A. A. Fanaroff, "Changes in the Delivery Room Care of the Extremely Small Infant," *New England Journal of Medicine* 314 (1986): 660–64.

53. B. Lo and A. R. Jonsen, "Clinical Decisions to Limit Treatment," *Annals of Internal Medicine* 93 (1980): 764–68; D. E. Johnson, "Life, Death, and the Dollar Sign: Medical Ethics and Cost Containment," *Journal of the American Medical Association* 252 (1984): 223–24; A. Griffin and D. C. Thomasma, "Pediatric Critical Care: Should Medical Costs Influence Clinical Decisions?," *Archives of Internal Medicine* 143 (1983): 325–27.

54. Johnson, "Life, Death, and the Dollar Sign."

55. International Code of Medical Ethics, London, World Medical Association, October 1949; reprinted in *The Encyclopedia of Bioethics,* 4 vols. (New York: Free Press, 1978), 4:1749–50.

56. N. G. Levinsky, "The Doctor's Master," *New England Journal of Medicine* 311 (1984): 1573–75.

57. See Johnson, "Life, Death, and the Dollar Sign."

58. N. Daniels, "Why Saying No to Patients in the United States Is So Hard," *New England Journal of Medicine* 314 (1986): 1380–83.

59. R. Gillon, "Ordinary and Extraordinary Means," *British Medical Journal* 292 (1986): 259–61; M. Swartz, "The Patient Who Refuses Medical Treatment: A Dilemma for Hospitals and Physicians," *American Journal of Law and Medicine* 11 (1985): 147–94.

60. Lo and Jonsen, "Clinical Decisions."

61. See Daniel Callahan, *Setting Limits: Medical Goals in an Aging Society* (New York: Simon and Schuster, 1987).

62. Kuhse and Singer, in reflecting on the application of their own personhood philosophy to public policy, make an enlightening admission: "It is one thing to have a defensible philosophical theory, however, and another thing to decide what to do in practice" (*Should the Baby Live?,* 139). The adequacy of any single philosophical theory, finally, is questionable. "There is no logic as such," states Jean Bethke Elshtain in criticizing the "logic" of personhood thinking. "Rather, there are many forms of thinking that bear the stamp of human reason" ("Commentary," in *Abortion: Understanding Differences,* ed. Sidney Callahan and Daniel Callahan [New York: Plenum Press, 1984], 142). At times moral theory points in one direction but a more compelling moral judgment and common sense point in another and must be followed, argues Thomas H. Murray. The relationship between moral judgment and moral theory is ultimately a dialectical one of mutual learning and correction ("Why Solutions Continue to Elude Us," *Social Science and Medicine* 20 [1985]: 1103–7).

63. I am indebted to Clifford Grobstein for suggesting this terminology as a substitute for an earlier, more clumsy approach to the topic.

64. Rorty, *Philosophy and the Mirror of Nature.*

65. Anthony Battaglia, "Sect or Denomination: The Place of Religious Ethics in a Post-Churchly Culture," *Journal of Religious Ethics* 16 (1988): 128–42.

66. George P. Fletcher, "The Right and the Reasonable," *Harvard Law Review* 98 (1985): 949, 971.

67. Editorial, *New York Times,* 27 April 1982, sec. A, p. 22, col. 1.

68. Shelp, *Born to Die,* 26–49; Kuhse and Singer, *Should the Baby Live?,* 98–117. See also Stephen G. Post, "History, Infanticide, and Imperiled Newborns," *Hastings Center Report* 18 (1988): 14–17.

69. Sissela Bok, *Lying: Moral Choice in Public and Private Life* (New York: Vintage Books, 1979), 96.

70. Roderick Firth, "Ethical Absolutism and the Ideal Observer," *Philosophy and Phenomenological Research* 12 (1952): 317–45.

Chapter 4: Humans, Animals, and Morality

1. Tom Regan, *The Thee Generation: Reflections on the Coming Revolution* (Philadelphia: Temple University Press, 1991).

2. Ibid., x–xi, 3.

3. Willard Gaylin, *Adam and Eve and Pinocchio: On Being and Becoming Human* (New York: Viking Press, 1990), 5.

4. Ibid., 12.

5. Ibid., 7–8.

6. Ibid., 258–59.

7. Singer, *Animal Liberation,* 8.

8. Ibid., 3.

9. Ibid., 21–22.

10. Tom Regan, "An Examination and Defense of One Argument Concerning Animal Rights," *Inquiry* 22 (1979): 208–9, 212.

11. Tom Regan, "Animal Rights and Human Wrongs," in *Ethics and Animals,* ed. H. B. Miller and W. Williams (Clifton, N.Y.: Humana Press), 39.

12. Tom Regan, *The Case for Animal Rights* (London: Routledge and Kegan Paul), 240–41.

13. Tom Regan, "Introduction," *Animal Sacrifices: Religious Perspectives on the Use of Animals in Science,* ed. Tom Regan (Philadelphia: Temple University Press, 1986), ix.

14. Raymond Gillespie Frey, *Interests and Rights: The Case against Animals* (Oxford: Clarendon Press, 1980).

15. Frey, *Interests and Rights,* 5.

16. Ibid., 119.

17. Ibid., 90, 118.

18. Steven Sapontzis, *Morals, Reason, and Animals* (Philadelphia: Temple University Press, 1987), 127. Sapontzis devotes a full chapter to refutation of Frey's book. I am indebted to Sapontzis's analysis for certain insights.

19. Ibid., 133.

20. Ibid., 8.

21. Ibid., 7.

22. Apparently Frey has changed his mind on the pivotal issue of whether animals can possess interests, but he has not published this revised view. See David DeGrazia, "The Moral Status of Animals and Their Use in Research: A Philosophical Review," *Kennedy Institute of Ethics Journal* 1 (Mar. 1991): 52.

23. Keith Tester, *Animals and Society: The Humanity of Animal Rights* (London: Routledge, 1991).

24. The primary source for animal trials in medieval times is Edward P. Evans, *The Criminal Prosecution and Capital Punishment of Animals* (New York: E. P. Dutton and Co., 1906). For the Falsise pig trial, see ibid., 140–41. For discussion of these practices based on Evans's work, see Tester, *Animals and Society,* 72–93, and Michael P. T. Leahy, *Against Liberation: Putting Animals in Perspective* (London: Routledge, 1991), 167–69.

25. Evans, *Criminal Prosecution,* 18.

26. See René Descartes, "Animals Are Machines," reprinted in *Animal Rights and Human Obligations,* ed. Tom Regan and Peter Singer (Englewood Cliffs, N.J.: Prentice-Hall, 1976), 60–66.

27. Evans, *Criminal Prosecution,* 66–69, 80–86, 88–92. Evans concludes his account of Bougeant's book with this intriguing comment: "Bougeant's ingenious dissertation has a vein of irony or at least a strain of jocundity in it, approaching at times so perilously near the fatal brink of persiflage, that one cannot help surmising an intention to render the whole thing ridiculous in a witty and underhand way eminently compatible with Jesuitical habits of mind; but whether serious or satirical, his treatise is an excellent example and illustration of the kind of dialectic hair-splitting and syllogistic rubbish, which passed for reasoning in the early and middle ages of the Christian era" (ibid., 89).

28. See Bernard E. Rollin, "The Moral Status of Research Animals in Psychology," *American Psychologist* 40 (Aug. 1985): 920–26.

29. Andrew Linzey, *Christianity and the Rights of Animals* (New York: Crossroad, 1987), 16.

30. Keith Thomas, *Man and the Natural World: Changing Attitudes in England, 1500–1800* (London: Penguin, 1984), 29.

31. "Hereby is refuted the error of those who said it is sinful for a man to kill dumb animals: for by divine providence they are intended for man's use in the natural order. Hence it is not wrong for man to make use of them, either by killing or in any other way whatever. For this reason the Lord said to Noe (Gen. ix. 3): 'As the green herbs I have delivered all flesh to you'" (Thomas Aquinas, "Differences between Rational and Other Creatures," reprinted in *Animal Rights and Human Obligations,* ed. Regan and Singer, 58–59).

32. Aquinas quoted in Linzey, *Christianity and the Rights of Animals,* 56.

33. Quoted in ibid., 56.

34. See Rollin, "Moral Status of Research Animals," 923.

35. See Linzey, *Christianity and the Rights of Animals,* 16–21.

36. Mary Midgley, *Beast and Man: The Roots of Human Nature* (Ithaca: Cornell University Press, 1978), xiii. I am significantly indebted to Midgley's fine volume for the neo-naturalistic argument that I develop in this chapter.

37. Ibid., 261.

38. Ibid., 262.

39. Alfred North Whitehead, *Process and Reality* (New York: Macmillan, 1929), vi.

40. See Ian Barbour, *Religion in an Age of Science* (San Francisco: Harper, 1990), 218–42. Barbour gives an excellent summary of Whitehead's metaphysics, particularly as it relates to recent scientific insights. I have used his convenient layout of process thought in my brief summary of this important school of thinking.

41. See James Rachels, *Created from Animals: The Moral Implications of Darwinism* (New York: Oxford University Press, 1991).

42. See Midgley, *Beast and Man*, 332.

43. Konrad Lorenz, *On Aggression,* trans. M. K. Wilson (New York: Harcourt, Brace and World, 1963), 33.

44. Konrad Lorenz, *King Solomon's Ring,* trans. M. K. Wilson (New York: Crowell, 1952).

45. Midgley, *Beast and Man*, 326.

46. Ibid., 325.

47. Iris Murdoch, *The Sovereignty of Good* (New York: Schocken Books), 84.

48. See Midgley, *Beast and Man*, 226.

49. Ibid., 226.

50. See ibid., 204.

51. Tester, *Animals and Society*, 30.

52. I am indebted to my colleagues in Loma Linda University's Ethics Center, Gerald Winslow and David Larson, for pressing me to be more explicit in addressing the naturalistic fallacy than was the case in an earlier draft of the manuscript.

53. Philip Lieberman, *Uniquely Human: The Evolution of Speech, Thought, and Selfless Behavior* (Cambridge: Harvard University Press, 1991), 113.

54. Ibid., 155.

55. Ibid., 150.

56. Ibid., 25.

57. Ibid., 21.

58. Tooley, *Abortion and Infanticide*, 405–6.

59. See Engelhardt, *Foundations of Bioethics*, 116–20.

60. Richard A. McCormick, "Proxy Consent in the Experimentation Situation," *Perspectives in Biology and Medicine* 18 (1974): 14.

61. See Rollin, "Moral Status of Research Animals," 926.

62. Robert Steinbrook, "Organ Retrieval Methods Spark Debate," *Los Angeles Times*, 4 July 1992, p. A30.

63. T. Kushner and R. Belliotti, "Baby Fae: A Beastly Business," *Journal of Medical Ethics* 11 (1985): 178–83.

64. Thomas Starzl, *Experience in Renal Transplantation* (Philadelphia: W. B. Saunders, 1964); Keith Reemtsma, "Heterotransplantation," in *Human Transplantation*, ed. F. Rappaport and J. Dausset (New York: Grune and Stratton, 1968), 357–66.

65. Council on Scientific Affairs, "Xenografts: Review of the Literature and Current Status," *Journal of the American Medical Association* 254 (1985): 3353–59.

66. A. M. Sadeghi et al., "Cardiac Xenotransplantation in Primates," *Journal of Thoracic Cardiovascular Surgery* 93 (1987): 809–14.

67. Sadeghi et al., "Cardiac Xenotransplantation"; C. Hammer, "Isohemagglutinins and Preformed Natural Antidotes in Xenogeneic Organ Transplantation," *Transplantation Proceedings* 19 (1987): 4443–47; D. C. Cooper, P. A. Human, and A. G. Rose, "Is ABO Compatibility Essential in Xenografting between Closely Related Species?," *Transplantation Proceedings* 19 (1987): 4437–40.

68. F. Patterson, "Conversations with a Gorilla," *National Geographic* 165 (1978): 438–65; J. Vessels, "Koko's Kitten," *National Geographic* 172 (1985): 110–13.

69. For an excellent review of the animal liberationists' debate on this topic, see DeGrazia, "Moral Status of Animals," 48–70.

70. Singer, *Animal Liberation,* 7.

71. Kushner and Belliotti, "Baby Fae."

72. Arthur Caplan, "Ethical Issues Raised by Research Involving Xenografts," *Journal of the American Medical Association* 254 (1985): 3339–43.

73. Singer, *Animal Liberation,* 92–162.

74. James W. Walters, "Minnesota Bioethics Retreat and Conference," *Update* 5 (Nov. 1989): 8.

75. The Multi-Society Task Force on PVS, "Medical Aspects of the Persistent Vegetative State" (pt. 1), *The New England Journal of Medicine* 330 (26 May 1994): 1499–1508; (pt.2), ibid. 330 (2 June 1994): 1572–79. Also see Bonnie Steinbock, "Recovery from Persistent Vegetative State? The Case of Carrie Coons," *Hastings Center Report* 19 (July–Aug. 1989): 14–15.

76. James W. Walters, "Yes, the Law on Anencephalic Infants as Organ Sources Should Be Changed," *Journal of Pediatrics* 115 (Nov. 1989): 825–28.

77. The notion that self-absent individuals do not share identical moral standing with readers of this volume and should be used as organ sources—before animals—is not as provocative as it may first appear.

There are circumstances in which particular human lives are not viewed by society as warranting the protection routinely given to animals. As was indicated earlier, only recently has it been openly recognized that physicians ethically may withdraw all life-support from certain patients. However, organized societal protection for animals is of long standing. Its history is even longer than statutes protecting children.

The Society for the Prevention of Cruelty to Children was founded in New York City in 1871 in reaction to a girl's legal rights that were less recognized than those of dogs and cats. Mary Ellen was regularly beaten by her adoptive parents. Although concerned neighbors reported the incidents to the police, nothing could be done because no legal mechanism existed to temper parents' sacred right to chastise their children. Finally, under the auspices of the Society for the Prevention of Cruelty to Animals, Mary Ellen was removed from her parents on the grounds that she belonged to the animal kingdom. See L. Armstrong, *The Home Front: Notes from the Family War Zone* (New York: McGraw-Hill, 1983), 17.

78. President's Commission for the Study of Ethical Problems in Medicine and Biomedical and Behavioral Research, *Defining Death* (Washington, D.C.: U.S. Government Printing Office, 1981), 58, 75.

Chapter 5: The Moral Status of Anencephalic Infants

1. "Report of the New England Regional Infant Cardiac Program," *Pediatrics* 65, no. 2 suppl. (1980): 436–39.

2. J. D. Lloyd-Still, "Mortality from Liver Disease in Children: Implications for Hepatic Transplantation Program," *American Journal of Diseases of Children* 139 (1985): 381–84.

3. M. Boyer, *End-Stage Renal Disease in Children* (Philadelphia: W. B. Saunders, 1984), 9–15. See P. W. Eggers, R. Conerton, and M. McMullan, "The Medicare Experience with End-Stage Renal Disease: Trends in Incidence, Prevalence, and Survival," *Health Care Financing Review* 5 (1984): 69–88.

4. Stephen Ashwal and Sanford Schneider, "Brain Death in the Newborn: Clinical, EEG, and Blood Flow Determinations," *Annals of Neurology* 24 (1988): 337.

5. Kenneth R. Swaiman and Francis S. Wright, eds., *The Practice of Pediatric Neurology* (St. Louis: C. V. Mosby, 1982), 410.

6. P. A. Baird and A. D. Sadovinich, "Survival in Infants with Anencephaly," *Clinical Pediatrics* 23 (1984): 268–71; By the editors, "Anencephalic Newborns and Organ Transplants: New Case, Further Reflections," *BioLaw* 2 (May 1992): S831–33.

7. J. M. Elwood and J. H. Elwood, *Epidemiology of Anencephalus and Spina Bifida* (New York: Oxford University Press, 1980).

8. W. E. Goodwin et al., "Human Renal Transplantation: Clinical Experiences with Six Cases of Renal Homotransplantation," *Journal of Urology* 89 (1963): 13–24.

9. Ibid.; see also Lester W. Martin, Luis L. Gonzales, Clark D. West, Robert A. Swartz, and Darryl J. Sutorius, "Homotransplantation of Both Kidneys from an Anencephalic Monster to a 17-Pound Boy with Eagle-Barrett Syndrome," *Surgery* 66 (Sept. 1969): 603–7; Kikuo Iitaka, Lester W. Martin, Joseph A. Cox, Paul T. McEnery, and Clark D. West, "Transplantation of Cadaver Kidneys from Anencephalic Donors," *Journal of Pediatrics* 93 (Aug. 1978): 216–20; Donald I. Moel and Khalid M. H. Butt, "Renal Transplantation in Children Less Than Two Years of Age," *Pediatrics* 99 (Oct. 1981): 535–39; Wolfgang Holzgreve, Fritz K. Beller, Bernd Buchholz, Manfred Hansmann, and Kurt Köhler, "Kidney Transplantation from Anencephalic Donors," *New England Journal of Medicine* 316 (1987): 1069–70.

10. Shinichi Ohshima, Yoshinari Ono, Tsuneo Kinukawa, Osamu Matsuura, Kazuo Tsuzuki, and Shigemitsu Itoh, "Kidney Transplantation from an Anencephalic Baby: A Case Report," *Journal of Urology* 132 (1984): 546–47.

11. Holzgreve et al., "Kidney Transplantation"; personal communication, 5 May 1995, from Prof. Dr. Hans-Martin Sass, Institute für Philosophie, Ruhr-Universität, Bochum, Germany.

12. Iitaka et al., "Transplantation of Cadaver Kidneys."

13. The first attempt to transplant an anencephalic heart occurred in 1966. See Adrian Kantrowitz, Jordan D. Haller, Howard Joos, Marcial M. Cerruti, and Hans E. Carstensen, "Transplantation of the Heart in an Infant and an Adult," *American Journal of Cardiology* 22 (1968): 782.

14. J. C. Fletcher, J. A. Robertson, and Michael R. Harrison, "Primates and Anencephalics as Sources for Pediatric Organ Transplants: Medical, Legal, and Ethical Issues," *Fetal Therapy* 1 (1986): 150–64.

15. Michael R. Harrison, "The Anencephalic Newborn as Organ Donor: Commentary," *Hastings Center Report* 16 (Apr. 1986): 21–22.

16. James W. Walters and Stephen Ashwal, "Organ Prolongation in Anencephalic Infants: Ethical and Medical Issues," *Hastings Center Report* 18 (Oct.–Nov. 1988): 19–27.

17. James W. Walters, "Loma Linda University's Protocol on Anencephalic Infants as Organ Donors," *Hastings Center Report* 18 (Oct.–Nov. 1988): 22–23.

18. Joyce L. Peabody, J. R. Emery, and Stephen Ashwal, "Experience with Anencephalic Infants as Prospective Organ Donors," *New England Journal of Medicine* 321 (1989): 344–50.

19. The Medical Task Force on Anencephaly [Child Neurology Society, American Academy of Neurology, American College of Obstetricians and Gynecologists, American Academy of Pediatrics, American Neurological Association], "The Infant with Anencephaly," *New England Journal of Medicine* 322 (1990): 669–74; Ronald E. Cranford, "Organ Retrieval from Infants with Anencephaly," *Transplantation Proceedings* 22 (1990): 1040–41.

20. Norman Fost, "Organs from Anencephalic Infants: An Idea Whose Time Has Not Yet Come," *Hastings Center Report* 18 (Oct.–Nov. 1988): 5–10.

21. Council on Ethical and Judicial Affairs, American Medical Association, Report 14: *Anencephalic Infants as Organ Donors* (Chicago: American Medical Association, 1988).

22. Council on Ethical and Judicial Affairs, American Medical Association, *Code of Medical Ethics: Current Opinions with Annotations.* Report 2.162: *Anencephalic Infants as Organ Donors,* updated, June 1994 (Chicago: American Medical Association, 1994). In "The Use of Anencephalic Neonates as Organ Donors," *Journal of the American Medical Association* 273 (1995): 1614–1618, the Council gave its reasoning for the earlier opinion. The Council modified its opinion by adding that the diagnosis of anencephaly must by confirmed by two physicians with special expertise and that the parents of the anencephalic neonate must initiate any discussion about organ retrieval. The *New York Times*

reported the *JAMA* article on its front page (24 May 1995), quoting leading bioethics critics and supporters.

23. Council on Ethical and Judicial Affairs, American Medical Association, *Code of Medical Ethics: Current Opinions with Annotations. Report 1-I-95: The Use of Anencephalic Neonates as Organ Donors: Reconsideration* (Chicago: American Medical Association, 1995).

24. Cranford, "Organ Retrieval."

25. Bioethics Committee, Canadian Paediatrics Society, "Transplantation of Organs from Newborns with Anencephaly," *Canadian Medical Association Journal* 142 (1990): 715–17.

26. T. C. Frewen et al., "Anencephalic Infants and Organ Donation: The Children's Hospital of Western Ontario Experience," *Transplantation Proceedings* 22 (1990): 1033–36.

27. Personal communication, 21 Feb. 1991.

28. D. Alan Shewmon, Alexander M. Capron, Warwick J. Peacock, and Barbara L. Schulman, "The Use of Anencephalic Infants as Organ Sources: A Critique," *Journal of the American Medical Association* 261 (1989): 1773–81.

29. Medical Task Force on Anencephaly, "Infant with Anencephaly."

30. George Annas et al., "Bioethicists' Statement on the U.S. Supreme Court's Cruzan Decision," *New England Journal of Medicine* 323 (1990): 686–87.

31. Aubrey Milunsky, "Harvesting Organs for Transplantation from Dying Anencephalic Infants," *Pediatrics* 82 (Aug. 1988): 274–76.

32. Shewmon et al., "Use of Anencephalic Infants"; D. Alan Shewmon, "Anencephaly: Selected Medical Aspects," *Hastings Center Report* 18 (Oct.–Nov. 1988): 11–19.

33. Donald N. Medearis Jr., and Lewis B. Holmes, "On the Use of Anencephalic Infants as Organ Donors," *New England Journal of Medicine* 321 (1989): 391–93.

34. S. T. Fry, "Ethical Issues in Organ Retrieval from Anencephalic Infants," *Issues in Comprehensive Pediatric Nursing* 12 (1989): 437–45.

35. See the excellent study by S. Shinnar and John D. Arras, "Ethical Issues in the Use of Anencephalic Infants as Organ Donors," *Neurologic Clinics* 7 (1989): 729–43.

36. See, for example, Fletcher et al., "Primates and Anencephalics"; Norman Fost, "Removing Organs from Anencephalic Infants: Ethical and Legal Considerations," *Clinics in Perinatology* 16 (1989): 331–37; B. J. Taylor, W. M. Chadduck, M. Kletzel, J. E. Rush, and B. Moore, "Anencephalic Infants as Organ Donors: The Medical, Legal, Moral and Economic Issues," *Journal of the Arkansas Medical Society* 87 (1990): 184–87; Frewen et al., "Anencephalic Infants"; Cranford, "Organ Retrieval"; Walters, "Yes."

37. See James F. Childress, "Reasons Not to Use Anencephalics' Organs for Transplantation prior to Death," *BioLaw* 2 (May 1992): S845–47. Childress states: "My main reasons for opposition are rule-consequences, particularly when there are certain conceptual difficulties, dangerous social pressures, and symbolic disvalues of disrespect and indignity" (S847).

38. R. W. Evans, letter, *New England Journal of Medicine* 322 (1990): 332.

39. May, "What Makes a Human Being."

40. William E. May et al., "Feeding and Hydrating the Permanently Unconscious and Other Vulnerable Persons," *Issues in Law and Medicine* 3 (1987): 203–17

41. Gilbert Meilaender, "The Anencephalic Newborn as Organ Donor: Commentary," *Hastings Center Report* 16 (1986): 22–23.

42. Gilbert Meilaender, *The Limits of Love: Some Theological Explorations* (University Park: Pennsylvania State University Press, 1987).

43. Shewmon et al., "Use of Anencephalic Infants." See also Fletcher et al., "Primates and Anencephalics."

44. Lecky, *History of European Morals*, 2:21–25.

45. Immanuel Kant, *Foundations of the Metaphysics of Morals*, in *Philosophical Writings*, trans. Ernst Behler (New York: Continuum Publishing Co., 1986), 94.

46. The undergirding ethical perspective of this argument or of the Loma Linda University protocol on anencephalic infants itself was not debated by the protocol committee. The committee focused on pragmatic legal, clinical, and ethical considerations. Although the committee members agreed on the basic planks of the protocol, the reasons for doing so likely were various. Stephen Toulmin's reflection on serving in the late 1970s as a staff member with the National Commission for the Protection of Human Subjects of Biomedical and Behavioral Research is illuminating here. After indicating that argument and reasoning could bring consensus in consideration of specific *cases*, he explains: "Only when the individual members of the commission went on to explain their own particular 'reasons' for supporting the general consensus did they begin to go seriously different ways. For, then, commissioners from different backgrounds and faiths 'justified' their votes by appealing to general views and abstract principles which differed far more deeply than their opinions about particular substantive questions" (Toulmin, "How Medicine Saved the Life of Ethics," *Perspectives in Biology and Medicine* 25 [1982]: 736–50).

47. See the helpful essay by Ronald E. Cranford, "The Persistent Vegetative State: The Medical Reality (Getting the Facts Straight)," *Hastings Center Report* 18 (Feb.–Mar. 1988): 27–32. Cranford distinguishes the two states into which permanently unconscious patients are divided: eyes-closed unconsciousness (coma) and eyes-open unconsciousness (persistent vegetative state and anencephaly). The author cites one PVS patient who survived for thirty-seven years, 111 days.

48. Council on Ethical and Judicial Affairs, *Current Opinions of the Council on Ethical and Judicial Affairs of the American Medical Association—1986* (Chicago: American Medical Association, 1986), 2.18, 12–13.

49. President's Commission, *Deciding to Forego Life-Sustaining Treatment*, 212–19. For a comparison of the best-interests and four other approaches to decision making, see James W. Walters, "Approaches to Ethical Decision Making in the Neonatal Intensive Care Unit," *American Journal of Diseases of Children* 142 (Aug. 1988): 825–30.

50. Arras, "Toward an Ethic of Ambiguity." This ethical analysis of the best-interests criterion is unsurpassed.

51. See, for instance, Charles Krauthammer, "No Such Thing as 'Living' Dead" (editorial), *Dayton Daily News,* 17 Dec. 1987.

52. See David Ross, *Kant's Ethical Theory: A Commentary on the Grundlegung zur Metaphysik der Sitten* (Oxford: Clarendon Press, 1954), 48–57.

53. Patrick A. E. Hutchings, *Kant on Absolute Value* (Detroit: Wayne State University Press, 1972), 293–48.

54. My colleague Gerald Winslow helpfully points out that the cultural sources for a maxim like Kant's are varied and deep: the Talmud, natural law, and the biblical-prophetic tradition of protecting the vulnerable. People with no Kantian knowledge hold to ideas similar to the categorical imperative.

55. See James W. Walters, "Transplant of (Anencephalic Infants') Organs Can Save Lives" (editorial), *Los Angeles Times,* 10 Dec. 1987.

56. "Pittsburgh Transplant Foundation: Post-Mortem Organ Procurement Protocol" (available from 1038 J. Scaife Hall, Pittsburgh, PA 15261). Fletcher et al., "Primates and Anencephalics," use this analogy as a key in their case for the appropriateness of "cooling" an anencephalic to preserve its organs although death may be hastened.

57. The widely publicized case of Marie Odette Henderson is illustrative (*San Francisco Examiner,* 17 June 1986).

58. Leslie S. Rothenberg and D. Alan Shewmon, "No Life Should Be Traded for Another" (editorial), *Los Angeles Times,* 10 Dec. 1987.

59. Peabody et al., "Experience with Anencephalic Infants."

60. "Report of Special Task Force: Guidelines for the Determination of Brain Death in Children," *Pediatrics* 80 (1987): 298–301. For an elaboration of the determination of brain death in children, see Walters and Ashwal, "Organ Prolongation."

61. Loma Linda University Medical Center had inquiries from over fifty families of anencephalic fetuses or newborns during the two months following the transplant of an anencephalic heart to baby Paul Holc in October 1987.

62. McCormick, "Proxy Consent."

63. "Additional Protections for Children Involved as Subjects in Research," *Code of Federal Regulations,* 1983, Title 45, chap. 46, p. 406.

64. Ibid., 406–7.

Chapter 6: Anencephalic Infants and the Law

1. *In the Matter of Baby K,* 832 F. Supp. 1022 (E.D.Va. 1993).

2. *In the Matter of Baby K,* 16 F. 3d 590 (4th Cir. 1994). See George J. Annas, "Asking the Courts to Set the Standard of Emergency Care: The Case of Baby K," *New England Journal of Medicine* 330 (26 May 1994): 1542–45.

3. Quoted in "Anencephalic Newborns and Organ Transplants," S831.

4. *San Francisco Chronicle,* 5 May 1986.

5. See Alexander Morgan Capron, "Anencephalic Donors: Separate the Dead from the Dying," *Hastings Center Report* 17 (Feb. 1987): 5–9, for an insightful critical analysis of Senator Marks's bill and related issues.

6. Andrea Scott, "Death unto Life: Anencephalic Infants as Organ Donors," *Virginia Law Review* 74 (1988): 1527–66.

7. Council on Ethical and Judicial Affairs, *Anencephalic Infants as Organ Donors*, 1994.

8. James W. Walters, "Are Anencephalic Infants Monstrosities?," *BioLaw* 2 (1989): S211–19.

9. Gerald Winslow, "Anencephalic Infants as Organ Sources: Should the Law Be Changed? Reply [to Walters]," *Journal of Pediatrics* 115 (Nov. 1989): 828.

10. Quoted in Paul Ramsey, *Patient as Person* (New Haven: Yale University Press, 1970), 108–10.

11. President's Commission, *Defining Death*, 36, 41.

12. Paul Ramsey, *Ethics at the Edges of Life* (New Haven: Yale University Press, 1978), 190.

13. Childress, "Reasons Not to Use Anencephalics' Organs," S845.

14. Ibid., S846.

15. Council on Ethical and Judicial Affairs, *Anencephalic Infants as Organ Donors*, 1994.

16. Ad Hoc Committee of the Harvard Medical School to Examine the Definition of Brain Death, "A Definition of Irreversible Coma," *Journal of the American Medical Association* 205 (1968): 377.

17. Robert M. Veatch, a long-time critic of the whole-brain-based definition of death on clinical and conceptual grounds, favors a higher-brain-oriented definition. See Veatch, *Death, Dying, and the Biological Revolution*, rev. ed. (New Haven: Yale University Press, 1989), and "Brain Death and Slippery Slopes," *Journal of Clinical Ethics* 3 (Fall 1992): 181–87.

18. Some physicians today see no pressing need to refine society's definition of death but just want to update the medical criteria for organ donation. Specifically, the issue is whether brain stem death must necessarily be present before organ donations are allowed. Although the certified death of the neocortex would be sufficient for many in regard to donation of their own organs, such thinking only begs the issue of whether a person must be dead before vital organs may be procured. See Robert M. Arnold and Stuart J. Youngner, "The Dead Donor Rule: Should We Stretch It, Bend It, or Abandon It?," *Kennedy Institute of Ethics Journal* 3 (June 1993): 263–78.

19. I join others who have suggested increasing the choices of a definition of death to include permanent cessation of consciousness. See Robert M. Veatch, *Death, Dying, and the Biological Revolution*, 1st ed. (New Haven: Yale University Press, 1976), 72–76, and the 1989 revised edition, 53–58; R. D. Truog and J. C. Fackler, "It Is Reasonable to Reject the Diagnosis of Brain Death," *Journal of Clinical Ethics* 3 (1992): 80–81.

20. See Dworkin, *Life's Dominion*, x. A central point in this important book

is that basic and debatable decisions about such topics as abortion and euthanasia are essentially "religious."

21. M. S. Pernick, "Back from the Grave: Recurring Controversies over Refining and Diagnosing Death in History," in *Death: Beyond Whole-Brain Criteria,* ed. R. M. Zaner (Dordrecht, Netherlands: Kluwer Academic Publishers, 1988), 17–74.

22. Ibid.

23. Pius XII, "The Prolongation of Life," *The Pope Speaks* 4 (1958): 393–98.

24. Frank Harron, John Burnside, and Tom Beauchamp, *Health and Human Values* (New Haven: Yale University Press, 1983).

25. Shewmon et al., "Use of Anencephalic Infants."

Index

tory of, 20–22; rationally compelling, 25

Personhood, 35–41; and Down syndrome newborn, 35; in Great Britain vs. U.S., 61; insensitivity and impracticality of, 63; low standard vs. high standard, 24; minimal conditions for, 69–70, 73; and moral beliefs, 24; and moral decision making, 61–62; and particularism, 43–46; philosophical value of, 25; and proximate personhood, 63–64, 74

Person/human dilemma. *See* Human/person dilemma

Persons: and Bantus, 46; Bernardin's ambiguous use of, 33–34; defined, 2, 26; future persons, 38; and higher brain capacity, 26; newborns as, 37; normal adult humans as, 38; possible, 22; as seekers of meaning, 48; sleeping, 39; as social beings, 47–48; Tooley's definition of, 36

Phenomenology, 20

Physical development: of fetuses and disabled newborns, 69; moral importance of, 68; and neonatal decisions, 69; as proximate personhood criterion, 68–70

Physicalism, 4, 15, 18–19; defined, 9, 17; importance of, 25; May and Ashley as leading proponents of, 28; and people of varying ideologies, 24; and Roman Catholic Church, 27

Pig trial. *See* Falsise pig trial

Pius XII (pope), 27

Plato, 17, 18, 58, 93, 95, 100

Postmodernism: and historical conditionedness, 10; open to religion, 10; and personhood, 20, 75; and religious claims, 16; softened by pragmatism, 14–15

Potentiality: mental over physical, 67–68; moral significance of, 66; as proximate personhood criterion, 66–68

Pragmatism, 15

President's Commission on Bioethics, 58–59

Process philosophy, 20, 94–95

Protestant work ethic, 11

Proximate personhood: argument developed, 62–77; argument summarized, 4,

5, 63; and dominant social ethos, 74–77; and Down syndrome, 64–65; and high moral status, 104; and moral status of marginal "persons," 64; potentiality, physical development, and bonding as criteria of, 63

Puritans, 20–21

Quasi-persons, 27, 61

Quinlan, Karen Ann, 2, 149

Ramsey, Paul, 12, 15, 56, 68, 106, 145

Rape, 14

Rational argumentation, 12–17 passim; and Engelhardt's ethics, 40–41; and religion, 49

Rationality: and affectivity, 96–97; in animals, 85–86; cleverness and integration in, 93; and humans, 87–88; and laudable ends, 93; and nature, 19; and self-absent individuals, 112

Reasonableness, 76

Reemtsma, Keith, 109

Regan, Tom, 78, 82–84, 87

Religion: and American values, 8, 11; contributions of, 10–11, 14; ethos and worldview provided by, 17; and humankind, 48–50; influenced by society, 16; and law, 14; as life-informing ultimate belief, 7, 14; and logical positivism, 15; and moral status, 7; normative claims of, 12–14; and postmodern era, 10; and public debate on social issues, 14–17; relation to philosophy, 14; and secularists, 13–15

"Respect for Human Life in Its Origins," 18–19

Roman Catholic Church: and physicalism, 27

Rorty, Richard, 75

Rose, Eric, 111

Ross, W. D., 133

Rousseau, Jean-Jacques, 58

RU-486, 1

Rushdie, Salman, 50

Sanctity of life, 12; and seamless garment ethic, 30; as simplistic slogan, 46

JAMES W. WALTERS, PH.D., is a professor of ethical studies at Loma Linda University, where he also directed the Ethics and Aging Project in Southern California. He has published numerous articles and is the author or editor of six books, including *Facing Limits: Ethics and Health Care for the Elderly* and *Choosing Who's to Live: Ethics and Aging.*

LAWRENCE J. SCHNEIDERMAN, M.D., is a professor of family and preventive medicine at the University of California, San Diego. He serves as an ethics consultant at UCSD's medical center and at Children's Hospital and Health Center, San Diego. He has over a hundred medical and scientific publications, including *Wrong Medicine: Doctors, Patients, and Futile Treatment.*